5-95

L ꓼ Y CC
ꞌY

Greek Tragedy
in Action

Greek Tragedy in Action

by Oliver Taplin

METHUEN & CO LTD

First published in 1978 by
Methuen & Co Ltd
11 New Fetter Lane, London EC4P 4EE

© 1978 Oliver Taplin

Printed in Great Britain
at the University Press,
Cambridge

ISBN 0 416 76320 0 (hardbound)
ISBN 0 416 71700 4 (paperback)

To the JACT Greek Summer School,
past and future

Contents

List of plates   viii

Preface   ix

1   The visual dimension of tragedy   1

2   Stage management and stage directions   9

3   Introduction to nine plays   22

4   Exits and entrances   31

5   Actions and gestures   58

6   Objects and tokens   77

7   Tableaux, noises and silences   101

8   Mirror scenes   122

9   Scenic sequence   140

10   Emotion and meaning in the theatre   159

11   Round plays in square theatres   172

Notes   182

Select bibliography   194

Index of passages discussed   199

General index   202

List of plates

(between pages 86 and 87)

1 View of the theatre at Epidaurus (reproduced by kind permission of the Greek National Tourist Office)
2 Spectators' view of the theatre at Epidaurus (Greek National Tourist Office)
3 Tragic chorus dancing (Basel Antikenmuseum BS1415)
4 Oriental pyre (American School at Athens, Corinth T1144)
5 Actors dressing (Boston Museum of Fine Arts, 98.883)
6 The Pronomos Vase (Naples National Museum 3240)
7 Andromeda (Staatliche Museen zu Berlin, 3237)
8 Actor and mask (Martin von Wagner Museum, H4600)
9 Sophocles *Oedipus* (Syracuse 66557, author's own photograph)
10 *Oresteia*, death of Agamemnon (Boston Museum of Fine Arts, 63.1246)
11 Death of Ajax (Bareiss Collection, New York, L.69.11.35)
12 Death of Pentheus (Boston Museum of Fine Arts, 10.221)

Preface

This book is about ancient Greek culture and about the theatre, and it is meant for the 'general reader' who is interested in either or both. I hope professional Hellenists will read it, but it was not written primarily for them. Who for, then? I suppose I have had students in mind above all, students of drama or English literature or Classical civilization – any student who encounters Greek tragedy. But anyone who is fascinated by the Greeks, anyone who loves the theatre, anyone who is prepared to be enriched by the great literature of the past may find these pages worth while.

But there is a condition. The core of the book (chapters 3–9) demands and assumes that the reader already knows all, or at least some, of the nine tragedies it concentrates on (they are listed on p. 22). Furthermore, it is probably best read with a translation (or text) open to hand, preferably a translation which has the line numbers in the margin (there are recommendations on pp. 198–9). This book is in no way a substitute for reading the plays themselves – and, if possible, seeing them. Indeed, I should dearly like to think that the book might encourage theatres to stage these great dramas, and might help to find them audiences.

I quote from the tragedies liberally. All quotations are translated and all the translations are my own. I am only too aware how stilted and imperfect they are; but I thought it essential to translate high poetry into something which suggests its lofty and arresting style. The language of Greek tragedy was not that of everyday speech, and I had rather turn it into bad verse than into pedestrian prose.

It is a cliché to say in a foreword that so-and-so's help has incalculably improved the book. In this case it is quite honestly true of my friend Colin Macleod, who commented on my manuscript in the fullest detail. Thanks to him I have changed the text in literally hundreds of places, and I have incorporated whole sentences of his in literally dozens of places. His contributions are far too pervasive to be singled out. No doubt the book would have fewer flaws if I had taken his advice yet more often. I have also had some helpful suggestions from Peter and Lesley Brown. And I should say how much I have been stimulated and taught by my pupils over the last five years.

Finally, if anyone between the ages of 15 and 20 is stimulated by this book to want to read Greek literature in the original language, they should write to Joint Association of Classical Teachers, 31–34 Gordon Square, London WC1H OPY, and ask what my dedication means. I look forward to meeting them.

September 1977   Oliver Taplin

1 The visual dimension of tragedy

> *Behind the dialogue of Greek drama we are always conscious of a concrete visual actuality, and behind that of a specific emotional actuality. Behind the drama of words is the drama of action, the timbre of voice and voice, the uplifted hand or tense muscle, and the particular emotion. The spoken play, the words which we read, are symbols, a shorthand, and often, as in the best of Shakespeare, a very abbreviated shorthand indeed, for the actual and felt play, which is always the real thing. The phrase, beautiful as it may be, stands for a greater beauty still. This is merely a particular case of the amazing unity of Greek, the unity of concrete and abstract in philosophy, the unity of thought and feeling, action and speculation in life. (T. S. Eliot)*

This extraordinarily succinct and perceptive passage from T. S. Eliot's early essay, 'Seneca in Elizabethan Translations', puts the theme of this book in a nutshell. Behind the words of Greek tragedy there is action, behind the action emotion: the abstract and concrete are made one, the emotion and the meaning are indivisible. The actual and felt play is my subject. Greek tragedy is often thought of as static, verbal, didactic and irretrievably alien: I hope to show, rather, how it is theatrical, emotional, absorbing – and so can still speak directly to us.

Great playwrights have been practical men of the theatre, never mere scriptwriters – Aeschylus, Aristophanes, Shakespeare, Molière, Racine, Chekhov, Shaw, Brecht. . . . They have wrought, not just written, plays. They have supervised the rehearsal, directed the movement of their works, overseen their music, choreography and design, and often have acted themselves. They composed works to be performed before an audience. For them the play is realized, finds its finished state, in the theatre.

The text, which is inevitably all we have, is no more than a transcript, a scenario. The play's the thing. Shakespeare seems to have paid no attention to the publication of his plays: he put his energies into having them seen and heard and understood in the performance.

But this applies even more to the Greek dramatists of the fifth century B.C. The very word 'theatre' first occurs in the fifth century: *theātron* means a place where things are seen, the audience are *hoi theātai* – those who look on, the spectators. So, too, with the word *drāma*: something that is acted out, a communication through action. The Greek tragedians must have written their words down, but that was incidental; the verbs used were 'to make' (*poiein*), and, synonymously and no less commonly, 'to teach' (*didaskein*). The playwright himself instructed his chorus and actors, he was both director and producer. His task ended not with the script but with the performance.

'Euripides maligns us', complains a wife in Aristophanes' *Women at the Thesmophoria* (383ff.), 'wherever there are theatres, tragedies, choral songs . . . so that as soon as our husbands come home from the auditorium they look suspicious. . . .' Not 'whenever they read Euripides . . .': the book is not yet the paramount vehicle for literature (though it was for more prosaic writings). It is during the hundred years after the flowering of Greek tragedy that reading replaces performance as the primary mode of literary communication. Aristophanes and Plato take for granted the audience-directed nature of drama; it is not until Aristotle's *Poetics*, nearly a century later, that we first encounter the notion that plays might be best read. Though he is ambivalent on this – and he is unbalanced by his reaction against Plato who fiercely criticized the theatre – Aristotle sows the suggestion that the performance is a distracting encumbrance, the province of rude mechanicals; and since then this view has been widespread (especially in the nineteenth century). But these days all but a lunatic fringe of students of Greek drama would accept the primacy of performance, and I shall take it as read without labouring the argument.[1]

All students of the theatre – indeed anyone who has thought about human communication – must be aware that the written quotation of any spoken sentence is a very incomplete transcript of what was conveyed by the utterance itself. On one level we miss the tone of voice, nuance, pace, stress; and we miss facial expression, gesture and the physical posture and positioning of the speaker and addressee. Even more profoundly, the transcript does not convey the rôles and social or personal relationships of the real people involved, their past, their shared assumptions, the full circumstances of the speech-act. It lacks *context*. All these attendant circumstances conflow to turn a lifeless sentence, such as may be delivered thousands of times every day, into a unique and expressive communication. (Think how many different accentuations and contexts might be given to the four-word sentence 'Pass the knife, please' – some mundane, others a matter of life and death.) Such matters have recently become the object of intense study from psycho-linguists, social psychologists and philosophers of language. But, of course, dramatists – from Athens onwards – have always been fully, if instinctively, aware that the words are the mere tip of a vast rootwork of context. For the medium of the playwright is the bodies and the voices of his actors, and by these means he has, in a very limited space of time, to build up a complex of relationships and communications of sufficient depth and interest to capture his audience. So the meaning of the play, what it is about, is heard and seen; and the artist is going to have to use voice and action with all the skill he commands. When we read a play, what we are doing – or what we should be doing – is hearing and seeing the play in the theatre of the mind. If we do not, then we are failing to do justice to the appropriate genre – a possible but perverse and unproductive procedure.

This contrasts very obviously with other genres that we read – epic poetry, or at the furthest extreme, the novel. Most novels contain a lot of dialogue, but the accompaniments of tone, gesture, etc. have to be added in narrative form. Similarly the ramifications of setting, of background, and of reaction, are all filled out by expository narrative. This gives the novelist scope for complexity, particularly of internal psychology: the loss, compared with drama, is one of immediacy and concentration. 'He thought' or 'she felt' are the stock-in-trade of the novelist: the dramatist must constrict thought and feeling so as to convey them through dialogue and action. He has to contain himself within the 'two hour's traffic' of his stage; and he has to convey all that he wants to convey in the course of an unfaltering movement not much less rapid than the pace of ordinary speech – that is to say, he has to put across everything at the same time as the dialogue.

Another evident and fundamental difference from the novel (in fact, from most other literature) is the presence of a large audience. The novel is, as a rule, read silently, contemplatively, by the individual in privacy: the play is presented to a public, in the Greek theatre to an experienced, demanding and appreciative audience of more than 10,000. As we read we must also feel the presence of the audience: not only because every sound and movement is, ultimately, directed at them, but also because their shared experience is part of the play as a whole. The play is so designed as to take the thoughts and emotions of the audience along with it.

So we must do our best to see and hear Greek tragedy, and not in an arbitrary or uninformed way, but in the way that the dramatist him-self meant it to be seen and heard.[2] The performance, the play in action, is all part of his work, and is – as I hope to show – an important element in the way he conveys what he has to convey.

My subject is, then, the Greek dramatists' visual technique, the way they translated their meaning into theatrical terms. I hope both to establish as far as possible what was seen, and to indicate its significance. The approach is not novel; nearly all students of Greek tragedy would admit its validity and advocate its application. And yet there has been remarkably little sustained work on the subject. It crops up here and there in books and articles, but there are only two books, both in German, where it is a central concern (Reinhardt and Steidle). It is becoming a sour joke that classicists trail along about a generation behind the critical advances pioneered by their colleagues in English studies. In so far as I am attempting the same sort of thing for Greek tragedy as (if it is not too presumptuous a claim) Granville-Barker did for Shakespeare in his *Prefaces* (1927–47), this is true in my own case too. But this aspect has not yet advanced very far in English studies, and there is still much to be done.[3] I think I may claim that the application of some of my methods and principles to Shakespeare and other more recent dramatists would produce results which would not appear grossly unsophisticated and antique to the practitioners in those fields.

Now, when I urge that Greek tragedy must be visualized, must be seen to be believed, I am not talking about the mechanics of the staging. The permanent features of the theatre – the stage building, machinery, etc. – are interesting enough (see chapter 2); but my concern is not so much with *how* the play was stage-managed as with *what* is being acted out within it. It is the dramatized visible event, with the unique significance its context gives it, that I am after. This means, in effect, the movements and stances of the participants, the objects they hold and exchange, the things they do to each other, their shifting spatial relationships, and the overall shaping of these stage events into meaningful patterns and sequences.

First of all we have to extrapolate the stage-directions and other signals from the text (or other evidence, if any is available). Once that is done, we go on to ask what the dramatist meant by it. He has arranged his visual composition in this way rather than any other; this is the way he himself put his drama into action. Why has he done it this way? It is, surely, only fair (not to say humble) to suppose that a great playwright will produce his work purposefully, and use his scenic resources so as to communicate to his audience. So, communicate what? It is here that the critic has to call on every resource at his disposal: the whole dramatic context, the conventions of the genre, the literary background, the social, legal, religious and intellectual background. For it is, I take it, the task of literary criticism to elucidate what the author communicates; and hence ultimately to show why anyone should – or should not – spend time and trouble on a certain work of literature.

My approach through the *visual* or active dimension is not a rival or an alternative to *literary* criticism, it is only a part of literary criticism, perhaps more rightly termed 'dramatic' or 'theatrical' criticism. It is only one approach. And if I have seemed to depreciate the 'mere' words of Greek tragedy in my attempt to highlight the importance of what is seen, then that impression should be redressed. I hope the central chapters, and the quantity of direct quotation, will do that in any case. The *words* – which are, after all, almost all we have – contain and explain the visual dimension: there could be no play and no meaning without them. Aeschylus, Sophocles and Euripides are also great poets. But they are not just great poets with a certain theatrical facility – that is an inapplicable disjunction. Visual meaning is inextricable from verbal meaning; the two are part and parcel of each other. They are the vehicles of the dramatists' meaning.

I have spoken of the dramatist's meaning, of what he is trying to convey, in full awareness that the concept of 'the author's intention' is a battleground of literary critical theory.[4] What I am talking about is the author's intention to communicate that which has found expression in the work in question. All art, indeed all writing and speech, is communication (except in some marginal and negligible circumstances). The artist communicates with his audience; the good artist communicates things which are worth communicating, and he does it well. So it makes obvious and elementary sense to enquire into his meaning. The existence of the author's communicative intention is a precondition of the existence of his work. While it is possible to take no notice of it, to do so would be not only blind and arbitrary, it would be ungrateful, arrogant and egocentric.

But while the author's meaning remains necessarily unchanged, the audience is no less necessarily always changing. *We* are now the audience of Greek tragedy, but it was others yesterday and will be others again tomorrow. But is *the* audience the author's original audience, in this case the Athenians at the first performance? That audience certainly has special claims on our attention because the dramatist took them for granted, and so they became from the beginning inextricable from his meaning. But they are long dead: we are now *the* audience; and we are not, and never can be, fifth-century Athenians. Just as it seems to me quite pointless to say 'Shakespeare' (or whoever) 'would have said . . . if he were alive today' – he is not – so it seems pointless to pretend that one can become an Elizabethan or an Athenian. It is not just that the exercise is doomed to failure; it is to turn our backs upon ourselves.

There are then the two parties: the author's immutable meaning and his new, unforeseeable and ever-changing audience with all its different expectations and preoccupations. And it is the critic's task to attempt to reconcile these two parties. It is also very important that

that latter party (us) is not unchangeable. One way we may be changed is by being brought into close contact with great works of genius; and so it is desirable for us to learn from the original audience. We will appreciate the work – and life in general – better if we are to add to our experience the sensibility of a particularly gifted audience from the past.

One further theoretical point. Faced with the suggestion of some new point in a work of literature, particularly if it is a point of some subtlety, sceptics – particularly classical scholars – are inclined to ripost 'I don't believe any such thing crossed the author's mind'. This betrays a naive view of human consciousness and of the creative process. The human mind does not work on two rigid and mutually exclusive levels, the fully conscious and the rest. There is, rather, a multiplicity of overlapping levels. And the mind of the great artist is one that sorts out experience and gives it expression in a particularly subtle and complex way. Much surely goes into the artefact – is part of its meaning – beyond what is expressly formulated in the mind on a fully conscious level. (That is the reason why the artist's own explication of his work, while important, is not definitive.) The only question we can ask when faced with some alleged critical point is this: is it *there* or is it not?

'Is it there?' If the point is to be accepted, it should (broadly speaking) meet three conditions: it should be *prominent*, *coherent* and *purposeful*. There is no definitive court of appeal on this (though time and the community of informed opinion form a lower court). Ultimately the interpretation of art is subjective and personal; it is not verifiable. But this does not in any way diminish its interest and value: on the contrary it is the need for the exercise of judgement, of taste and of thoughtfulness that makes it so worth while.

And just as the author does not consciously articulate everything he puts into a work, so an audience does not explicitly formulate everything that it gets out of it, particularly not a theatre audience. You have only to think of what it is like to go to a play for this to be clear. And yet the sceptics are for ever complaining that 'an audience could not possibly think of (or notice or appreciate) . . .'. When in an audience one does not consciously analyse everything in the play which is having an effect on one's reaction; that would be a completely inappropriate, as well as impracticable, thing to attempt. Many levels of consciousness are involved; much that one is not fully aware of will be having its effect. And yet it is precisely the critic's task to spell out in longhand what makes the audience respond during the performance. The result is nothing in the least like a re-creation of being at a performance, since it has to spend whole pages over what is felt and thought in a single moment.[5] None the less the critic does hope to clarify and enrich his readers' appreciation when they next experience the drama.

To look at Greek tragedy in action is an approach which, I think, *both* interprets the author's meaning *and* brings home his communication to us, his present audience. The test of whether it really does throw light on the author's own meaning, created and fixed nearly 2,500 years ago, rests in the central chapters (4–9) of this book; and I must leave it to the reader to decide whether the meanings which I extricate are prominent, coherent and purposeful – whether they really are *there* or not.

So that must wait: but I shall offer, finally, some reasons for thinking that this is an approach which may have much to offer to us now. The discriminating theatre-going public is larger than ever before. The scenic aspects of drama come in for more and more attention in literary studies; and practical performance has become the central concern of burgeoning departments and schools of drama. Also non-verbal communication is a developing subject in various fields, including anthropology, philosophy, and social psychology.[6] There is everywhere a more sensitive awareness of the crucial place of action (in the broadest sense) in human relationships.

Furthermore, humanity shares much more than just 'birth, copulation and death', and this is especially clear in the irreducible physical aspects of life whose dramatization are my chief concern. Much of the visual dimension of Greek tragedy is immediately accessible to us with little qualification or adjustment. Thus, it could be transferred to the contemporary stage with little apology or explication. While I hope I have done justice in this book to the deep and manifold differences between Greek culture and our own, it is, by the very nature of my subject, the similarities that I shall be emphasizing.

The nineteenth century tended simply to assimilate the ancient world to its own: our own less self-confident century has been more relativist and less innocent, and there has been a healthy reaction against such a naive equation. The chief catalyst to this more detached vision of the Greeks has been the rise of the comparative anthropology of primitive societies, which has made us ever more aware that other societies have coherent and valid social structures and world pictures, yet quite other than our own. And it is clear that the ancient Greeks shared a great range of cultural features, alien to us, with various 'primitive' societies that still exist (or existed until recently). The re-examination of the Greek world in this relativist light has been an invigorating and valuable movement. But to lay exclusive stress on the *differences* is no less of a distortion than to assume unqualified similarity. Difference is a matter of degree and quality. And ultimately it is the almost uncanny similarity or timelessness of the Greeks which demands our attention. How can poets of so long ago have understood so deeply the human condition of the twentieth century?

Great drama makes universals concrete, and portrays the human condition through the voice and the actions of the human body. Let me compile some facts of life that are tied to the human body, to the eyes, hands, organs, dimensions and senses. Must we not all have parents, eat and sleep; all cry, laugh, feel pain and pleasure? We can all hear, speak or keep silent, may be killed, kill ourselves, have our life spared. We can all hold objects, keep them, give them away; we can follow others, depart from them, sit, lie down, stand up. We are all male or female, young and then old, closely attached to some people and not to others; we all have hopes, fears, feel sorrow and joy – live with bread, feel want, taste grief, need friends. These are the surface-pickings of human experience. And human experience is the field which Greek tragedy cultivates, and which finds expression, among other ways, through its visual dimension.

To present that catalogue without qualification would be deceptive; even in those universal experiences there will be differences of attitudes and associations and values between cultures and sub-cultures in various places and times, differences which may go deep. None the less ancient Greek culture was in many ways the archetype of European culture. Moreover it constantly attempted to look behind or through life to human universals, or, rather, seize on the universals within the multifariousness of life – Eliot's 'unity of Greek'. Greek tragedy is not all foreign; much is very close to home, often too close for comfort.

2 Stage management and stage directions

O, pardon! since a crooked figure may
Attest in little place a million;
And let us, ciphers to this great accompt,
On your imaginary forces work. (Shakespeare, Henry V)

The theatre of the mind has no shape, no conventions, no stage-management, except any that may be imposed, consciously or unconsciously, from time to time. If we imagine Greek tragedy with a proscenium arch or artificial lighting or detailed facial expressions then we shall both add much that is not to the point and lose much that matters. Now, I have argued in the previous chapter that much of the visual dimension is unaffected by such temporal externals: none the less, if we are to pay due respect to the dramatist's own original realization of his work, then we cannot neglect the actualities of his theatre, its layout, its facilities and so forth. This book is a critical study of certain tragedies in action, not another antiquarian reconstruction of the Athenian theatre; I shall, therefore, give only the barest and most dogmatic account of the theatre (with the help of some photographs), and refer the reader elsewhere for the evidence and the controversies, and for what there is to be said about the arrangements of the festivals and so forth.[1] I shall then go on to aspects of stage-management which are less familiar: the style of acting and the relation of stage action to the text.

Here, suppressing the controversies, is a very brief sketch of the Athenian theatre itself, which I shall assume did not change substan-

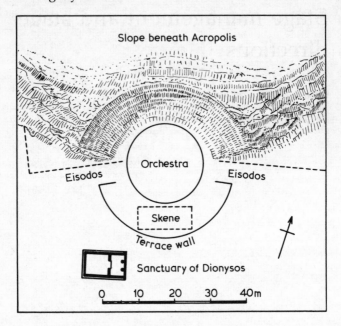

Fig. 1

tially between Aeschylus' *Oresteia* in 458 B.C. and Euripides' *Bacchae* at the very end of the century. The place is the south-east slope of the Acropolis at the annual festival of Dionysus in late March.[2] There is room for up to 15,000 to sit between the foot of the citadel walls and the actors, mostly on the ground, though there may have been some seating of stone or wood near the front. As for the focus of attention, the acting area, we can get no idea of this from the Theatre of Dionysus as it is today since it was greatly altered in the following centuries: a much better idea is given by Epidaurus (plates 1, 2), though that architectural showpiece is far more shapely and monumental than Athens ever was. Figures 1 and 2 show a ground-plan and an imagined audience's eye-view of the original acting-area at Athens. The centrepiece is the huge, round dancing floor, some 20 meters in diameter, the *orchēstra* (it looks rather like the threshing-floors which may have been its origin). Leading up to it from either side are the broad ramps – *eisodoi* – by which many of the audience will have arrived and which will be the route of most of the plays' entrances and exits. On the far side of the *orchēstra*, at a tangent to it, is the stage-building, *skēnē*, whose inside is the actors' changing-room, and whose front outside stands for a palace or temple or whatever is called for by the world of the play. Made of wood, perhaps some 12 metres long and 4 metres high, the *skēnē* had a large double-leaved door. The roof could be used, and painted scenery or architectural features could be fixed along the front (perhaps including smaller side-doors). This was a period of great interest in the painting of landscape and of perspective (the origins of the kind of painting familiar from Pompeii), and the *skēnē* was no doubt decorated, though the painting may well not have been changed to suit each play but each year drama was, in the fifth century, one of Athens' great cultural showpieces, and its accoutrements will not have been barely utilitarian.

These are the fixtures, so to speak. There may also have been a low, wooden stage-platform in front of the door, but if so, it was easily negotiable, and it was small enough not to encroach on the orchestra circle.[3] Various large stage-properties might be brought on – altars, statues, a cave mouth, chariots and so on. There were also two pieces of stage-machinery which, to judge from the parodies in comedy, were especially associated with tragedy. The *ekkyklēma* (literally

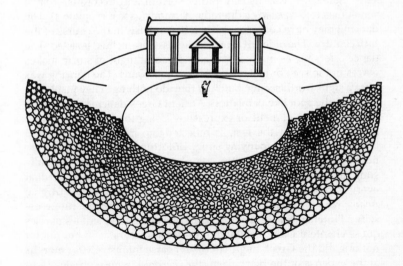

Fig. 2

'something which is rolled out') was a low platform on wheels which could be extruded from the central doors. On it would be arranged a tableau which the audience is to imagine is still *indoors*, though as the scene progresses the indoor/outdoor distinction tends to be neglected (for examples of its use see chapter 7 on 'tableaux'). The other contraption is the *mēchanē*, some kind of crane which could swing a flying character round into sight and set him down on stage. It is uncertain whether the *mēchanē* was used in fifth century for divine epiphanies (*deus ex machina*, see p. 186 n. 20), but it was certainly used for the not very common occasions when someone was meant actually to be flying, e.g. on the winged horse Pegasus.

These sticks and stones must be peopled. In the *orchēstra* were the *chorus*, an anonymous group of fifteen, who normally stayed there throughout the entire play after the opening scene. Their chief function was to sing and dance the choral odes which divide the acts of tragedy. However, they also on occasion sang or chanted in lyric dialogue with the actors; and their leader, the *koryphaios*, probably distinguished slightly by costume, might also speak in the dialogue. (For a fuller account of the elements of the formal structure of Greek tragedy see pp. 19–21.) The chorus's musical accompaniment was on the *aulos*, a double pipe with reeds (see plates 4, 6); and the *aulos*-player stood in the *orchēstra*, also in tragic costume. The choral dancing was normally in formation, either rectangular or circular in basis, and, while it might occasionally become quite wild and rapid (consider plate 4), it was usually rather solemn and decorous, a style sometimes called *emmeleia* (literally 'harmony', see e.g., plate 3). The dancing may have come to receive less emphasis in the course of the fifth century. The older rival of Aeschylus, Phrynichus, boasted 'The dance offers me as many forms as a dreadful night of storm makes waves in the sea'; but later a comedian complains 'The dancing was once a sight worth seeing: but now they do nothing. They just howl, stuck on the spot like paralytics!' Ancient Greek dancing was, in the broadest sense, mimetic or expressive. Using the hands, arms and body no less than the feet, it reflected the mood, emotions and character of its accompanying song. Unfortunately we know next to nothing of the music,[4] but the complex lyric metres were normally sung in unison with one note to each syllable. I have no doubt that every word was perfectly audible. Corneille may have written (*Arg.* to *Andromède*) 'je me suis bien gardé de faire rien chanter qui fût nécessaire à l'intelligence de la pièce, parce que communément les paroles qui se chantent étant mal entendues des auditeurs . . .': but not for nothing did the Greek tragic chorus rehearse intensively for months at the expense of the rich citizen (the *chorēgos*), whose privilege – or liability – it was to finance most of the production. Between their

songs the chorus will have stood (or knelt or sat) as still and incon-
spicuous as possible: their role was to dance and sing, not to be a
naturalistic stage crowd.

Anyone who has seen or heard a Greek tragedy will know what a
prominent and important place the chorus has in the performance as
a whole (however obliquely related their songs may be to the plot of
the play). If we find this hard to come to terms with, that is, I think,
above all because choral singing and dancing has no equivalent place
in our life to that it held in the Greeks' life (although the opera chorus
and church choir provide some weak analogy). For the Greeks a
chorus was an integral part of many communal occasions, religious
and secular – festivals, weddings, funerals, victory celebrations, for
example. A chorus lent ceremony and depth to all 'festive' occasions
in Greek life. And yet the chorus will inevitably receive comparatively
little attention in this book, since it is not as a rule closely involved in
the *action* and plot of the tragedies. There are exceptions, especially in
Aeschylus, but it is – to put it very roughly – the place of choral song to
move into a different world, a different register, distinct from the
specific events of the plot. The lyrics are not tied down in place and
time, in language, in the reasoned sequence of speech and thought,
as the dialogue is: they swerve through a sequence of associative,
often emotional, links into a highly coloured world of more wide-
ranging, universal and abstract trains of thought by deserting direct
'humdrum' relevance for the poetic connections of imagination and
universality.[5] If only we knew more of their choreography and music,
then the tragic chorus might find a larger place; but, as it is, my glass
will inevitably focus on the actors.

Three male actors, professionals in effect, took all the speaking
parts between them. This often meant 'doubling' several parts within
a single play – even from a god to a slave or from a warrior king to a
girl. Though they were helped by the mask and full costume, this is a
tribute to their remarkable vocal and physical versatility (and not a
token of some metaphysical notion of the fluidity of personal identity). One reason for the restriction on the number of actors was
probably that there were very few who were good enough for the
great city festival; and another that they trained at state expense.
However, all characters of high social status would be accompanied
by some appropriate attendants, all in grand tragic costume (at the
expense of the *chorēgos*). (The Greeks sometimes used the same slang
for these silent extras as the modern theatre: *doryphorēmata* – spear-
carriers!)

The tragic outfit was much the same for chorus and actors alike. The
costumes were lavish and ornate, though their splendour may have
increased with time from relative plainness (cp. pls 3, 5 with 6, 7). Spe-

cial parts called for special costumes: thus warriors wore armour (see plate 3), barbarians had trousers (plate 4), mourners were in black and so on (see further chapter 5). But the standard tragic dress, for both male and female parts, was a colourful robe from the neck almost to the ground with long sleeves, which was covered with decorative patterns of the kind especially associated with oriental weaving – whorls, stars, circles, zigzags, even animal figures (see plates 4, 6, 7). These special splendours were as far from everyday dress as they are from the monochrome 'togas' of modern productions or adapted bedlinen of Isadora Duncan. Characters would also wear or carry extra stage properties, some merely formal or decorative, others crucial tokens within the drama itself (see chapter 6).

Some actors may have had bare feet (see plates 3, 7), but the characteristic tragic footwear was the *kothornos*, a calf-length boot. They did not, as is widely supposed, have the clumsy and stilted high soles of the later Greek theatre, they had a thin flexible sole and were more than anything like the slippers of Athenian women (pls 5, 6, 8).

The common picture of the tragic mask with piles of hair and gaping grimace is equally anachronistic. The masks, which were made individually by a skilled craftsman, covered the whole head. They usually had plenty of hair, and, naturally, an open mouth; but fifth-century vase-paintings show that they were on the whole rather naturalistic and good-looking, solemn, but in no way grotesque or sinister: see plates 3?, 5, 6, 8. Now, the mask is an integral feature of the Greek theatre which we may find it difficult to accommodate ourselves to. It must direct attention, not to the unexpressed thought inside, but to the distant, heroic figure whose constant ethos it portrays. The mask will present a person in a role rather than the changing aspects of a fleeting personality. This ties in with the way that passion and suffering are not introvertedly wrung out through tiny, intimate gestures and facial movements, but are put directly before the audience's sympathetic concentration. The characters may still weep and even refer to facial expressions; but the emotions of Greek tragedy are presented openly in word and action, they are not left to be inferred or guessed at. The mask is in keeping with this broad explicitness.

The causes and effects of this masking are indivisible from the plain fact of the size of the *theātron*. Facial expressions and small physical movements would simply not be visible to the audience – not even the nearest, let alone the furthest away. In some respects we have a theatre not unlike Shakespeare's: a bare open-air acting-area with the audience on three sides, rich costumes and so on. But at the Fortune or the Globe no-one would be much more than 10 metres from the actors: and that is the distance at Athens from the front row to the middle of the orchestra, while some would be 50 metres away up the hill. In fact the entire Fortune theatre would almost have fitted inside the orchestra circle of Dionysus. Yet I do not believe it is impossible for anyone to imagine what every willing spectator at Epidaurus has memorably experienced: that those miniature figures down there in the orchestra may with their large, firm movements and their clear, ringing voices entrance the whole imagination and engage our every capacity for emotion and thought.

The whole style of acting will have been appropriate to the vast size of the theatre. This assertion is an inference rather than a known fact; but still there is clear evidence of the emphasis which was laid on the clarity and projection of the actors' voices. Thus Sophocles, it is said, had to give up acting in his own plays because of his weak voice. Just as the language of tragedy is in the high style, often employing vocabulary, phrasing and even prosody which was foreign to ordinary speech, so the delivery was, no doubt, given a timbre and tone in the grand manner – one reason why it was such an obvious target for parody by the comedians.

So actions and gestures must have been large and distinct. There is no place in this theatre for fidgeting, for the idiosyncratic twitch and reflex: stance, large use of the arms, and the whole style of movement must convey both the ethos of the characters and the significant action of the play. The Greek theatre has sometimes been characterized as 'statuesque'. There certainly were long periods when the actors would remain more-or-less motionless (this is, indeed, true of almost any theatre); but there is also quite a lot of movement in Greek tragedy, even if less than in most more recent drama. Indeed, one actor was able to overdo it enough to earn the nickname of 'the monkey'. It is safe to say that the text 'indicates' a great variety of movement.[6] Apart from exits and entrances, the range extends from the simple gestures which emphasize speech – movements and positioning of hands, feet or head – to rapid and fluent actions such as running, fainting or raving in madness. In between come kneeling, embracing, veiling, drawing swords, handing over objects, approaching, fleeing and so on and so forth (see especially chapter 5).

Every age seems to think that its actors are unprecedentedly 'natural' or 'true to life'. But this should not be taken to mean that the acting is cinematographically realistic: it means simply that the actors are able entirely to capture their audience's imagination. All acting must necessarily be more-or-less artificial and stylized (*pace* the 'Method' school), though the conventions and mannerisms change with fashion. But it is generally supposed that the Greek tragic theatre was particularly non-naturalistic and stylized. In so far as the acting had to be appropriate to the size of the theatre this is no doubt right.

But was the acting, within those limits, as naturalistic as possible? Or might there have been a whole range of conventional gestures and movements which were special to the tragic stage and which did not really resemble those of everyday life, rather like the modern mime – one thinks of Marcel Marceau? Modern productions often handle Greek tragedy this way (though my experience is that it alienates rather than involves the audience). Might we not go even further and argue that the action of Greek tragedy had *no* significant resemblance to real life, but developed a symbolic and highly formal code? The analogy of the traditional Nôh and Kabuki theatres of Japan might appear to offer some encouragement to such a supposition.[7]

Can we settle on any point between the two extremes of broad realism and of the totally non-naturalistic formality of the Nôh? Strictly speaking we lack the evidence. But I think there are reasons for inclining in the direction of the former rather than the latter extreme. The aesthetic theory of the fifth century, which applies to tragedy as well as the fine arts, uses the notions of imitation (*mīmēsis*) and illusion (*apatē*). This concern may be seen in the practice of sculpture and painting: the results are far from photographic, of course, but they are even further from a highly formalized non-naturalistic art. Also, vase-painting gives, so far as I know, no evidence of highly conventional tragic movements and gestures totally different from those of life.[8] The range of realism and convention in the Greek theatre might be gauged by the two pieces of stage machinery discussed on pp. 10–12. The *ekkuklēma* is a highly conventional and non-naturalistic device. On the other hand the dramatists wanted characters who are supposed to be flying to come literally through the air (even if on the end of a rope!). One would have thought that in any non-naturalistic theatre flying would be represented symbolically: yet the Greek theatre went to the trouble of inventing the *mēchanē*. Working within this range I should guess that an earthquake, for example, would be presented entirely in verbal and choreographic terms, or that the *skēnē* could without any additional scenery represent a wood, if required: on the other hand I suppose that when characters say they are coming or going or embracing or falling or carrying something, then they would actually be doing so in a fairly realistic manner.

The whole question of the relation of the text to the action on stage can be postponed no longer. We have, to all intents and purposes, no evidence besides the texts for what happens in the action of the plays. And, bearing in mind that the text is far from a record of the whole production, does it tell us enough to fill a book on Greek tragedy in action? There are virtually no marginal stage-directions in the transmitted texts, and there is no reason to think that there ever were.

Similarly, only a few of the stage-directions in our texts of Elizabethan
and Jacobean drama go back to the author's hand. Lengthy and
explicit stage-directions are a comparatively modern phenomenon;
and in some extreme cases, e.g., Ibsen, Shaw or O'Neill, they seem to
verge on an attempt to blend the written version of the drama with the
novel.[9] One reason for their absence in earlier dramatists will be the
fact that the playwright was his own director, and so conveyed his
stage-directions in rehearsal. But there is more to it than that: in
Greek tragedy, as in Shakespeare, the stage-directions are incorporated in the words of the play (with the notable Shakespearean
exception of dumb-show). People say what they are doing, or they
are described doing it, or in one way or another the context makes it
clear what is happening. Chapters 4–9 will illustrate this fully
enough. So there is no call for extra stage-directions because they
would add nothing worth adding to what is already contained in the
words themselves.

This is perhaps an over-generalization, and we are occasionally left
in uncertainty. None the less I take it as a fair rule of thumb that the
significant stage action is implicit in the text. I say *significant*, because
there undoubtedly were many formal and decorative visual details
which are not indicated by the text. Thus, for example, vase-paintings
indicate that stage kings carried sceptres and that Trojans wore
Phrygian caps; yet these are not usually referred to. Similarly, noble
characters do not often refer to their attendants, nor old men to their
white hair; but we need not doubt they had them. And speech was no
doubt reinforced by suitable gestures. But the point is that such
details, while important for the overall economy and impact of any
production, are not really *significant* within the particular action of the
particular play. My claim is that if they are to be significant attention
will be drawn to them by the words.

This leads on to two awkward, and ultimately unanswerable, questions. How are we to know that there was not much significant action
which is given no indication in the words? And how do we know that
the action implied in the words was actually translated into action on
the stage?[10] To take the first question first, we cannot *know* for certain
that there was not all sorts of extra unsignalled stage business which
would have completely altered the meaning of the tragedy. Indeed
the interpolation of stage business which is not indicated by the
words is the chief weapon of modern reinterpretations of old plays – a
subject I shall return to in the final chapter. But the fact remains that
all the action *necessary* for a viable and comprehensible production of a
Greek tragedy is, as a matter of fact, included in the words. I chal-
lenge the reader to find from Greek tragedy one single indispensable
stage-direction, without which the play does not make sense, and

which is nevertheless not verbally signposted. You will not find one easily: and yet in any play of the last hundred years such actions, indicated solely by added stage-directions, are two a penny.

The point may be reinforced by a consideration of what such unsigned action would mean in practice. There are necessarily only two ways in which it might be incorporated: it would either have to be performed in dumb-show without words, or it would have to be acted out simultaneously with words which say nothing about it. But we have no evidence whatsoever of anything like dumb-show in Greek tragedy. And when most action is undeniably indicated in the words, why should there occasionally be silent goings-on which leave no trace? And, again, when it is perfectly normal to talk about actions as they are performed, why should occasional sequences be admitted which have no direct bearing on the words and no commentary from them? This would make for a confusing and purposeless duplication of attention. If the accompanying actions are merely decorative or formal, then well and good: but if they are unique and significant, then, far from having nothing to do with the words, they should be united with them. And the more significant the action, the more attention it should receive in the words. This argument does not claim to be logically flawless: it is an argument from elementary dramatic sense.

In general, then, an action which has attention drawn to it will be significant; and an action which receives no attention is insignificant. But how do we know, in the first place, that the characters actually did what they say they are doing? If earthquakes and landscapes can be left to the imagination, then why cannot actions, props, even exits and entrances? Again I cannot *prove* that they were not. And if the action was not translated into the visual dimension, then the thesis of the book is considerably impaired – yet not totally ruined since the things are still happening in the imagination of the audience even though not before their eyes. But I can seen no good reason for doubting that ordinary practicable actions were in fact performed. It may help to draw a rough distinction between 'passive' staging, that is large non-human effects like earthquakes and sunrises, which are best left to the imagination, and 'active' staging, which covers the small practicable actions, things which happen on the individual human level and involve the actor's personal participation. I should argue that 'active' staging was fairly literally performed on stage.

The arguments deployed against extreme non-naturalism (p. 16) may be revived and extended. As well as the fifth-century emphasis on illusion, the evidence of vase-painting and of the mēchanē, there is the parody of tragic performance in Aristophanes, and the evidence that dancing was mimetic. For if the chorus and actors imitated actions as they sang and danced, then there is all the more reason to think they acted out their words as they spoke. And there is a stubborn question from basic dramatic method: what is to be gained by *not* putting the words into action? All the aspects of Greek tragedy in action which are discussed in the following chapters gain enormously from the blending of the visual and the verbal, and they would be pointlessly impoverished if the movements and props and so on were not concretely represented. *Agamemnon* with an imaginary purple cloth? *Philoctetes* with no bow?

In conclusion, I shall assume throughout that virtually all the significant action is signposted by the words, that all practicable 'active' stage-directions were put into concrete terms on stage, and that the actions were generally performed in a large and formal yet fairly fluid and naturalistic manner. I admit that all three of these assumptions are unprovable; but this admission does not cause me serious misgivings. Let anyone who doubts these assumptions return to the question after reading the following chapters.

The formal construction of Greek tragedy

I shall have to give some account of the formal structure of Greek tragedy here, so that the basic modes of delivery and the constructive framework may be taken as read during the chapters that follow.

Everyone who has read, let alone seen or heard, a Greek tragedy must be aware that it falls into constituent parts. But without the familiar breaks of scene divisions, house lights, etc., it may well not be clear just how these divisions work. This is a surprisingly neglected subject, and, since there is no standard handbook to refer to, I shall have to begin by outlining the fundamental types of delivery.

At one pole there are the actors, whose basic medium is iambic speech. This may take the form of long speeches (*rhēsis*), or of dialogue, which, while it may be divided into contributions of any length, tends to fall into the rhythm of one line each (*stichomythia*). Actors may also on occasion speak or chant the less solemn trochaic metre or chant the more strongly rhythmical anapaestic metre. They may also sing lyric metres, either solo (monody), or duets, or in interchange with the chorus (lyric dialogue).

At the other pole is the chorus, whose basic medium is choral lyric sung in unison and arranged in sets of pairs of stanzas (strophe and antistrophe). But it may also sing short astrophic stanzas, or chant in anapaests, or (as already mentioned) it may sing in lyric dialogue with the actors. There are also spoken lines attributed by our texts to the 'chorus'; but, although there is no clear evidence, it is generally and reasonably supposed that such spoken lines were delivered by the chorus leader (*koryphaios*) only. Such lines are largely in stichomythia, but also include brief comments, though they never extend to a proper *rhēsis*.

These are the basic ingredients. What structural conventions and expectations govern their use? There is no agreed answer to this question, though I think it may be answered quite simply. The barrier to the truth has always been a chapter (12) to be found in Aristotle's *Poetics* (though it is probably not, in my view, the work of Aristotle). This chapter gives a set of structural terms and definitions which simply do not reflect the true situation once they are applied to tragedy of the fifth century.[11] So I shall simply discard this time-honoured aberration.

As I see it, the structural framework is based on the interaction of (i) the two main modes of delivery (actors' speech/choral song) with (ii) the articulation of the action through exits and entrances. The fundamental form is, then: enter actors – act – exeunt actors/strophic choral song/enter actors – act – etc. Within this frame (which is far simpler than the practice) everything except the strophic choral songs would properly come *within the acts* – that is to say, all kinds of speech, monody, duet, lyric dialogue, astrophic lyric, etc. all come within the acts. Even this oversimplified pattern would be far from monotonous, thanks to the wide variety of kinds of delivery permitted within the acts. Also the acts may vary greatly in length (we have, in fact, acts ranging from about 20 to 500 lines), and so might the choral songs between the acts (from some 20 lines up to 200 or so); also there may be exits and entrances during the course of the acts, though very seldom in rapid sequence.

In practice not one single surviving tragedy follows the framework laid down above without any variation or adaptation whatsoever (though Sophocles' *Antigone* comes very close to it). However, the variations and adaptations work within this framework and do not invalidate its underlying form. Thus, there are act-dividing songs which are not preceded by an exit or are not followed by an entry. Also, more importantly, astrophic choral lyric can occur in the act-dividing position, so can chanted anapaests, so can lyric dialogue between actor and chorus; and even occasionally the act division may be marked by nothing except the sequence of exit and entry. That is to say that the act-dividing function of the pure choral song may be varied and broken down in different ways and to differing degrees; similarly the sequence of action marked by exits and entrances is varied and broken down. The framework I have offered is both persistent and flexible: the exceptions prove the rule. This flexibility is found in the earliest tragedies; but some of its extreme manifestations, in particular the occurrence of lyric dialogue in an act-dividing position, became less and less uncommon towards the end of the century.

These indigestible technicalities may seem remote from the appreciation of particular Greek tragedies. But it is important to consider the structural sequence, or scenic form, of tragedy, and this will be a recurrent concern, especially in chapter 9; and I think this formal framework is needed before we can really get to grips with the plays themselves.

3 Introduction to nine plays

I keep six honest serving-men
(They taught me all I knew);
Their names are What and Why and When
And How and Where and Who. (Kipling)

This chapter aims to give a foundation on a factual and inquisitive level to the next six chapters, which will discuss various aspects of the theatrical realization of nine Greek tragedies, three by each of the great three authors, Aeschylus, Sophocles and Euripides. The restriction to nine is in the interests of depth at the expense of breadth; for in this way some view of each play as a whole may begin to emerge.

The nine plays are numbered thus: Aeschylus: (1) *Agamemnon* (abbreviated as *Agam*), (2) *Choëphoroi* (*Cho*, in English *The Women Bearing Libations*), (3) *Eumenides* (*Eum*, *The Gracious Goddesses*); Sophocles: (4) *Aias* (*Ajax*), (5) *Oidipous Tyrannos* (*OT*, *Oedipus the King*), (6) *Philoktētēs* (*Phil*); Euripides: (7) *Hippolytos* (*Hipp*), (8) *Iōn*, (9) *Bakchai* (*Ba*, *The Bacchant Women*). The sections on each play carry the number of that play (1–9) after the number of the chapter (4–9): thus *Ion* is discussed in 4.8, 5.8, 6.8, etc. A third figure distinguishes the sections of the discussion of each play, thus 4.8.1, 4.8.2, etc. The piecemeal discussion of each play necessitates a lot of cross-reference, and this is marked by square brackets as [see 5.8.1]. It also means that the plays are not treated sequentially from start to finish; but anyone who wishes to take the discussion of any particular tragedy in the sequence of performance may do so by using the 'index of passages discussed' and jumping back and forth at its command.

Before I briefly introduce each play and pose some of the questions which are to be encountered in the following chapters, two words on the origins of Greek tragedy: unknown and irrelevant. The theory that if we know the origin of something then we somehow know its essence has kept an extraordinary grip on human enquiry; but it is surely unwarranted. I can see no reason for thinking that, if we knew about the forerunners of tragedy in the eleventh or eighth or seventh century B.C., they would share anything significant with the fifth-century works, or that they would throw any light on them. It was during the 530s, in the days of the semi-legendary Thespis, that the tyrant of Athens, Pisistratus, gave tragedy an official blessing by bringing rural mumming to the city and making it an important part of his newly instituted Great Festival of Dionysus. For Pisistratus to have done this, 'tragedy' must already have developed far from anything crude and primitive: it was already a source of national pride worthy to demand everyone's attention for three festive days each year and to a considerable expense to the city and its leading members. Yet this is still 60 years and more before our earliest surviving tragedies. The art will have developed enormously during that time, maybe almost beyond recognition (consider vase-painting during the same period). Why should it not have developed even more during that time than it did during the 66 years spanned by our surviving tragedies?

Aeschylus may never have seen a tragedy produced by Thespis. He was born in the 520s and produced his first set of plays in 499 B.C. In his 43 years of productivity he created more than 60 tragedies.[1] Of these we have just 7, the 7 selected for pedagogic purposes in late antiquity (and the vagaries of transmission almost lost us a couple of those). All come from the second half of Aeschylus' output, and the earliest is his *Persians* of 472 B.C.; so we have no early Aeschylus and no early Greek tragedy. In 472 B.C.; it is already a highly developed and accomplished art-form. Aeschylus may not have the deftness and facility of Sophocles or Euripides, but he has a richness of expression, especially of imagery, a sure sense of theatre, and a depth of insight into human hopes and fears, which make him for some (including myself) the greatest of the Greek tragedians.

Agam, *Cho* and *Eum* were all performed as a trilogy on a single day in 458 B.C., just two years before Aeschylus' death. The *Oresteia*, as it was already known in the fifth century, may well have been Aeschylus' masterpiece: fine as the other plays are, especially the neglected *Seven against Thebes*, it certainly is so for us. Its vision of human destruction and restoration is realized on such a scale and with such

thematic depth and theatrical boldness that a worthy performance is
emotionally and intellectually an exhausting, and yet elating, experience with few comparisons. And yet the monumental framework
does not in the least diminish the intensity and integrity of each
particular play and each scene within each play. The trilogic construction is masterly, and yet each play within it might be (and has been)
performed separately.[2]

Agamemnon centres on the return home of Agamemnon from his
ten years at Troy, the return to his murder at the height of his
triumph. And yet Clytemnestra is the dominant figure of the play:
Agamemnon is on stage for under 200 lines (783–972),[3] and much
even of that scene is dominated by Clytemnestra. Why has Aeschylus
arranged things in this way; and what does he mean by the purple
cloth which so stains Agamemnon's scene? At the end of that scene
we know that Agamemnon must die: what bearing on his death have
the first 782 lines, over half of them choral lyric? And what about the
long Cassandra scene (1035–330) which comes in between Agamemnon's one and only exit and his actual death? This inevitably distances
Agamemnon's death from us, but is this in return for some extra
perspective? And the play does not end with the murder, far from it.
What is the purpose of the long and apparently inconsequential
confrontation between Clytemnestra and the old men of the chorus
(1348–576); and why is Aegisthus brought into the play so late, and
almost incidentally, less than 100 lines before the end? Given the basic
facts of his story, Aeschylus has made his drama in a far from obvious
way.

Choephoroi also concerns a return to kin-murder, yet it is a very
different play. The differences are, of course, grounded in the new
situations: Orestes has to approach very differently from Clytemnestra; and she, no longer the victorious wife, becomes the defeated
mother. But they also emerge in the whole construction of the drama.
A much shorter play, *Cho* is made in two distinct halves. The first,
which is set at the tomb of Agamemnon, is dominated by a huge
23-stanza lyric dialogue lament and invocation (306–478); and before
and after it Orestes and Electra hatch their plot. Why such a monolithic scene? What bearing does it have on what is to follow? Then,
with a change of scene to the palace, the pace changes radically: four
separate acts culminate in the murder, all within the space of 300 lines
(653–935). Why the *two* confrontations between Orestes and Clytemnestra? What is the point of the nurse and of the very short Aegisthus
scene in between? Unlike in *Agam* the murder follows directly on the
battle of words and wills, and the end of the play soon after that.
Orestes is driven back into exile with horrifying promptness. Is this
unexpected? And are there, after all, also similarities with *Agam*?

Eumenides is utterly unlike the other two plays. Gods walk the stage, the chorus itself is made up of ancient terrifying goddesses, the judicial standards of a great city are established, a primeval cult is instituted. How does all this relate to the rest of the trilogy? Firstly, there is something of the rapidity of *Cho* about the opening scenes at Delphi (which include a vindictive dream of Clytemnestra, the only character who appears in all three plays). Why this shifting series of clashes? Why the unique change of place and lapse of time at 234/5? And why still further delay before Athena arrives at 397? The trial scene (566–777) is tense and portentous; yet does it really resolve any problems? Has it something more than a 'purely antiquarian purpose', as one scholar (D. L. Page) has put it? And, finally, there is the great struggle and reconciliation that close the play (778–1047). Orestes and Apollo are wiped out from the mind: this is a matter for the City, Athena, and these strange goddesses who command blight and fecundity. Why has Aeschylus misled our response to the Furies, and how are we to accommodate this new view of them? Is this scene a purely Athenian issue? 'The last 350 lines of *Eum* are not an integral part of the trilogy. They are a loosely connected episode, stitched on its outside' (R. Livingstone). Are they merely a chauvinistic and political imposition, as he supposes; or does the end somehow resolve and summate the whole trilogy?

Sophocles, born in the 490s, produced his first tragedies in 468 B.C., only four years after the earliest surviving play of Aeschylus, and still twelve years before his death. But Sophocles lived on and continued to produce for another 50 years. Among the statutory 7 tragedies which we have out of a total of about 90,[4] only 2, *Philoctetes* and *Oedipus at Colonus*, are securely dated, and they are both products of his last five years, when he was well over 80. Yet I am not alone in thinking them perhaps the finest of the seven. *Electra* and *Oedipus the King* may well also be the work of a man over 70; and it is quite possible that we have no work by Sophocles before he was 50. For the other three (*Antigone, Ajax* and the *Trachinian Women*) have all been dated by scholars at various times between 460 and 420. The one I have chosen, *Ajax*, might be comparatively early (440s?), but I should not be dumbfounded if it turned out to come from the 420s.

It is rash to try to sketch Sophocles' talent on a thumbnail; but compared with Aeschylus he is plain. That is not to say that he is simple or straightforward, but that the issues are presented in a dramatic manner which is concentrated and severe. He is perhaps the most abstract of the three great tragedians in that the bare bones of his tragedies may be anatomized in terms of abstract nouns: and yet, at the same time, he is supreme in giving his thematic structure human shape, in making it immediate through the behaviour of people, and in presenting that behaviour through the medium of the theatre. It is, I think, above all because he is such a craftsman of the stage that he touches most directly and most painfully the very sources of human suffering. George Eliot was asked how Sophocles influenced her and went straight to the point: 'in the delineation of the great primitive emotions'.[5]

Ajax has reduced critics to bewilderment. For in Ajax himself we have one of the most powerful figures in heroic poetry; yet he seems to compromise his own uncompromising greatness, and, worse, he is dead too soon, leaving the play to drag on for another five hundred lines. Despite the critics, I have always felt that this is a great – not necessarily flawless – tragedy. Working on the assumption that Sophocles was in control of his art, the purpose of the sublime poetry of the (so-called) 'deception' speech (646–92) becomes at once the great problem and the key to the play. How does it relate to the heroic resolution that has preceded; and how does it bear on what follows it, especially on Ajax's unflinching death speech (815–65)? And then what are we to make of the last third of the play (866–1420)? 'Sophocles has more time than he quite knows what to do with', patronizes one critic (A. J. A. Waldock). Why is so long spent on the crude wrangling with Menelaus and Agamemnon? What are we to make of the changed attitude of Odysseus? And is anything solved by the end of the play? Whence this feeling that out of despair and meanness there is a rightness, a fitness to the scheme of things in the final funeral procession?

OT presents no such blatant problems of unity. The whole play revolves around the great will of Oedipus and around the very greatness that makes his fall all the more terrible. Often since Aristotle's *Poetics*, *OT* has been cited as the epitome of tragedy. And yet, while the reversal which hinges on appearance and reality may exemplify the tragic movement, the exciting 'jigsaw' or 'detective story' element of the play is certainly not typical. And there are plenty of problems. What are we to make of Tiresias, and of Oedipus' apparent inability to pay attention to him? Why the virulent clash with Creon? Why Oedipus' great distress at 726ff., too soon for the play to have reached its catastrophe? And this play also has closing scenes which are not straightforwardly related to what has preceded. For the moment which the play has been leading up to – Oedipus' realization of the whole truth – comes at 1185, still 350 lines before the end. Why the protracted recriminations, the final scene with Creon, the daughters? And what happens at the very end? But here, as much as anywhere, the most urgent problem is to ask what questions the play itself is and is not raising. Does Sophocles ask why Oedipus suffers, whether he deserves to suffer? Is Oedipus uniquely unfortunate? Or an archetype for Man?

It may be that *OT* has suffered from adulation since Aristotle singled it out as the flower of tragedy's growth: *Philoctetes* on the other hand has been generally underrated, though it has recently attracted more of the attention it deserves. It is easy to see why readers have been put off: there is no death, no thrilling action, no women characters at all – in fact the drama is largely made out of the interplay of only *two* characters, Philoctetes and Neoptolemus. But in performance there is a great deal of action, on a small but none the less telling scale. And Philoctetes and his bow stand for an entire world view, also represented by Achilles and Heracles, both dead: Neoptolemus is torn between their values and the very different world of Odysseus and the Greek generals. Out of this conflict Sophocles draws a supremely tense and subtle series of shifting relationships. Questions well up: What is the place of the bow? Of the oracle of Helenus? When and why does Neoptolemus first waver? Why the new start at 1222? Is Philoctetes too stubborn? Why does Sophocles press him on until an external intervention is required? Is Odysseus vindicated by the outcome, or is he utterly discredited? But the question which subsumes them all is – how does Sophocles wring so much tension and such profundity out of such spare material?

Euripides did not, as is often carelessly implied, come after Sophocles. He was a younger contemporary, and, what is more, his influence on Sophocles is clear (and vice versa). Born in the 480s he first produced plays in 455, the year after the death of Aeschylus (though no doubt he saw the original performance of the *Oresteia*), and thirteen years after Sophocles' first production. He died in 406, a few months *before* Sophocles (whose death so soon after seems to have been a problem for Aristophanes in composing his *Frogs* of 405). Euripides composed about 65 tragedies; but in his case, as well as the usual selection of 7, a single manuscript fortunately survived containing another 10 tragedies. So we have about a quarter of his output.[6] Nine plays can be dated for sure, and the rest within a few years; and it emerges that only 2, *Alcestis* (438) and *Medea* (431) – 2 of the best – come from the first half of his 49 years of activity in the theatre, and 8 at least date from his last decade.

It may be misguided to attempt to arrange our random sample of plays into periods. But the earlier plays, e.g., *Medea, Andromache, Hecuba*, fit best a 'classic' idea of tragedy. Noble figures struggle and endure in a world that gravitates towards destruction and waste. Sometimes they endure with dignity; sometimes they become savage, though none the less with a strength that gives them tragic stature. A blacker period seems to follow, including, e.g., *Heracles*, *Trojan Women*, and *Electra*: here the sheer intensity of human anguish sometimes seems to be the only grace in a pointless universe, in a cruel anarchy where human friendship and kindness persist but are not redeemed. Between this stage and three final and problematic sagas of melodrama and pathos (*Orestes, Phoenician Women* and *Iphigenia at Aulis*) come three curious 'romances' with happy endings, *Ion, Helen* and *Iphigenia among the Taurians*. These are clever, poignant plays, in which fate harmonizes with luck instead of misfortune, and discovery leads to integration instead of the desolation more charac- teristic of Euripides. Whether or not there is anything to this crude chronological ordering, I have chosen one earlier play, *Hippolytus*, first produced in 428, and one romance *Ion*, dating from about 413. My third play, *Bacchae*, does not fit the scheme, for although it was one of Euripides' last plays, first performed after his death, it does not go with the three late 'melodramas': rather, its tight structure and balanced catastrophe align it with *Hippolytus* and the earlier plays. But its theatrical qualities command its inclusion.

Now I will not disguise the fact that I find Euripides the least great of the three great tragedians. His oeuvre is uneven in quality, and several of the tragedies are very uneven internally; but I have chosen what I take to be three of his very best plays. He is the most explicitly intellectual of the three, and sometimes contrives set-piece conflicts for the sake of the issues themselves rather than integrating those issues in a convincingly human setting. These may be brilliant; but judged by the highest standards they are still flawed. There is (as has often been said) a resemblance to Shaw in the vigorous pursuit of verbal conflict. But Euripides is also (like Shaw) a great dramatic technician; and he is able to extract the last twist of pathos from tragic situations. More tears, I suspect, have been shed over Euripides than over Aeschylus and Sophocles together. Above all he excels in the lyric expression of emotion in aria and duet. His weaker plays lack the sustained and integral theatricality of Aeschylus and Sophocles, since they tend to disengage the dramatic effects from the intellectual stuff and to lapse into monotony or dissipated diversity; but, even if this is true of some plays, it hardly applies to the three I have chosen.

Hippolytus was not the first play which Euripides produced that concerned Phaedra's adulterous passion for her stepson. But in the earlier tragedy (now lost) she had brazenly importuned Hippolytus to his face. This prompts the questions: Why in this play does she attempt to hide her passion? Why does she fail? Why does Euripides studiously avoid a face-to-face meeting of the two, and shift culpabil- ity on to the Nurse? There are four major characters in the play, and yet not once is there an open full-scale clash between them. Then, granted that Hippolytus must suffer, why must his fall drag down Phaedra and Theseus as well? What is the place in all this of the two goddesses who appear at the very beginning and end? How do they compare with the struggling humans? This is very clearly a two-part tragedy: Phaedra is dead (786) before Theseus ever arrives (790). What unites the two halves? Hippolytus himself is the overt link, of course: a self-righteous prig, or a model of youth so pure that he cannot be allowed to live?

Ion has usually been noticed for two aspects, neither of which do the play full justice in my view. First, it has been seen as a forerunner of New Comedy and hence of the mainstream of European comedy. Certainly we must take account of the paraphernalia of exposed babies and recognition tokens, and we must ask how much of this odd play is meant to be laughable, bizarre, or in some way not in earnest. But it is much more rewarding to ask how far the play *is* serious; whether Euripides contrives to heighten emotion and poignancy by means of a fanciful setting and an impending happy ending. Second, *Ion* is seen as some kind of theological propaganda, either an exposée of Apollo's unworthiness to be a god, or as a vindication of his providence against human faithlessness. Certainly we must ask why Apollo's scheme goes awry, and why he has caused a woman like Creusa such anguish: does the ending make up for the suffering that has gone into it? But the damnation or defence of Apollo is not the central point, surely. Human vicissitudes, Creusa's and Ion's, are the core of the play; and it is the setting of these in a distant fairy-tale world that gives them their piercingly touching qualities. What drives Creusa on? What does *she* feel about Apollo? What dilemmas tear Ion? Does he develop in the course of the play? And why is so much of the play in one way or another about *Athens*?

The problems of *Bacchae* tend to be similarly reduced to a decision between the damnation or vindication of Dionysus. There is rather more reason in this case, since the god takes an active part in the play, disguised as a human, and hence invites assessment in human terms. But in the end it is the sheer fact of Dionysus' power, rather than any moral assessment of it, which impels the play. But what are we to make of his opponent Pentheus? Does he have any control over his behaviour? If he does, then when does he lose it, and what are we to feel about his humiliation? Fascinating though the god himself is, I find the final scenes (1165–392, but originally some 300 lines), the scenes with Agave and Cadmus, no less powerful, no less what the play is 'about'. What are we to make of their calamity and of their attitude to the kindred-god who is responsible? And how does this fit with the sublime lyrics of the bacchant chorus, now virtually reduced to silence? The play is much more than a simple clash of ecstatic liberation with repressive authoritarianism. Does the emotional sequence and theatrical scoring help us to sort out its ambivalence? Or is that ambivalence intractable to analysis?

A chapter of questions. All of them are no more than tendentious elaborations of a single one: why has the playwright made his play in exactly the way that he has? Now, to ask the right questions is to be half way to the right answer: but by raising certain questions and putting them in certain terms the critic is, of course, begging many others. I do not pretend that my questions are the only ones; and the following chapters do not pretend to provide definitive answers. But perhaps they are a start.

4 Exits and entrances

*'Pshaw! What the devil signifies how you get off! Edge away at
the top, or where you will. . . .' (Sheridan, The Critic)*

It may seem odd to start with the moments when people are on the
verge of absence, but a second glance sees that entrances and exits
mark key junctures in a play – the beginnings and ends of acts, the
engagement and disengagement of characters, the changes in the
combination of the participants which alter the whole tone and direction of the drama. The timing, manner and direction of these comings
and goings are fully in the control of the playwright, and his disposi-
tion of them may well signpost the way to our understanding of what
he is about. The precise event, seen in its larger context, draws
attention to the relationships on either side of it. Entries which come
late in an act, exits which coincide with entries, arrival and departure
in silence, the first entry and final exit of the play – all these are special
junctures which reveal the alignment and re-alignment of interest.
An entry provides the first impact of features of person, dress,
stage-properties and so on; the manner and destination of an exit
conjure up the future, the consequences of the scene we have just
witnessed. All these potentialities depend on the context which is
built up, especially by means of preparation, anticipation and predic-
tion.

My special concern in selection has been with what Maynard Mack has called 'the emblematic entrance and exit'.[1] It is not hard to find illustrations throughout Shakespeare, from the sobering shock of the unforeseen arrival of Marcade (*Love's Labours Lost*, V.ii.706ff.), which suddenly overcasts affairs of state, of responsibility and of death to cloud the long holiday of idle quibbling, to the long-awaited final mission of Ariel, who speeds off at Prospero's command, as so often before, yet this time away to his freedom in the elements (*The Tempest*, V.i.316ff.). But Shakespeare, by comparison with Greek tragedy, is a hurly-burly to and fro – there are so many more characters, so many scenes, often short. The measured pace and large-jointed construction of ancient tragedy means that there may be as few as five entrances (and hence five exits) in a whole play; and there are seldom as many as twenty. This throws even more weight onto the structural cruces; and they are often prepared for repeatedly, sometimes hundreds of lines in advance, so that the mere paces on stage become vital, focal events. Moreover, these are large eye-catching movements, especially in the Athenian theatre, where a character might traverse 15 yards or more. This provides the dramatist with an obvious opportunity to emphasize whatever dramatic aspects he wishes to bring out. And the two side-ramps – *eisodoi* – are treated as part of roads leading to and from the place of action; entrances and exits are hardly ever a matter of simply stepping into or out of the action, they are proper arrivals and departures.

[4.1.1]   In many Greek tragedies the stage-building represents a royal palace, and this convention is not usually given any prominence. But in *Agam* Aeschylus exploits the association in Greek society between the house and the household, the family and the family property, to make the house itself a brooding presence, an integral and fixedly disturbing background to the drama.[2] The *skēnē* is the house of the kings of Argos, the Atreidai; and the home should represent the secure central hearth of the family, the storehouse of its prosperity, the core of its religious life, fertility and joy. Above all, at the beginning of peacetime after war it should stand for all that is good in life. Yet the watchman on the roof of the palace at the very beginning of *Agam*[3] sounds the discord which will reverberate through the trilogy: he rejoices to see the beacon of victory and yet

> the house itself, could it but get a voice,
> would speak out all too clear. (37–8)

In the *Oresteia* there is no cause for gladness which is not somehow flawed or perverted or stained, not until the end of *Eum* [9.3.2]. This house, which has all the appurtenances of a prosperous palace, will, in the penetrating visions of Cassandra, be exposed awash with blood and corpses, the slaughterhouse never left by the Furies, where children sit clutching the meat of their own vitals. Even Clytemnestra is brought eventually to see that it is the dwelling of the evil demon of the Atreidai [9.1.2].

The *threshold* demarks the frontier of the house, and it is no surprise to find that the doorway in and out of the palace has an important place within the play. Cassandra sees these doors as 'the gates of Hades' (1291). And the watchdog of the gates is Clytemnestra (the image is explicit in 607, 1228). She controls the threshold and everyone in *Agam*, with the exception of Cassandra [9.1.1], uses the door on her terms and under her supervision. This is the key to three entries she makes at very different moments, but each when all attention is turned to the closed doors which she lurks behind.

Up to the point when the advance messenger has delivered his good news only Clytemnestra has used the door. But the chorus has no sooner advised him to go in and tell the Queen –

> This should concern the house, and Clytemnestra
> above all, as well as reward me. (585–6)

– than Clytemnestra enters and stands there in the doorway, almost as though she knows that all thoughts were turned to her. Agamemnon's mere herald shall not encroach on her dominion. She has no need for news, she knows everything already; she gives the man a message of false comfort to take to his master, and she goes back into her kennel (614). The messenger stays to give his bad news of the loss at sea of Menelaus and the other Greeks. Clytemnestra's entry is like rennet to the freshness of his joy at coming home.

Next Agamemnon's own scene is soured by the entry of his house- [4.1.2] keeper. His triumphant return home is carried off with due gravity and decorum, until the point when he prepares to enter his own house.

> I now enter my halls, my hearth and home,
> where I shall first give greetings to the gods,
> who sent me far, and now have brought me back.
> Victory has followed me; so may she remain. (851–4)

Clearly he means to go in; the great victor, after ten years away, is about to regain his own threshold. But before he can even leave his chariot, Clytemnestra faces him in the doorway: he can only go in on her terms, and those terms mean defeat and death. At the very moment that the triumphant king prays for victory to stay with him, his conqueror stands before him – not on the battlefield, but on his own doorstep. The great scene which is inaugurated by this master-stroke of sinister irony will be considered in 6.1.1.

Next I turn to Clytemnestra's final entry in *Agam*, her fifth, the [4.1.3] zenith of her deadly day. After Agamemnon's death cries have rung out from behind the doors [7.1.2], the chorus of Argive elders is at a loss what to do, and in a series of twelve couplets (1348–71) they dispute one by one whether they should rush inside or wait and see. The second even urges 'I think that we should break in at once . . .', but as they prevaricate they move away from action towards stupefied anticipation. Then, suddenly, Clytemnestra is revealed in the doorway, standing by the corpses [8.1.3]. Now, the twelve couplets, which are quite without parallel,[4] are often criticized as betraying Aeschylus' embarrassment over the convention that the chorus cannot leave the stage. But their uncomfortable inactivity is purposely protracted in order to lead up to and contrast with the incisive entry of Clytemnestra: the fifteen men dissipate their resolution in doubt and argument, just as in their earlier choral songs, while she is sure. Throughout *Agam* the men waver and dither, while Clytemnestra decides and acts.

[4.1.4]   And, finally, at the very end of the play Clytemnestra shows once more her control of the threshold, this time implicating Aegisthus in a way that visually ratifies his fatal complicity. Clytemnestra speaks the final couplet:

> Forget the yelping of these doddering fools: we two,
> you and I, shall rule this house, and we shall make all well.
> (1672–3)[5]

With these words she takes Aegisthus into the palace. He has come late into the play (1577); and he presents himself as an exile who has returned to righteous revenge – he thus foreshadows, in some ways, the role which Orestes is to assume against him [9.1.3]. Aeschylus has deliberately thrust Aegisthus back from the central actions of the play, where Clytemnestra alone takes the initiative and rules the roost. He took no practical part in the murder, as he himself admits:

> And so I gripped him, though I was not there,
> by catching every rigging of the plot. (1608–9)

Aegisthus has come from outside, in terms of stage direction as well as dramatic function; and it is only at the very end that Clytemnestra takes him, hustles him almost, in through her doorway, and we see him inextricably entangled in the evils of the house, spotted by its bloodshed, tarnished by its wealth. He triumphs for the time being – 'like a cock strutting by its hen' (1671); but in the next play he will pay the price.

Notice also how the old men leave in silence. This is most unusual, since the chorus normally sang, or chanted, a lyric, often very brief, as they followed the *aulos*-player off stage (this was known as an *exodos*).

It is possible that some closing lines have been lost from *Agam*, but, assuming that they have not, this silent dispersal must show their dejected, yet hostile, subordination to Clytemnestra and Aegisthus.[6] To some extent they represent the city as a whole which suffers a humiliation by the regicide. But for the moment they are powerless to do, or even say, anything more: they can only steal home and wait in surly silence for Orestes.

In the light of all this we can detect an irony and pointedness in [4.2.1] Clytemnestra's exits and entrances in *Cho*. The contrast with *Agam* brings out her disablement, her defeat: this is considered more fully in 8.1.1/8.2.1 and 8.1.2/8.2.2. The tables are already turned when Clytemnestra first meets Orestes at the door (668ff.), but the full implications of the staging come into focus when Orestes and his mother confront each other the second time (892ff.), all deceit stripped away. They both of them face the stark prospect: for 38 dogged lines they dispute for Clytemnestra's lifeblood. The outcome is also given a spatial dimension, in which the threshold of the ancestral palace is the line which divides life and death, as it was in *Agam*. Orestes means to kill his mother inside, where he has already killed Aegisthus: 'Come with me: I want to cut your throat right over him' (904). So the dispute is over whether Clytemnestra will be taken in through the door: if she can stay outside, she lives; if she once goes inside, then that very action means her death. She battles for control of the doorway, but it is a lost cause. When Orestes takes her in at 930, she has finally lost her domination over the frontier of the palace, and with it her life [see further 8.2.1/8.2.2].

Orestes' first entry and last exit in *Cho* make a telling pair of [4.2.2] converse stage-movements. His return opens the play, and his initial entry is a positive action within the drama: 'For I have come to this land, and come home . . .' (3) (as Aristophanes' Aeschylus rightly explains at *Frogs*, 1152ff. the two verbs are not pleonastic since Orestes' arrival is also his return). The beginning is hopeful and correct; and the cleansing righteousness of the revenge-return carries us through the play with a vague optimism as to its consequences – perhaps Orestes really will be securely re-established in his own house, as the chorus hopes in its song at 783–837. Once the deed is done, however, the scales of naive hope fall from our eyes, the mother's curses can no longer be glossed over, the looming aftermath of bloodshed must willy-nilly be acknowledged – and not faced, but fled. Orestes begins to go out of his wits as he sees Clytemnestra's hounds, the Furies, who will pursue him to Delphi, and beyond.

> You cannot see them, but I can, all too well,
> I am hounded, and can no longer stay. (1061–2)

And suddenly the ancestral heritage, Argos, the palace are all abandoned, and Orestes is gone. When Cassandra in *Agam* prophesied
that she would be avenged, she predicted that Orestes would return,
'a vagrant, an outlander from this his home ground' (*Agam*, 1282). But
Cassandra did not look beyond the death of Clytemnestra; when
Orestes sees that he must flee Argos he uses exactly the same unusual
words of himself (*Cho*, 1042). He entered into the play a homeless
wanderer, and he departs at the end still a wanderer; his return and
his flight frame the entire play. His vagrancy is not yet over, he is not
yet restored to his house – his trials have but begun [8.2.3].[7] As
Orestes goes the chorus wish him well; but in the final *exodos*
(1065–76) they wonder whether this repetitive chain of bloodshed can
be broken. And the play ends with a question:

> O where shall it be completed,
> how shall it be brought to rest,
> and cease, this raging destruction? (1075–6)

[4.3.1]   A Greek tragedian might always, if it served a special purpose, take
his chorus off and bring it back on within the course of a play; but the
weight of convention was against it, and it was, in fact, rarely done
(five instances survive in all; for Sophocles' *Ajax* see 4.4.2). In *Eum* the
chorus of Furies leaves Delphi after 231, and re-enters, now at
Athens, a mere twelve lines later. There is not only the change of
place, but also a lapse of time, unique in surviving tragedy – it is not
made clear how long has passed, but it seems to be weeks rather than
hours, see 286 'Time, as it ages, purifies all things'[8] (cf. *Eum*, 75–9,
235–42, 248–51 [quoted below], 276–86, 451–2). Now, one often reads
that 'Aeschylus takes the chorus off in order that he may change the
scene'; but it is much more helpful to say that Aeschylus changed the
scene in order that he might take the chorus off and bring it back on
again. The pursuit of Orestes by the Furies began back in *Cho*, though
they were then visible only to him; then we see Orestes flee from
Delphi (93), and then the chorus set off after him:

> Led on by mother's blood, I press my case
> against this man, and shall run him to earth. (230–1)

Orestes has scarcely arrived at Athens when the Furies re-enter, hot
on his tracks (on the staging of this entry in scattered disorder see
8.3.1):

> Aha! Here are clear traces of our man.
> Follow the clues of our dumb informer.
> For, as a hound seeks out a wounded fawn,
> so we keep to the dripping track of blood.

> My lungs heave at our many killing toils:
> every region of earth has been explored,
> and I have pressed my chase over the sea
> flitting without wings, swiftly as a ship.
> And now he is somewhere cowering here;
> the scent of human blood tickles my senses. (244–53)

Their relentless coursing is not something we have to take on trust; we see it with our very eyes. It was a daring stroke to make the Furies themselves the protagonists, even the chorus, of a tragedy; now Aeschylus takes them off during the play so as to impress on us their merciless harrying of Orestes.

The Furies' re-entry at Athens embodies and welds together several of the recurrent complexes of metaphor in the *Oresteia*. Images of enfolding cloth or netting, prominent in *Agam* [see 6.1.1] connect through the hunting-net with images of *dogs* (compare and contrast the watchdog of *Agam*) – hunting-dogs who track their quarry until it is ensnared. The Furies are 'a mother's angry hounds' (*Cho*, 924, repeated verbatim at *Cho*, 1054). When, in *Eum*, the dream of Clytemnestra reproaches the sleeping Furies, she extends the metaphor to take in Orestes:

> But he is off; escaped you like some fawn,
> one that has slipped from the thick of your snares,
> he has sprung off leering over his shoulder. (111–13)

(cf. *Eum*, 131–2, 147, 230–1 quoted above). When the Furies re-enter so close behind Orestes the metaphor becomes personified as a horrifying reality. And they do not track Orestes by scent only, they follow a trail of *blood* (see 244–7, quoted above). With each successive murder blood has been spilt on the ground, and an insistent choral motif through all three plays is that blood which has once been shed cannot be recalled nor washed away – see, especially, *Agam*, 1019ff. [6.1.1], *Cho*, 48, 66ff.; and at this entry the Furies sing:

> A mother's blood once spilt upon the soil
> can't be recovered, no.
> Liquid poured on the ground, it seeps away. (261–3)

The theme of blood on the ground will be taken up again in the trial (647ff., 653ff.), and will find its final resolution only in the civic benediction of the Eumenides:

> And I pray that the insatiable evil of civil strife
> may never rumble in this city.
> May the dust never drink the dark blood of fellow-citizens
> and greedily quaff retribution
> murderous within the single city. (976–83)

The 'dumb informer' whose trail the Furies follow must be the blood of murder dripping from Orestes' hands (not, as one pedestrian scholar supposed, from his sore feet). The blood is on his hands at the end of *Cho* (see 1055), the Delphic priestess saw blood dripping from his hands (*Eum*, 41f.), and it leads the Furies on (233, quoted above). Yet Orestes proclaims to Athena no less than three times that he has been purified: 237–42, 276–87, 443–53 (see especially 280 'for the blood is drowsy and is faded from my hands'). He has been purified, and yet the Furies still follow the reeking trail: to resolve this contradiction Athena and her city have to take upon themselves the responsibility of a new civil way of arbitration. But that is yet to come. When at 235ff. we witness the re-entry of Orestes followed by the Furies, the stage picture brings to a head the motifs of the hunt, the quarry, and the irretrievable blood of the vendetta spilt on the life-giving earth. The images are made literal and yet retain all their associative metaphorical power. Poetry becomes drama.

[4.3.2]   As soon as the verdict of the trial is announced, Orestes makes his farewell speech of thanks, and departs for Argos (754–77):

> O Pallas, you are saviour of my house;
> I was deprived of fatherland, and you
> have settled me at home once more. . . . (754–6)

With his exit the '*Oresteia*' in the narrow sense is ended [but see 9.3.2]. We have seen Orestes as a wandering outcast, unable to do anything but to run and to put himself in Apollo's hands: but now that he is free and repatriated he can stand on his own feet, he can promise the eternal alliance of his city to Athens and even his own supernatural aid after death. His purposeful, confident exit marks the reversal of his former desperation; and shows his true return home in contrast to his 'return' at the beginning of *Cho* [4.2.2]. It also marks a watershed in the play, which is now to be concerned exclusively with larger issues. The transition at 777/8 is abrupt – it is bound to be, since the chorus is too closely involved to sing an interlude-song [see 9.3.2] – but it is by no means unprepared for. Already at 476ff. Athena foresaw that the Furies, if frustrated, would pour their poison on the soil of Athens. In his farewell speech and exit Orestes sums up the meaning of the trial for himself and for Argos, though not for Athens and the world at large. When he leaves the stage, the saga of his house leaves the play, or rather takes its place in a larger pattern.

[4.3.3]   And what about Apollo after the trial? His exit, though it has been neglected by scholars, poses a difficult problem: when does he go, and what does his departure tell us about his dramatic function? After the verdict Apollo is mentioned rather incidentally in Orestes' speech at 758, and indirectly by Athena at 797–8; and that is all.[9] His silent and unnoticed departure, whether at 753 or 777, would be extraordinary. There is nothing else like it in all surviving Greek tragedy; and far from being negligible, the audience would dwell on it, and search for its meaning. Zeus has used Apollo to ensure the acquittal of Orestes: Apollo has played his part in this (see 797–9), but now, it seems he has no further part to play, no more to offer. The final part of the play concerns the reinstatement and solemnizing of the Furies. This is at odds with Apollo's attitude towards them, since he has insistently, and mistakenly, dismissed them as merely outmoded ghouls. For him they are vampire monstrosities, and he thinks he can 'ride over them roughshod' (the verb *kathippasdesthai* occurs in Greek only at *Eum*, 150, 731 and 779–809). Can it be that the play now dismisses him? I ask this to sow the seeds of doubt whether Apollo in *Eum* is above reproach in the obvious way that Zeus and Athena are above reproach. His partial vision of the place of the Furies, his low abuse and tricky rhetoric at the trial – these might be taken to reduce his stature low enough for Aeschylus to push him from the stage without any attempt to justify him or to integrate him in the final scheme of things.

The marvellous procession at the end of *Eum* concludes the whole [4.3.4] trilogy. Athena leads (see 1003f.), followed by the chorus of Furies, now transformed into Eumenides or *Semnai* (1041, 'the August Goddesses'). Their movement is accompanied by the *exodos*-song, sung by a second chorus of escorts, who are, in my view, the Athenian jurors of the trial scene, the fathers of Athenian justice, and the 'men who hold the city' (*polissouchoi*, a word usually used of gods, in 775, 883, 1010f.). The accoutrements of the cult of the Eumenides also go to make up the procession: sacrificial victims, flaming torches, red robes [6.3.2], and female attendants. But this pageant would be far from gratuitous show: no less an event could convey the full weight of the final dispensation. This is a united, civic reconciliation in which all the tragic distortions of the previous trilogy are put to rights – fecundity, weather, wealth, blood, victory, the ritual cry (*ololygmos*), sacrifice, song itself, are all restored in their true form.[10]

The place of the exit itself may be brought out if we see the change of the function of the Furies in the context of the shape of the play as a whole, since the play has elements of a 'suppliant-plot'. We have five tragedies with this plot-pattern:[11] an outcast suppliant is pursued by vicious enemies and is rescued by a pious city, the pursuers are sent packing, and the plot tends to be rounded off by a procession in which the grateful suppliant is escorted off to the security of the city. But in *Eum* the suppliant, Orestes, has gone to Argos [4.3.2]: it is the cruel pursuers, the Furies, who have nowhere to go. They too have wandered, they too have suffered (see 248ff., etc.); but they are homeless and dishonoured. After the trial their destructive attention is turned from the individual to the city, and they are prepared to blight Athens with their poison, although they will suffer for it. If they blight the city, then they will wander homeless again; so Athena must persuade them to do the opposite – to bless and to stay.

> I shall not tire of offering you honours,
> so you may never say that you, old gods,
> by a new god and by these citizens
> were cast away dishonoured from his land. (881–4; cf. 851ff.)

So the long-term issue is also put in terms of theatrical space: will the Furies depart from a poisoned land, or will they stay? In return for a home, a cult, and an honourable function they decide to withhold their withering poison and to grant instead unblighted fruitfulness to their new home [see further 9.3.2]. Earlier Apollo drove them from Delphi and told them that by pursuing Orestes they would only find more pain (226), and that their proper home was a blood-lapping lion's den (193f.); but in fact, they find a civilized home and an end to their thankless wanderings. The trial of Orestes founds Athenian justice; and the solemn and benevolent procession at the end of the trilogy inaugurates Athenian prosperity. The justice of the civilized city must incorporate an element of fear, even the Furies [cf. 6.3.2].

[4.4.1]   Sophocles' *Ajax* opens with a most unusual dumb-show whose significance is only revealed in the ensuing dialogue between Athena and Odysseus. First, Odysseus enters cautiously, looking closely at the ground, then looking about, prowling tensely, approaching the doors of the *skēnē* with great wariness. After him comes Athena, who watches him calmly. Her opening lines at last clarify this puzzling charade:

> I have for ever found you, Odysseus,
> hunting to snatch some chance against your foes:
> so now I've long watched you beside
> the tent of Ajax at the camp outpost,
> long watched you following and scanning round
> his fresh tracks to see if he is in or not.
> And your searching, like some keen-scented hound's,
> has surely brought you to your prey. (1–8; cf. 36–7)

This explanation is furthered by Odysseus' reply, which follows a similar sequence of expression:

> Athena speaks, closest to me of gods,
> how well I know you, even when unseen . . .[12]
> so now you have well understood that I
> am on the track of a dangerous enemy,

> Ajax of the famous shield. It is Ajax,
> no other, I have long been hunting down. (14–15, 18–20)

Odysseus is, then, the wary dog *par excellence*, the hunter who tracks his enemy to the death, and no difficulty or danger will stop him from getting his man. Athena is a goddess of marked friendships and hatreds: Odysseus is her special favourite and she enjoys watching his skill. Ajax is a special enemy. Not only does she protect Odysseus and the Greeks from Ajax, she openly exposes his fatal madness for Odysseus to see and to tell all (see 66ff.). The dumb-show, inexplicable until put into words, presents the audience vividly with the dispositions and gambits which open the play.

Gods do not, or need not, change their purposes and their [4.4.2] enmities: mortals must, when appropriate, shift their ground and give way. But Ajax is too unyielding to change until too late; and in the end he has to yield and to die [see 8.4.1]. Odysseus will live and prosper, for he is a lesser man; but he is the wisest of the lesser men. He immediately takes the lesson of the prologue:

> Yet I still pity him, although my foe,
> seeing him yoked with cruel disaster –
> in this I am thinking of myself no less.
> I see that we are nothing more than wraiths,
> we mortals, insubstantial shadows. (121–6)

We do not see Odysseus again for nearly 1200 lines, but Sophocles has already prepared for the role he will play at the end, when he is responsible for the rehabilitation of Ajax. Compare his second entry (1316) with his first. When he returns there is nothing cautious or devious about him; there is not even the formality of an entrance-announcement, instead the chorus suddenly addresses him (1316–17) 'have you come to tangle or to loosen?'. Odysseus' entry is abrupt and forthright, and accords with his vision of the truth: 'I too shall come to this' (1365). On this firm ground amid the shifting sands Odysseus takes his stand.

Odysseus is perhaps the most obvious of the many interlacing [4.4.3] fibres which bind together a tragedy which is clearly and deliberately split in two by the death of Ajax [see 9.4.1]. Another visible and concrete bond is made by the two exits of the chorus. *Ajax* is another of those few plays in which the chorus leaves the stage during the course of the play and then returns [on *Eum* see 4.3.1]. As soon as Tecmessa hears from Teucer's messenger that Ajax should not have gone off alone, since his death is prophesied for this very day, she takes immediate action and organizes the chorus to search for him:

> Alas, my friends, protect me from this fate.
> Some of you hasten Teucer's coming back,
> and some go to the western coves, and some
> the east, to seek his fatal sortie out . . .
> Ah, what am I to do, my son? Not stay;
> I too will go wherever I am able.
> Come on, let's hurry. This is no time to rest.
>
>   (803–6, 809–11)

In a few more moments the scene is cleared; the chorus hurry off by either *eisodos*, and Tecmessa and the boy presumably go within. Suddenly the world of Ajax's tent, which has become familiar through the first 800 lines, is dissolved, scattered: the scene is set for Ajax alone. Quickly and unceremoniously the entire setting, including even the chorus, is dispersed in a last desperate attempt to save Ajax, the man round whom this miniature society was built.

[4.4.4]   With this hopeless dissolution in mind consider now the second exit of the chorus at the end of the play. Ajax's corpse has long lain there in full view (see p. 189 n.5). It has been the subject and the stage-focus of the preceding scenes, while its treatment has been contested: will it be moved and taken off to proper burial, or will it be left to lie there in the open for carrion (see 830 etc.)? At last the matter is settled, and Teucer gives the final instructions:

> Enough. Too much time has been let slip already.
> Some hurry and dig out the hollow grave,
> some set a lofty tripod over the flames
> ready for the last ablutions,
> and let one group fetch his armour from the tent.
> And you, boy, take hold with love your father's frame
> and lift him up to the best of your strength.
> The warm ducts still spout up dark gore.
> But come everyone, any here who claims the name of friend,
> hurry, go, and do your final service
> for this best of men, when he was one. (1403–16)

So all the close dependants of Ajax – Teucer, Tecmessa, the boy, and the faithful sailors from Salamis – take the mighty corpse off in a funeral procession. The purposefulness and unity and decorum of the action puts its meaning in clear visible terms: Ajax is saved, his honour is preserved, and his dependants live on together under his protection. Earlier the chorus had dispersed in disarray on a lost cause: now they march together on a mission which leads to a secure success, even as it marks the final fate of the tragic hero.

[4.5.1]   *OT* is by no means one long crescendo building up to the moment when Oedipus sees the truth about his past: on the contrary, it is a tempest of emotion, as Oedipus' self-confidence now rises, now sinks. He is at his most vigorous and elated, though most vulnerable, shortly before the truth strikes him in all its clarity [9.5.2]. A series of entrances and exits by secondary characters articulates the ups and downs of his state. When in the prologue Creon returns from the oracle at Delphi, Oedipus is eager for his news, which seems to be good. The king seems to have been almost superhumanly provident in his care for Thebes. Creon returns pat on his cue, and Oedipus eagerly addresses him even before he has a chance to speak (78ff.). Later, Oedipus has with similar foresight sent for the blind seer, Tiresias, who, it seems, cannot but help in the search; and when his approach is announced (297–9), Oedipus similarly importunes him to speak out, and addresses him for no less than fifteen lines, as Tiresias silently approaches (300–15). Quickly Oedipus' goodwill turns to exasperation, and then his fury turns to disquiet, so that the scene ends on a very different note [see 4.5.2 below]. And there is another entry in the play which seems to bring good news, while it serves, in truth, to take Oedipus one step nearer disaster: the messenger from Corinth at 924ff. [see also 6.5.1]. At the end of the previous scene Oedipus had reached a low ebb of foreboding and distress, consoled by a single hope; but when he hears that Polybus of Corinth, whom he supposed his father, is dead, he relaxes in giddy ridicule of his own fears (964ff.); and as more and more of the truth is revealed he becomes still more elated [9.5.2].

When Tiresias arrived Oedipus spoke while he remained silent: at the end of the act there is a reversal, and Tiresias has the last speech while Oedipus stands in silence (447–62). At the end Tiresias goes down the *eisodos* and Oedipus into the palace (he must go, since he comes back on at 531). It is unusual for any character in Greek tragedy to go off in silence, let alone one as dominant as Oedipus. It is so strange that some scholars have conjectured that Oedipus must go off at 446, and that the blind Tiresias speaks to thin air; but, apart from the fact that a theatrical trick of this sort is unlike the straightforward technique of Sophocles and that it would serve no purpose beyond its own ingenuity, this neglects the function of Tiresias' lines. Why should Sophocles have Oedipus stand silent and then go without a word?

[4.5.2]

> I'm telling you, the man you have long sought
> with threats and edicts, the murderer of King
> Laius, that man is here in front of us.
> Supposed an immigrant, he will emerge
> as native Theban; yet will take no joy

in that turn. For a sighted man will go
blind; a rich man become poor; and will walk
to an alien land, feeling with a stick.
He will emerge as brother and as father
to children, son and husband to the woman
who bore him, seed and slaughterer to his father.
Go in: work that out. If you find me false
then say my art of prophecy is nonsense.

[*exit Tiresias, exit Oedipus*] (447–62)

The point is that Tiresias is speaking in *riddles*. Not only is there a clear
allusion, in the stick, to the most famous riddle of all, that of the
Sphinx ('four feet, two feet, three feet . . .'), but much of the speech is
framed in the paradoxes characteristic of riddles.[13] It is repeatedly
stressed in *OT* that Oedipus gained the throne of Thebes because he
was the only man with the intellectual power to solve the Sphinx's
riddle (36, 130, etc.); and earlier in the scene Oedipus taunted Tiresias
with this very achievement (390ff.). But seers, like oracles, tended to
express themselves in a riddling way, and Tiresias often couches the
truth in more or less enigmatic words. The audience interprets him
easily; some of his speeches are plain enough, and all are transparent
to someone who knows the truth. But Oedipus does not take him at
face value, precisely because what the seer says is so monstrous that
he assumes that it cannot be literal – it must all be riddles. What
Tiresias says has so little evident contact with reality that someone
who does not hold the key will assume that it is enigma.

> *Oed*: Your words are all so dark and enigmatic.
> *Tir*: Aren't you the one who's best at finding answers?
> *Oed*: You taunt me just where you will find me great.
> *Tir*: Yet it was this same skill which ruined you. (439–42)

Oedipus' great achievement in the past was to see through the Sphinx
and that has seemed to bring him good fortune: now, in this play, his
mental strength is faced with another set of riddles, and this time the
outcome will be plain enough. It takes him toil and trouble to crack
them, but he does not rest until he has the answers [see 9.5.3].
Oedipus stands in silence and goes in silence at 447–62 because he
cannot yet make any sense of Tiresias' paradoxes – for if one cannot
see the solution to a riddle then it remains nonsense, and there is
nothing to be said.

[4.5.3]   At first Tiresias tried to restrain Oedipus' questions and to go
without revealing his knowledge, but Oedipus would not let him
(320ff., 332ff., 343): by the end of the scene Oedipus is only too glad to
see him go (430f., 444–6). This sets a pattern for the way that Oedipus

goes on to cast aside all well-wishing hindrances to his search. Creon is a moderate man, and all he wants is to be left in peace and ignorance: Oedipus rejects him even more vehemently than Tiresias. Once he is gone, Oedipus is left with Jocasta. As she comes to see the truth she too tries to hold Oedipus back from further enquiry (1056ff.); but he impatiently brushes her aside as obsessed with mere parentage. Now the king is stripped of his nearest links and is alone with two strangers (or rather links only of his earliest infancy). One last time the old shepherd tries to stop him from looking any further (1144ff.) – but the truth must out. First Tiresias, then Jocasta, even the old shepherd all try to restrain Oedipus from asking questions – as though ignorance were bliss. Ignorance would not, of course, change the awful truth, but the way that Oedipus overrules each of them accentuates his determination to know, the driving power of this play.

The final exit of *OT* seems to me to be one of the most problematic [4.5.4] stage-directions in Greek tragedy. I cannot fully gauge its significance; but, provided the end of the play is still as Sophocles meant it to be, then it certainly must be of great significance for a complete account. Someone who had read the play hastily might be forgiven for thinking that at the end Oedipus goes off into *exile*, since everything has been leading up to that. The Delphic oracle laid down that the pollutant murderer should be sent out of the land (96–8, 100; cf. 309), banishment is proclaimed by Oedipus (229, 241), Tiresias foretells that Oedipus will make his way blindly out of his fatherland (416f., 455f., quoted above). When Oedipus suspects that he was the killer of Laius he dreads that the doom of exile falls on him (917ff. esp. 923f.). And in the final scene he begs repeatedly to be cast out of the land (1290f., 1340ff., 1410ff., 1436ff., 1449ff.). Furthermore, it is clear where Oedipus should go when he stumbles from Thebes: to *Cithaeron*, the mountain between Thebes and Corinth.[14] It is, characteristically, Tiresias who first names it:

> What place shall not be harbour to your cry,
> where on Cithaeron not reverberate,
> when you find out your wedding . . . ? (420–2)

It was Cithaeron where the Corinthian 'found' the baby Oedipus (1026), and when the chorus sings elatedly of his origins, their words have the ironic second meaning that tomorrow Oedipus will return as a fellow citizen to the mountain, his mother and nurse (1086–93). The mountain is the link between the Corinthian and the old shepherd (1127, 1134); and when Oedipus, now blind, tells over the various links of Fortune, which have preserved him for this misery, he calls out

> O Cithareon, why did you harbour me?
> Why not kill me when first you took me? Then
> I might have never shown my birth to men. (1391–3)

And so, finally, exile and the mountain are brought together as
Oedipus pleads with Creon:

> Don't damn this city of my ancestors
> to suffer me alive within it. Rather
> let me be in the mountains, over there,
> Cithaeron, claimed my mountain, which my parents
> while still alive fixed as my proper grave.
> And thus, as they appointed, shall I die. (1449–54)

Yet the tragedy does *not* end with the final departure, so long and
ominously foreboded. Instead it peters out with a dialogue between
Oedipus and Creon (1515–23), which contradicts the emotional
power which has been collected in readiness for Oedipus' final exit,
his lone journey to Cithaeron, feeling his way with a stick. Instead he
is taken off into the palace where he will await a final verdict from the
gods. Creon had ruled back at 1432ff. that he would consult 'the god'
(presumably the Delphic oracle) before taking any action; and though
Oedipus justifiably protests that the original oracle was perfectly clear
(1440f.; cf. 1519), Creon insists on waiting for confirmation. And the
great cleansing final exit is abandoned. Why?
    In response to that question in an earlier draft Colin Macleod wrote
me an answer which I shall quote in full. 'Start from the last words of
the play, spoken by Creon [1522–3: "Do not desire to be master of all
things. Your past mastery has not stayed with you to the end of life"].
The point is that Oedipus, formerly the king, now cannot even
control his own destiny: he has to be in Creon's hands (Creon whom
he treated so sharply [532ff.]). The entry to the house is deeply
significant. Oedipus cannot escape from the place where he blinded
himself and Jocasta killed herself, to death or desolation: he has to go
on being humiliated and guilt-ridden where he belongs. I think this is
very fine: how Sophocles eschews the grand suicidal gesture (or even
exile), quietly "refuses" it to Oedipus, to bring out something far
more realistic, down-to-earth, and painful.' That is much more persuasive than any account I have read in print.[15]

[4.6.1]   Philoctetes first enters at line 219. Before that awesome moment his
arrival has been anticipated with apprehension, wonder and pity and
he is even heard off-stage slowly approaching. Odysseus cuts short
his account of Philoctetes' wound in case his arrival should be
detected (11–14); and he makes Neoptolemus search the cave. He
concludes from its squalid signs of life:

> Clearly this is the region where he lives;
> he must be somewhere near. For how could he
> get far, his limb infested with that old
> canker? He must have gone to fetch some food
> or some pain-killing herb he knows about. (40–4)

He then tells Neoptolemus to send his man as a look-out in case he is caught unawares (45–7). The alarm is never raised, but this precaution conveys the deadly fear that Odysseus has of a mere maimed castaway. The rest of the prologue (54–134) is taken up with Odysseus' instructions to Neoptolemus once Philoctetes should arrive. He persuades him that the end – the glory of the sack of Troy – must justify the means; and that the only means which will work on a man like Philoctetes are deceits, lies, false flatteries. The young man resists – 'I would rather do the right thing and fail than succeed by foul means' (94–5) – but Odysseus plays on his desire for advancement, and he agrees. Neoptolemus is then left to wait for Philoctetes, and the chorus of sailors enters to the first song. Sophocles has them know already about Philoctetes and his imminent return (though that does not mean they were present during the prologue), and they sing:

> Tell me, my lord, I am a stranger in a strange place,
> tell me what I am to hide and what to say
> to a man full of suspicion. (135–7).

In lyric dialogue they ask him anxiously how they are to behave when faced with the man himself, where he is, how he lives. Their anxieties alter to pity and to wonder (169ff.): 'How, how on earth could the poor wretch have survived?' (176).

Suddenly Philoctetes is heard approaching [see further 7.6.2]. For the whole of the last pair of stanzas (201–18) Neoptolemus and his men wait as the unmusical cries grow louder; and then Philoctetes stands there, squalid, crippled, in the doorway of his cave.[16] For a moment he must pause as he takes in the sight of the crowd of strangers on his desert threshold: this, then, is the man Odysseus cannot face, the victim, the dupe, once a great man, now maimed by suffering. Will his mind have become as savage as his appearance? The only evidence can be his speech. His first speech (219–31) is courteous, apologetic, open-hearted. He is in rags, but he recognizes their Greek dress (223–4); he is transparently noble and honest – are they?

> *Ne*: First, stranger you may be assured we are
> Greeks. That is what you wanted to find out.

> *Phil*: O lovely sound! To think that I should live
> to hear the voice of Greek after so long.
> What need, my son, has landed you? What mission
> has brought you here? What loveliest of winds? (232–7).

The scene is set for the rescue of the noble castaway. But what is
Neoptolemus' *mission*? These men in Greek dress have come to betray
him, as their compatriots had done in the past; and cruelest of all,
Greek is the language which is to be used to deceive him and to give
him false joy. Neoptolemus falters at first, but then presses on,
subservient to Odysseus [see 7.6.3]. Philoctetes' first entry presents
us with a man so racked, so lonely, so honest, that only the most
unscrupulous and ambitious could hurt him further. Odysseus, we
know, would do so if he could: but Neoptolemus?

[4.6.2]   I move on now to an entry which, far from being intensely
expected, is in many respects a surprise, though at the same time
thoroughly prepared for by Sophocles. Odysseus' insistence that
Philoctetes' bow can only be got to Troy by deceit is fully borne out by
events; and eventually it comes into Neoptolemus' hands [6.6.1], and
he himself falls in turn into Odysseus' hands [8.6.1]. The two of them
go with the bow, and leave the chorus with Philoctetes with instructions to follow them. In the ensuing lyric dialogue (1081–217) the
chorus makes a last attempt to persuade Philoctetes to come to Troy;
but it is bound to fail – at no point until the final epiphany of Heracles
does Philoctetes give way an inch in his determination to stay and die
on his island rather than help his hated 'allies' at Troy. Without his
bow he cannot get food; so he will go into his cave and there waste
away and be eaten clean to the bone by the very beasts on which he
would have fed:

> You birds of prey and you various fierce-eyed predators,
> all you who live and feed in this hilly island,
> no longer will you come my way as you flee from your lairs;
> for I no longer wield my former strength –
> my arrows – desolate as I am. . . .
> now is the time for you to glut your appetite,
> exact a bloody satisfaction on my discoloured flesh. . . .
> (1146–52, 1155–7; cf. 952ff., 1081ff. [quoted on p. 50],
> 1101ff.)

So his thoughts turn to death, and at the end of the lyric dialogue he
goes into his cave to die:

> O my city, my fatherland, would that I might set eyes on
> you.

What a sorry fool I was to leave your sacred streams,
and go to help the hateful Greeks.
This is the end of me.   [*exit*] (1213–17)

That is, it seems, the end. The will to win and the unscrupulous
ambition of the new men has prevailed: the stubborn honesty of an
outmoded generation of heroes is left to rot. The tragedy could well
close here; nothing which has gone before inevitably supplies the
momentum for a resumption. It will be made clear later that Philoctetes as well as his bow is needed if Troy is to fall; but up to this point
Sophocles has deliberately left this unclear, so that it seems perfectly
possible that Teucer or Odysseus himself might use the victorious
bow (1055ff.), and so that Philoctetes can be discarded and abandoned in earnest.[17]
    After Philoctetes' death-determined exit there is a pause, a void,
while it seems doubtful whether the play can continue. Then,
abruptly, Odysseus and Neoptolemus re-enter, already involved in
an argument (1222ff.).[18] Suddenly the play is off to a new start, and
the morbid, bitter ending, which seemed inescapable, is superseded.
The new energy is supplied by Neoptolemus' decision not to desert
Philoctetes, a decision which has been reached off-stage. Sophocles
has foregone the open presentation of this in order to make his
audience reconstruct it from what they have already witnessed. And
immediately it feels that it is right, indeed essential, that the heartfelt
pity and shame which Neoptolemus showed earlier should not have
been so perfunctorily overruled by Odysseus, that they must find
expression in action. The unsoftened juxtaposition of the exit of
Philoctetes and the return of Neoptolemus is highly original dramatic
technique, and it realizes in the theatre a deeply moving conception.
Sophocles fully explores the tragic consequences of the Odyssean
model of human relationships, before he supplants it with the Achillean.
    Finally, once more, the very last exit: Philoctetes leaves Lemnos.   [4.6.3]
His departure, so long delayed and so often frustrated [see 5.6.1], is at
last achieved in a few halting paces. After ten lonely years this is no
everyday departure. Sophocles has forged a strong bond between the
castaway and his habitat.[19] From the beginning in the detailed explo-
ration of Philoctetes' cave (15ff.; cf. also 152ff.) we are made aware of
the place as a place, rocky, comfortless, real. When Philoctetes first
tells of his painfully harsh life he is only too eager to leave it (285–313;
cf. 468ff.); and the chorus is so affected that they sing of the herbs, the
stagnant pool of water, the beasts he eats (676ff.) – and they temporar-
ily forget that his promised release from all this is merely a lie. But
when his saviour, the man he trusted, is found false, then Philoctetes'

attitude to his landscape changes its aspect. Betrayed and isolated, he
turns to those things which have stayed with him through his suffering:

> I call on you, you coves and promontories,
> you wild beasts who share my mountain habitat,
> you jagged crags, on you I call – I have
> no others to invoke, I cry out to
> my usual companions – see what
> this man has done to me, Achilles' son. (936–40)

His further pleas seem to meet with no response [see 7.6.4], and so he
turns back to his cave (952ff.), and acknowledges the ironic justice
that those he has fed on will now feed on him. It is in the lyric dialogue
at 1081ff. that this reciprocal intimacy with the landscape and its
fauna is most fully explored (cf. 1146ff., quoted above):

> So, you curved archway of my cave,
> hot or icy cold,
> I never was to leave you in the end, never;
> and you shall be with me at my death. . . .
> go, you birds, who used to cower down,
> go free through the whistling wind.
> I have no means to stay you any more. . . . (1081–5, 1092–4)

Mankind – not only the worst, Odysseus, but also the best, Achilles –
has let him down: so Philoctetes turns to the rocks and winds as more
constant.

   This, then, is the place he has to leave at the end of the play. The
most moving farewells in drama are naturally between two people:
yet this one between a man and a place can be ranked with them, for
those lame footsteps evoke a nine-year long intimacy ended. And his
final words say, and say convincingly, why it is that he must leave:

> Come now, I call upon this land in valediction.
> Farewell, dwelling which shared my watches,
> you nymphs of the water meadows,
> you broken-voiced booming of the sea and headland,
> where even in the inmost chamber my head
> was often drenched by the south wind's gusty spray,
> and Mount Hermaion returned an echoing groan
> as I hollered in the storm.
> And now, you springs of the Lykian stream, I leave you,
> leave you, as I never dared imagine.
> Farewell, o sea-surrounded land of Lemnos,
> and give me a calm and prosperous voyage,

where I am sent by mighty fate, the wisdom of my friends,
and the all-subduing god who brought these things about.

(1452–68)

Aphrodite and Artemis in Euripides' *Hipp* cannot be reduced to   [4.7.1]
elemental forces, which people may indulge or suppress, for there
they stand, visible and audible epiphanies, explaining their particular
angle on human affairs. Yet they are thrown by the vortices of human
passions and wiles to the beginning and end of the play. Their arrivals
and departures may indicate how much or how little they interact
with the drama as a whole.

Cypris (this is the name used for Aphrodite from line 2 onwards)
never shares the stage with a mortal. When she has just explained
how Phaedra must die, though honourably, so that she may punish
her enemies, she says:

But I can see Hippolytus approaching
from his hunting: I must leave these parts.
Along with him his festive followers
sing hymns of praise to Artemis. He sings,
and does not see the open gates of Death –
he does not know he sees his last sunlight. (51–7)

Now, this elementary device of having one character retreat before
the approach of another, though found throughout Greek tragedy
(cf. Aesch., *Cho*, 10ff.; Eur., *Ion*, 76ff.), was never common. It is
effective because it sets up a tense transition, and can provide a close
and suggestive link between two separate scenes; but it is, perhaps,
rather too hurried for the usual pace of Greek tragedy. Here we have,
obviously, the pathetic irony of Hippolytus' walking with unsuspect-
ing piety, without misgiving, into the trap, vigorously stepping into
the gaping gate of death. At the same time, there may be the suggestion that Cypris has to give way, to recede before his pure hymn to
Artemis. She can make any normal human being fall helplessly in
love, as she has Phaedra (27ff.), but Hippolytus is, it seems, imper-
vious to her designs; and the theatrical handling of the transition
insinuates that she cannot stand up to his presence. But, while there
may be these connections, there is also a vacuum between Cypris and
the play which is to follow. Although she has, in a sense, motivated
the whole tragedy, she takes no direct part in it: the struggling mortals
play out their roles independently.

Although Artemis is not similarly isolated, there is also in her scene   [4.7.2]
a strong sense of disconnection between the human and the divine
planes. In that she dispels ignorance, ties up loose ends, and explains
a future cult which will develop from the preceding tragedy, her func-

tion is like those other gods who appear at the end of Euripides' plays
– the so-called 'god from the machine'.[20] But, while all the others
make the very last entry of the play after the mortals have moved on
as far as they can see their way, Artemis appears to Theseus and
explains the truth, *before* the broken Hippolytus returns. It is he, not
Artemis, who will provide the resolution of the tragedy. When he
approaches (1342ff.), Artemis makes no response, and throughout
his agonized lament she remains unmoving and unmoved. And
when she speaks, she speaks with a detached sort of sorrow: 'Poor
wretch, bound to misfortune, your nobility of spirit has been the
death of you' (1389–90). Contrast Hippolytus, who, although he is too
disfigured even to see her, strains every failing sense to respond:

> Ah, divine fragrance! Even in my state
> I can still sense your presence, and my body
> feels relief. Artemis is near me here. (1391–3; cf. 85–7)

Artemis responds 'I see you; but my eyes are not permitted tears.' The
gods, unlike us mortals, are not allowed the consoling salve of tears:
instead, the goddess nourishes revenge (1416ff.), and offers the cold
comfort of a future cult (1423ff.). Her part played, Artemis goes:

> And so farewell. I may not look on death,
> nor blot my vision with a man's expiring.
> And I can see that you are close to it. (1437–9)

Again Hippolytus' last words to her have the extra pull of human
feeling:

> Fare you well too on your pure, blessed way.
> How easily you leave so long a friendship.[21] (1440–1)

It is the ease, the detachment, of Artemis' departure – no touch, no
mutual movement – which the scene conveys in performance; and
this sharpens the contrast with the brief final scene (1442–61), full as it
is of human love and regret [5.7.4]. Just as Artemis' arrival is over-
whelmed by that of Hippolytus, so her farewell pales before that of
the mere mortals. These are the Homeric gods, blessed, immortal and
thus untragic: a foil to the misery, and yet nobility, of the mortal
condition.

[4.8.1]   *Ion* is sometimes not taken seriously because it is set in a gilded
world of Delphic fairytale: yet much of its power derives from the
tension between that brightness and the dark struggles and seethings
of human feelings. An illustration is the slight entrance from which –
within Euripides' fiction – the play takes its name. The oracle told
Xuthus that 'the first man I met . . . as I came out (*exionti*) of this holy
temple . . . was born my son' (534–6). The boy he meets, since he has

no family, has no name ('I am simply called "Apollo's slave", and so I am' 309); so Xuthus, as his father, names him:

> 'Ion' I name you, fitting the event,
> since I first met you as I came out from (*exionti*)
> the holy shrine (661–3)

(*exionti* is compounded from *iōn*, 'coming'). At the end of the play Athena explains that the Ionians shall be named after Ion (1588f.). All this is pretty and petty enough; but the moment when Xuthus emerges from the oracle is also a turning point in a deeper sense. One of the central concerns of the play is the change which Ion has to undergo from carefree servant to the responsible heir of a kingdom and founder of a race. It is Apollo's gift of the anonymous boy to Xuthus which sets this process irreversibly in motion (as was laid down by Hermes in lines 69–75).

The difficulty of this development in Ion is conveyed in the scene at   [4.8.2]
576–675, after the first joy of the (false) reunion between father and son has subsided. When we first saw Ion he was the exemplar of childlike innocence [6.8.1]; and though his long scene with Creusa (237–400) introduces him to noble suffering, to the possible pains of parenthood, and to the notion that gods might be immoral tyrants, he is still able to return, with some misgivings, to his sacred servitude (434ff.). He still belongs to Apollo. But the apparent blessing of finding a father brings disquieting consequences close behind. He must, of course, go to his father's city and become his heir (576ff.). But his father is not an Athenian by birth, the kingdom goes with his wife, the Erechtheid Creusa, and should descend to her children: so he will be the usurping bastard of a foreigner. And Athens is a great city, full of ambition, faction, resentment (585ff.) – 'things do not keep the same aspect, seen from afar and from close to' (585–6). To exchange a father and a throne for carefree servitude under these conditions is a doubtful gain (633ff.); yet he must go (668).

In terms of plot most of the rest of the play is taken up with the attempt of Creusa and those who are loyal to her to prevent the new-found interloper from ever reaching the royal house which he has no right to. (Xuthus has played his part and is dismissed from the play.) Repeatedly their aim is put in terms of stopping Ion from making the crucial journey to Athens – see 719ff., 836ff., 1291ff. Through all this Ion (like the audience) learns much of the world, much of the emotional strength of legitimacy, heritage, jealousy, shame – of the dark motives which will drive people to impiety and to murder, if need be.

None the less, Ion will in the end go to Athens as the legitimate heir of the ancient line. Only, we are made to feel, after all these perilous vicissitudes can the temple boy go to become ruler of a great city. It is Athena who appears as the 'god from the machine', not Apollo; because she is the protector of Athens and it is the future of Athens that is at stake in these events:

> Creusa, take this man, your son, to the land
> of Cecrops, set him on the royal throne;
> for he's descended from Erechtheus' line,
> and it is right that he should rule my land. (1571–4)

After her speech the change of metre (1606ff.) marks the impending movement, and, as the lines are split between the three speakers, the mother and son begin their momentous journey to Athens under the protection of Athena:

> Cr: My son, let us go homeward now.
> Ath: Go and I shall accompany you.
> Ion: Propitious is our escort.
> Cr: And she loves our city well.
> Ath: Take the primaeval kingship.
> Ion: It is a fitting heritage.
>   [exeunt]   (1616–18)[22]

Ion leaves as a man the play he entered as a boy: he leaves the obscure innocence of his Delphic daily round for pan-hellenic fame (1576). A fair exchange? Whatever the loss, the gain is unquestioned.

[4.8.3]   However we are to regard Ion's farewell to innocence, the final departure of Creusa is undeniably moving. All these years she has lived with and relived the shame of her rape and the anguish of exposing her baby: she can tell over every detail, and she recalls the places and events of her ruin no less than four times, each time with a different emphasis (330–56, 881–922, 936–65, 1478–96). Her ordeals are now recompensed, and the divine scheme made clear. Whether or not her eventual happiness makes up for those years of misery, it is far better than no happiness at all. Creusa first entered weeping: she leaves as the fruitful link in a great dynasty. At the beginning she sent on her maids, the chorus, to wonder at the awesome beauty of the Delphic monuments (184ff.); but she herself follows after, dwelling as ever on the blighting of her life:

> The truth is, as I saw Apollo's house,
> I looked back upon an ancient retrospect;
> and so my mind was back at home, though here. (249–51)

Almost as soon as he sees her Ion sums up her contrariness, that she weeps in the setting where all others take delight (241–6). While Ion will learn that the world contains much suffering, even where Apollo moves in it, Creusa will learn that suffering is not pointless, not, at least, when the gods move it. At the end after Athena's speech she approaches Apollo's temple:

> Now I praise the Phoebus whom I formerly dispraised:
> he has restored to me the child he had discarded.
> And these doors to his oracle, once hateful in my sight,
> now look most lovely. And see, I cling to the fastenings
> in joy, and I greet these gates with love. (1609–13)

It is an irresistibly heartening moment, when the once weeping, childless queen becomes the devotee of the god, clinging to the merest external token of his providence.

Lastly, an illustration of the way that Euripides uses his theatre to convey the strength of emotion, in this case of loyalty and hatred. When Creusa's faithful old servant (her father's 'tutor', *paidagōgos*) first enters he is so decrepit that he can scarcely climb to the oracle and see his way (738ff.). The full depth of the disasters of his house reduce him to despair; he covers his head and weeps (967). This is the low point, and Creusa's consolatory cliché – 'that's life: nothing stays the same for ever' (969) – begins a revival of spirit, albeit destructive, in reaction against the blighting of prosperity. As his plan for revenge by the murder of Ion takes shape, the old man regains strength and enthusiastically grasps his part in the plot. He receives the poison and sets off: [4.8.4]

> Come on, my aged limbs, there's work to do,
> you must become youthful, if not in years.
> Stand by your rulers and against the foe:
> you too must kill and root him from our house.
>
> (1040–4)

As he goes, with much less business than he arrived, he is almost rejuvenated by his murderous mission – and he would have succeeded, had not the supernatural intervened.

In *Ba*, as often, the first entry and final '*exeunt omnes*' frame and, to some degree, sum up the tragedy. Dionysus himself opens, already disguised as a sort of oriental holy-man in complete bacchic regalia [6.9.1]; and while he has, strictly speaking, already been in Thebes some time (see 20ff.), his first entry is, none the less, made to give a strong impression of his arrival there. The first word is 'I come'; and shortly after 'I am arrived . . . , and I see . . .' (5–6), as he surveys the scene of his mother Semele's miraculous pregnant death. The play is concerned with Dionysus' arrival at Thebes in two senses: as a presence and as a cult. His arrival in person we see now; the acceptance of his cult he is determined to achieve before he leaves for elsewhere [4.9.1]

(48ff.). This divine prologue is different from the others in Euripides (e.g., in *Hipp* and *Ion*) not only because it is a true arrival and in disguise, but also because it does not *unconditionally* predict the outcome of the play:

> But *if* in anger Thebans try to bring
> the Bacchants from the hills by force of arms,
> then I shall lead my Maenads to the fight. (50–2)

While it is certain that Dionysus will be accepted at Thebes in the end, the strength and manner of the opposition remains unknown, and much of the suspense of the next 750 lines derives from this.

[4.9.2]   Although the emphasis in the prologue is on the city as a whole, the tragedy concentrates on the royal house of Thebes which was founded by Cadmus and which produced Dionysus' mother. Pentheus has been given the throne by Cadmus (43–4). He is, it seems, the only male descendant (1305f.): with his death the royal line is destroyed, extinguished. Cadmus laments:

> Through you, my daughter's child, the house retained
> its light; you kept my home intact; the city
> held you in awe. (1308–10)

Although Pentheus is punished the most obviously, life for those who survive is, as so often in Greek tragedy, a burden in many ways worse than the release of death; and so it is for Cadmus and Agaue. During the first part of Dionysus' final speech 'from the machine' he probably predicted the destruction and enslavement of Thebes, he certainly pronounced the inevitable exile of Agaue, polluted by kin-murder, and in the last lines he predicts the future wanderings and reptilian metamorphosis of Cadmus and his wife (1330–43).[23] There can be no shuffling: all that is left for father and daughter at the end is to set out on their comfortless exiles.

> *Ag*: Father, bereft of you I go to exile.
> [*she embraces him*]
> *Cad*: Why do you clasp me in your arms, poor child,
> like some swan with its white and helpless parent?
> *Ag*: I know not where to turn, cast out from my land.
> *Cad*: No more do I. Your old father is no help. (1363–7)

The play ends with the heavy departures, in opposite directions, of Cadmus, the heroic founder of a great city, and of Agaue, daughter and mother of kings – departures away from the palace, scene of their greatness, and off into the empty, friendless outside. One only has to contrast the end of *Ion* [4.8.2]. We see here the dispersal of a great house, a house great enough to breed a god: so dangerous is it to be mortal kin to the immortals. Thus Euripides uses the necessary clearance of the stage to demonstrate the frailty of human exaltation.

Last of all, a much less obviously dramatic entry. At 660 a herdsman [4.9.3] arrives from Cithaeron to tell Pentheus of the behaviour of the bacchant women out on the mountain. The entry of a messenger is so conventional and in itself so slight as normally to call for no special preparation or attention. But this one is announced by Dionysus himself, and with some interesting words:

> But first take in (*mathe*) the message of this man
> come from the mountains to tell you some news.
> (Don't worry about me, I shall not run.) (657–9)

The verb *mathe* has the range 'learn–notice–understand'.[24] Here in 657 it means little more than 'listen to', but there may be an undertone of 'learn the truth from'. And, in any case, how does Dionysus *know* that this is a messenger from the mountains? The hint is sown that Dionysus has 'arranged' this messenger-speech as an opportunity for Pentheus to see the truth, in fact one of a series of opportunities [see 9.9.1]. And, indeed, this herdsman gives unequivocal evidence that Pentheus' suspicions of the immorality of the cult are unfounded, that a real god has arrived, that he performs miracles, and that opposition by force is useless. The very poetry of the speech assures us of its authority. The man concludes 'and so accept this god into the country, master, whoever he may be . . .' (769–70) – and this imperative follows incontravertibly from what he reports. Furthermore the narrative contains, if only Pentheus would recognize it, a sort of miniature paradigm of his own situation. The herdsman and his neighbours witness the bacchants' miracles and are amazed (677–713). But 'a city idler with a glib tongue' (717) suggests that they should hunt the bacchants in order to please Pentheus (714–21). The countrymen agree and lie in ambush, but they are discovered and flee; and then the women go on the rampage, wreaking effortless destruction. This sequence of events foreshadows Pentheus' own ambush and destruction fairly precisely: but he will not learn. So it seems that Dionysus 'stage-manages' the arrival of the messenger to give Pentheus a chance to recognize the truth. This is a sign of the god's knowledge, a knowledge it is dangerous to scorn.

5 Actions and gestures

Then write again 'Faustus gives to thee his soul' . . .

                                                                    [he writes]

Consummatum est; this will is ended,
and Faustus hath bequeathed his soul to Lucifer.

                                             (Marlowe, Doctor Faustus*)*

This chapter needs little introduction. Faustus writes in his own blood, and at that moment, not before, but now beyond all cure, he is damned. My remarks earlier (p. 17) about the relative significance or triviality of stage acts and about their commentary within the text are here especially applicable. No doubt conventional gestures and small movements often accompanied the speech of Greek tragedy: even inhibited northern Europeans tend to gesticulate when they become emotional. An obvious example is the deictic, or 'pointing', pronoun, *hode* – 'this here'; this extremely common word was presumably accompanied by a gesture in the direction of whatever is being talked about. But these run-of-the-mill bodily movements, while they are a concern for the actor and producer and while their economy and appropriateness are essential for a good performance, are not my chief concern here. I am preoccupied with the unique action which is brought about by, and which often epitomizes, the dramatic impact of a particular moment. As when Coriolanus takes Volumnia by the hand, or Cordelia kneels to Lear, or Lady Macbeth cannot wash the stain and smell from her little hand. Some kinds of action and gesture in Greek tragedy are considered elsewhere, notably exits and entrances in the previous chapter, and those involving stage-objects in the next. But there is still a large residue: sitting and lying down, running, kneeling, supplicating, embracing, striking, bowing the head, looking away and so on. Such small deeds may be imbued with a meaning reaching far beyond the mere action itself – just as in familiar life a signature, the exchange of rings, the cutting of a tape, the shutting of a door may ratify and symbolize a momentous event. And small actions may loom very large when brought beneath the searching glass of the theatre.

Cassandra's part in *Agam* is punctuated by stage-actions in such a [5.1.1] way that the changeable choreography and movements give a physical dimension to the mobility of her visionary expression. Faced with Clytemnestra, who tells her to go inside, she has the bearing of an unbroken wild animal (1062ff.), but once the queen has gone she leaves the chariot with strange cries, and approaches the palace (1072ff.). As she reaches the sacred stone of Apollo Agyieus,[1] she stops:

> Apollo, Apollo Agyieus, my destroyer –
> ah, where on earth have you brought me?
> What sort of house is this? (1085–7)

She was going to go inside blindly, but the onset of her vision stays her; and when she does finally go 150 lines later it is in full knowledge of her fate [9.1.1]. And she not only sees the truth of the present and of her doom, but she also puts these into perspective against the grim vistas of the past and future. Her revelations also provide the relief of insight, which puts in its place the foreboding and self-doubt of the earlier choral songs. Relief and despair come together in a bold stage gesture. Having seen clearly that Clytemnestra is about to kill her (1258–63), Cassandra casts her prophet's trappings to the ground (1265); but this defiant rejection of Apollo, who has brought her to misery and death, far from spoiling her prophetic power, seems to unburden and sharpen it, as she goes on to foresee the vengeance of Orestes (1279–85).[2]

Cassandra knows she must go inside, and she knows that there she must die. The scene is now drawing to a close, and at the end of this third and final speech she prepares to leave the stage:

> Since I have seen Troy doing as it did,
> and its conquerors duly take their turn
> by the judgement of the gods, I shall go in
> and do what must be done. I can bear death.
> And I address these doors as the doors of Hades. . . .
>
> (1287–91)

But she cannot yet bring herself to go, as the chorus all too clearly put her plight:

> But if you truly know your doom, how can
> you face the altar boldly, like a heifer
> directed by a god to sacrifice? (1296–8)

Again Cassandra begins to make her way in at 1305, and again she turns back with a cry of revulsion:

> *Chorus*: Why cry out in disgust? What is this loathing?
> *Cass*: The whole house reeks of slaughter dripping blood.[3]

Cassandra senses her death with smell no less than sight, and she translates her plight into words which unerringly find their place within the themes and images of the play as a whole. Twice more, at 1314 and 1320, she begins to go, and both times she turns piteously back to speak once more. The inevitable is more, not less, terrible. Finally:

> So much for mortal life! The happy ones
> are like a shadow: and as for the wretched,
> the dash of a wet sponge blots out the picture.
> And this I find is far more pitiful. (1327–30)

And she is gone, erased. We have witnessed the confluence of fate, the gods and human will power. While we watch the sacred animal approach and turn back, approach and turn back from the sacrificial altar, as she senses her own slaughter with each physical and mental faculty, her words and actions take on all the extra power that the nearness of innocent death can give them. This scene, perhaps the finest scene in all Greek tragedy, not only has a central place in the sweeping lines of theme and imagery which mark out the monumental form of the *Oresteia*, it also has all the immediacy and concentration which only great stagecraft, a sure eye for theatrical, can achieve.

[5.2.1]   When Aegisthus' death-cry is heard at *Cho* 869, the chorus leader says:

> Listen! What has been settled for the house?
> Let's stand clear of this business till it's done,
> to appear innocent of all this trouble.
> For now the final battle has been reached. (870–4)

With these words the chorus of slave-women move to the fringes of the *orchēstra*, or perhaps right into the *eisodoi*; and they do not move or speak until they re-assemble for the song at 935ff. Thus the scene is cleared for the decisive confrontation of Orestes and Clytemnestra;

and though the chorus is not actually out of sight it should be right out of the audience's range of perception. Concentration is now exclusively on the family battle: Clytemnestra stands alone, Orestes alone but for Pylades at his shoulder [7.2.3]. Nothing must distract from the debate for life and death [see 4.2.1]. An important element in Aeschylus' tragedies is the central role given to his chorus: but he can, on occasion, make it so insignificant that it virtually disappears (compare the recession of the chorus during *Agam* 905–74).

One of the most tense crises in the final battle between Orestes and Clytemnestra comes almost at the beginning, as soon as she has heard that Aegisthus is dead and that she is to die with him: [5.2.2]

> Stop, son, respect the sight of this breast, child,
> the breast where you would drowsily suck out
> with pressing gums the health-fostering milk. (896–8)

At this point Clytemnestra cannot (as many commentators declare) bare her breasts – not only for the sake of decorum, but also because the part is played by a male actor. None the less, the deictic pronoun ('this', *tonde*) shows that Clytemnestra made some expressive gesture, presumably by laying her hand on her breast. This tense, almost shocking, action evokes other less tangible motifs of the play, for this is not the first allusion to Clytemnestra's nursing breasts. Electra and the chorus came to Agamemnon's tomb because of a dream which had alarmed Clytemnestra (32ff.); and Electra tells the details of this at 526ff. She dreamt that she had given birth to a snake and wrapped it as a child:

> *Or*: What food did this new-born vermin desire?
> *El*: In her own dream she offered it the breast.
> *Or*: But did the monster not bite at her nipple?
> *El*: It drew out clots of blood mixed with the milk. (530–3)

Orestes reads the dream and concludes 'I must myself become all-snake, and kill her, as this dream proclaims' (549–50), a grisly metamorphosis that captures the ambivalence of this play. So, when Clytemnestra later lays her hand on her breast, source of Orestes' first sustenance, she instantly conjures up the image of her dream – a connection she herself makes in her very last line before death: 'Ah, this man is the snake I bore and fostered.' Throughout the three plays, and especially in *Cho*, imagery of snakes and monsters is associated with Clytemnestra; but to kill his own mother Orestes cannot avoid also becoming viperous. It is in his blood, and he sucked it with his mother's milk.

The Delphic Pythia – the mouthpiece of Apollo, who is the mouthpiece of Zeus – piously sets about her daily routine, and tells how [5.3.1]

Apollo received his shrine as a gift from the older gods (*Eum*, 1–33); and it may seem we are given a glimpse of a peaceable solution to the questions which hang over the end of *Cho* [4.2.2]. But after her preamble she goes inside to take up her prophetic throne: for a few seconds the stage is empty, nothing happens, and then she bursts out again in horror (dramatic technique without parallel in the fifth century):

> Oh, terrible to tell of and to see:
> horrors drive me back from Apollo's temple.
> I have no strength to keep myself upright –
> I run on hands, not feet. A terrified
> old woman is no better than a child. (34–8)

Scholars have been reluctant to face the clear consequences of these words: the venerable priestess crawls out on all fours. What can Aeschylus mean by this crude and undignified stage-direction? The Furies within are quite beyond her comprehension and outside the scope of her everyday piety. Faced with this hideous disruption she is, for all her age and sanctity, no better than a child, mentally and *physically*. She can only leave the matter to Apollo to deal with (60–1). But the overthrow of her opening Delphic speech prefigures Apollo's own failure to understand the power and significance of the Furies [cf. 4.3.3]. It needs a god, Athena, of far deeper wisdom to accommodate this monstrosity ('Zeus has granted me, too, some intelligence' 850); and eventually her city, Athens, will receive the Furies as completely as Delphi had rejected them. By reducing the Pythia to her hands and knees, Aeschylus has characteristically embodied his meaning in the boldest physical terms and translated it into theatre. Some have felt that he here drives his inventiveness to the verge of the grotesque: but how is he to present more effectively the response of a world still without understanding to the repulsive aspect of the Furies?

[5.3.2]   The jurors have probably been sitting quietly on benches throughout the trial scene of *Eum*: at the end they rise to place their voting pebbles into two urns (708ff.). The voting is evidently completed by 734, and it seems highly likely that one juror cast his vote during each of the eleven couplets of dialogue 711–33.[4] Athena then announces that her casting vote goes to Orestes, and tells the officers of the jury to turn out the votes and count them (734–43). The votes are counted during lines 744–51, and then Athena pronounces the verdict: 'This man is acquitted of the charge of murder, since the votes are equal on each side' (752–3).

So the voting and counting is rather a long drawn-out piece of stage-business; and rather than putting this down to a mere desire for

spectacle or verisimilitude we should ask what else Aeschylus may be
trying to convey. It is only a partial explanation to say that the
suspense over the outcome is kept up as long as possible, since, while
this is the main concern of the dialogue during the counting (744–51),
it is nothing to do with the couplets during the voting (711ff.). The
dispute between Apollo and the Furies shows how the voting reflects
the conflict as well as resolving it. And perhaps a further point is that
this is a fixed procedure, and any effective law-court has to have a
dependable procedure. This court is, after all, presented as the fundamental precedent of the court of the Areopagus for all time. Note
how Athena opens her founding charter:

> Hear now my statute, men of Attica,
> who are to judge the first trial ever held
> for bloodshed: this council of jurors shall
> exist for all of future time among
> the folk of Aegeus. . . . (681–4)[5]

A further point to the stage-business may be the crucial importance of
the way the court votes: the votes are *equal* on both sides. The rights
and wrongs of the case are so evenly balanced that half vote one way
and half the other; and Athena's vote is based on an external,
miraculous and 'irrelevant' factor (see 736ff.). Now it is stressed that
the jurors are the choice representatives of the city, and that they
scrupulously vote according to their best judgement (see 481–9, 573,
674–5, 704–6, 881ff.). This means that, although Orestes is acquitted,
the city has not actually rejected or dishonoured the claims and rights
of the Furies. This is the first point that Athena must make in her
attempt to win round the Furies from blighting the city to blessing it
[see 4.3.4, 9.3.2]:

> Be ruled by me: do not complain so harshly.
> You did not lose: the judgement was honest,
> the votes were equal, and your honour saved. (794–6)

Ajax's young son, Eurysakes, was played by a boy with no speak-   [5.4.1]
ing lines at all; nevertheless he has his part in the tragedy, indeed he is
in some ways a vital nerve. Ajax sees his son as his successor and
replacement, and his safety, which he repeatedly commits to the
protection of Teucer, is one of his chief concerns. Indeed, before we
even see Ajax after he has recovered his sanity, we hear him call 'Ah,
boy, boy' (339) and then call on Teucer (342f.). Before the son is
actually summoned on stage Ajax has made in 430–80 an irrefutable
case for suicide – his conclusion is compressed into two lines: 'The
noble man must either live well or die well. That is all I have to say'
(479–80). So when he calls for his son (530ff.), it is evidently to make

his final farewell to him. He takes him to his arms as he still sits among the futile slaughtered cattle:

> Bring him here to me. He will feel no fear
> at the sight of such new-shed blood as this,
> not if he is really mine, his father's son. (545–7)

He goes on solemnly to entrust the boy to Teucer's care, and adds that he shall be a comfort to his aged parents in his stead. He bequeaths to his son his strength, his bravery, all his great qualities except his misery; and finally gives him his shield, the mark of the great warrior Ajax of the *Iliad*:

> But you, my son, take what you are named after,
> my seven-hide impenetrable shield (*sakos*),
> and wield it by the strap, Eurysakes.
> The rest of my arms will be buried with me. (574–7)

(The text leaves it uncertain whether the shield is actually brought on stage – perhaps not.) Then, abruptly, without any sentimentality or further farewell, he thrusts the boy away from him:

> Now quickly, take the boy away, and shut
> the building – and no mournful tears outside. (578–80)

This is the end of the last embrace; his son is cast off into the world without his protection, at least without his living protection.

Ajax is apparently at this point bent on killing himself immediately, inside among the cattle, almost in the presence of Tecmessa, the boy and the chorus. Yet he enters again at 646, and makes a speech which Tecmessa and the chorus take to mean that he has decided to live on, even though subservient to his former enemies. This 'deception speech' is at once one of the greatest problems of the play, and necessarily, one of the cornerstones of its interpretation [see further 8.4.1]. Whatever its point, this previous scene with his son is clearly and irreversibly his last contact with his son, his final testament and blessing. What should be noted in it, and in his previous justification of suicide, is its *finality*: Ajax evidently has everything arranged and has demonstrated the inevitability of suicide in such a way that we can never doubt it, whatever he may say in the next scene. What we should remember from the apparently insensitive way that Ajax lets go of his son is the sureness and resolution with which he sets about what has to be done: this same decisiveness is also the keynote of the 'deception speech', for all its ambiguity.

[5.4.2]   Eurysakes will, however, touch his father again before the play is done. Tecmessa went on the search for Ajax without him and so left the boy at the mercy of his enemies. Almost as soon as he enters

Teucer, true to his trust, realizes this and sends for him (983ff.). Once he arrives (1168ff.) Teucer tells him to kneel with his hand on the body of Ajax as a suppliant, thus treating Ajax as a sort of asylum or sanctuary. This is discussed in 7.4.2; what I observe here is the symbolic action with which Teucer ratifies this sacred tableau. For the Greeks an oath or a curse was activated, or at least strengthened, if it was associated, as it was uttered, with some concrete object or action. Thus, for example, in the first book of the *Iliad* (233ff.) Achilles swears that the Greeks will miss him as surely as the sacred sceptre in his hands will never again put out foliage, and he flings it on the ground; and in Aesch. *Agam* (1598ff.) Thyestes at the feast of his own children is said to have kicked over the banquet-table with the curse 'thus perish the whole race of Pleisthenes'. So too Teucer, as he cuts a lock from his hair to give to Eurysakes, says:

> If any from the army tries to tear
> you from this corpse, then may he vilely die
> and lie unburied, cast outside the land;
> and may his race be hacked down at the root,
> even as I now shear off this lock of hair. (1175–9)

When Jocasta tells the story which seems to show that he was the murderer of Laius (711ff.), Oedipus flinches. She asks 'what is the worry that makes you turn and say this?' (728); and it may be that Oedipus physically turned away from her for a moment – away from the truth. Oedipus even comes to regret the vigour with which he has searched and laments that he has cursed and outlawed himself (817–20; cf. 767–8, 1381–2), and at the end of the act he goes inside, almost a broken man (862; cf. 914ff.). Later on, however, when he is near to discovering the truth of his parentage (though he does not yet suspect the enormity of it), he does not flinch, but approaches the truth full-face. When the old shepherd arrives (1110ff.), even before he speaks, Oedipus has the Corinthian identify him (1119f.), and then says 'Hey you, old man, here, look me straight in the eye and answer everything I ask you . . .' (1121–2). As the scene progresses, the old man desperately tries to stop the truth from coming out, but Oedipus does not falter [4.5.3]. At one point he even threatens him with torture:

Oed: If you won't talk willingly, you'll regret it.
Shep: No, by the gods, don't maltreat an old man.
Oed: Seize his arms immediately. . . . (1152–4)

It is likely that Oedipus raised his hand but did not actually strike the old man, and his attendants did not, perhaps, actually lay hands on him. None the less, the threat of force wrings out the truth, and

Oedipus' readiness to resort to it shows the strength of his will to find out the truth above all. Not many lines later the old shepherd will speak one of the most moving words in the play 'from pity' (*katoiktisas*) –

> *Oed*: Why did you give the child to this old man?
> *Shep*: From pity, master. For I thought he would
>   take him away to his own land. In truth
>   he saved him for the worst . . . (1177–80)

– the old man will be cursed for that act of kindness (1349ff.). Oedipus shows no pity to himself, nor to the old man, in his determination to know the worst.

[5.5.2]   Oedipus is a polluted man, polluted by the two most heinous crimes, patricide and incest. Now, anyone who touches a polluted man, even talks with him or looks at him, is in danger of infection by the miasma. Yet there is something about Oedipus which makes his state almost, it seems, incommunicable. Thus he begs the chorus to take hold of him and cast him out (1410ff.):

> See fit to lay hand on a wretched man.
> Come on, don't be afraid. No human being
> is able to sustain my ills but me. (1413–15)

It may even be that the old men of the chorus did obediently move forward and touch him. For it may be them, rather than some extraneous attendants, that Creon addresses when he enters soon after (1424ff.), reproaching them for letting such a pollution outside in contact with earth, rain and light, and telling them to take Oedipus indoors. Despite Creon's rigour here, when Oedipus later begs him to let him touch his daughters (1466–9, quoted on p. 111), Creon grants the request and Oedipus takes the girls into his arms (1466f., 1480ff.; cf. 1521f.). Furthermore Oedipus pleads with Creon to touch him in token of his agreement to look after the daughters – 'mark your consent, my noble lord, by touching me' (1510); and Creon presumably does so. I am unable to account with confidence for the apparent contradiction between Oedipus' terrible pollution and all this contact with others, bodily contact as well as visual and aural exposure. It may be that Sophocles simply allows the demands of emotive pathos to override meticulous religiosity – pollution is bound in any case to be an intuitive matter to some extent. Or is the immediate family somehow exceptional (cf. Creon in 1430–1), either immune or already tainted? Or is Oedipus somehow isolated, so extreme and so strong in his enormity that others are safe from sharing it (as he himself seems to imply in 1415, quoted above)?

The touching of these final scenes is important in that it is the blind man's only contact with the world, a world which is no longer at his command. At the end he even has to let go of his own daughters [1515ff; cf. 4.5.4].

Phil ends with the departure for Troy [4.6.3]. We have had to wait a   [5.6.1] long time for this simple, voluntary, unimpeded movement: the action of the play has been a long series of frustrated beginnings, of journeys which have never got under way, of movements which have been hindered or spoilt in one way or another. To show how these theatrical techniques take their place throughout this study in deceit and stubbornness I shall make a rapid survey of this unparalleled series of *delayed or frustrated exits*.

The first is, appropriately, a sham. At 461ff. Neoptolemus pretends that he must be off to Skyros; he says farewell and makes as if to go. He does this to increase Philoctetes' eagerness to leave and get on board ship, and, since the old hero does not dream that the son of Achilles might tell a lie, the ploy is completely successful. By 533ff. he is keen to depart just as soon as he has gone within his cave a final time. At this point the 'false-merchant' arrives (539ff.). Although this proxy for Odysseus delays their immediate preparations to go, he also succeeds in still further sharpening Philoctetes' desire to depart at once (see 635–7, 645, etc.); and finally at the end of this long act they go inside (675).

When Philoctetes and Neoptolemus re-emerge at 730ff. they seem set on immediate departure; but now they are delayed by a new and unforeseen compulsion.

> *Ne*: Come on then. What is it? Silent for no
>   reason? You seem paralysed. What is it?
> *Phil*: [cries of pain – in Greek *ā, ā, ā, ā.*]
> *Ne*: What is it? *Phil*: Nothing serious – go on
> *Ne*: Is it an attack of your old trouble?
> *Phil*: No, no. It feels a little better now . . . ah, you gods! . . .
>
> (730–6)

The pain, a recurrent agony caused by the snake-bite in his foot, is too excruciating to allow Philoctetes to continue on his way; and eventually he sinks to the ground in a coma (821). Neoptolemus now rejects the chorus' urgings to make off with the bow and to leave Philoctetes [7.6.1]. Almost as soon as the sufferer recovers, his thoughts turn again to their departure:

> And now there seems to be some breathing-space
> from my pain: so, my child, you lift me
> up and put me on my feet, so that, as soon
> as this throbbing subsides we may set off
> for the boat and delay our voyage no more. (877–81)

A few lines later Neoptolemus helps Philoctetes to his feet, and they begin to go once more – but once more they stop (895). Again the impediment is pain: but this time it is Neoptolemus who feels it, a mental anguish, scarcely less than Philoctetes' physical agony. Philoctetes' pitiful disease, his long-suffering nobility, his open gratitude and trust have all been made a mockery by cruel deception; they have all built up to such a pitch of torture that Neoptolemus stops in his tracks, unable to move further [see further 8.6.2].

It needs Odysseus to enforce once more the departure for Troy:

> *Phil:* I say no. *Od:* And I say yes; and what I say is to be done.
>
> (994)

Now Philoctetes turns away from the ship and back towards his old rocks: rather than go to Troy under Odysseus' power he would make a final swift journey. He threatens to throw himself to death on the rocks of Lemnos, but is quickly restrained by force (999–1003). In the end Odysseus goes with Neoptolemus and the bow, and Philoctetes is left behind. The chorus tries to persuade him to come to Troy, but he is adamant. He tells them to leave him alone (1177ff.); but when they take him at his word and begin to go, he calls them back – he cannot bear yet to be left alone again. But his determination is now hardening on a short last journey into his cave, where he will wait to die; and finally at 1217 he goes in – 'This is the end of me' [see 4.6.2]. Once Neoptolemus has returned to give the play a new start, and has rebutted Odysseus, Philoctetes is called out once more (1261ff.). Now Neoptolemus brings to bear on him the persuasive power of the oracles of Helenus and of the promised cure, but Philoctetes' stubbornness and hatred is so strong that he would rather die on Lemnos than help his enemies, however gloriously, at Troy (1316–96). He utterly rejects every argument, he will not budge an inch. Suddenly he presses an alternative, the journey home which he holds Neoptolemus to have promised him (strictly speaking, he made no such promise). If Neoptolemus is to stand by Philoctetes and to reject Odysseus and Troy – and this is the stance which the whole play has been leading towards – then he must agree. He makes no resistance, and with his decision the metre changes to one of movement (trochaic):

> *Ne:* Very well, let's go.　　*Phil:* That's nobly said.
> *Ne:* Lean on me as we step.　*Phil:* I will do my best. . . .
>
> (1402–3)

Once more they are on a journey, a real journey without deceit, to Greece and not to Troy. And once more their footsteps are halted before they leave the stage [see further 8.6.2]. But this is the last time that Philoctetes' exit will be frustrated: Heracles brings new and decisive forces into the play; and he is soon followed by the final and successful departure. Philoctetes' departure from Lemnos is not easy. It must be made in the right way, for the right reasons and to the right destination. This long series of false departures explore all the flawed alternatives before the true outcome is achieved.

Phaedra is determined to starve herself to death rather than reveal [5.7.1] her shameful lust. Her overriding concern is with her honour and good name (see lines 47, 329, 331, 419ff. etc.). And yet her old Nurse somehow elicits the truth from her – and disaster follows. Already before she is even seen the chorus-women have addressed to her their frantic curiosity over the nature of her ailment (141ff.). As soon as the Nurse enters with Phaedra she is pressing her with questions (177ff.), and these continue unrelentingly for 150 lines. But when Phaedra says 'let me alone in my wrong: I do you no wrong' (323), she has still made very little headway. Yet at 335 Phaedra begins to reveal all. One might argue that Phaedra simply gives in through exhaustion, or that she secretly desires to reveal her passion all along and has only made a show of reluctance. But what actually tips the balance is the Nurse's appeal to Phaedra's honourable reputation combined with her physical supplication.

The socio-religious procedure of supplication is often vaguely alluded to, but it is not easy to give a precise account of it.[6] Zeus protected the suppliant, just as he protected the stranger and the victim of a broken oath – all instances of the weak who lack worldly protection. A suppliant is one whose state is so desperate that he throws himself completely at the disposal of another in return for his protection. Usually this means taking asylum at a sacred place; and as long as the suppliant remains in contact with the sacred object or precinct then another harms him at his peril. Similarly, if it is a person who is supplicated this physical contact is vital – the relationship only holds good as long as the physical grip on the knees (and usually beard or hand) is maintained. So here in *Hipp* it must be just before 325 that the Nurse grasps Phaedra:

Pha: Would you force me by gripping on my hand?
Nurse: And your knees – and I never will let go. (325–6)

Phaedra makes a show of resistance, but the Nurse attacks her obsession with her reputation:

Nurse: By speaking, then, you will enhance your honour.
Ph: For god's sake go and let my hand alone.
Nurse: No, not while you withhold the gift you owe me.
Ph: I give in – I respect your suppliant clasp. (332–5)

It may be that the Nurse releases her hold at this point; or it may not be until her despair at 353ff. when she throws herself on the ground ('my body I cast down, let fall', 356).

Now it may be doubted whether the Nurse has legitimate grounds for supplication: she is not, after all, in direct physical danger. None the less she is utterly dependent on Phaedra: if her mistress dies, she has no function in the world. In any case, the awesome physical action levers the turning-point from reticence to revelation, which is essential for Euripides' purposes. In an earlier *Hippolytus* play he had Phaedra indulge her lust and openly solicit Hippolytus on stage. In this play, on the contrary, he makes Phaedra's concern for her good name and for her children override even her desire for life. She is determined to die rather than even say, let alone do, anything shameful. Somehow this barrier must be breached, and the Nurse's supplication combines with her clever playing on Phaedra's pride to effect this swiftly and convincingly.

[5.7.2]   In her later scene with Hippolytus the Nurse will make another attempt to exploit the suppliant's touch to avert frustration –

> *Nurse*: Yes, by this strong right hand of yours. . . .
> *Hipp*: Keep your hands off. Don't even touch my clothes. (605–6)

– but this time she fails as Hippolytus retreats out of her reach. Not only does he characteristically avoid any bodily contact, his moral rigour is more wary of such tactics. The Nurse has already tricked him into an oath of silence [7.7.4], and he is on his guard. Phaedra falls because she lacks moral rigour: Hippolytus falls because he has it even to excess.

[5.7.3]   When the Nurse has gone inside to do whatever she has in mind to medicine Phaedra's passion, the queen stays on stage while the chorus sings a hymn to Desire, *Erōs* (525ff.). It is quite common for an actor to stay on during a choral ode; sometimes he is addressed or given some function during the singing, but usually, as here, he is not directly integrated, and he would, presumably, have stood as inconspicuously as possible, so as not to distract the audience at all. It is, therefore, a great surprise when after two strophic pairs Phaedra bursts out 'Silence, woman! Oh no, I am undone!' (565) – a surprise not only because of the alarming interruption, but also because we are suddenly to suppose that Phaedra is eavesdropping at the door. And an extraordinary scene follows (565–600). Phaedra stands at the door straining to hear the violent altercation within between the Nurse and Hippolytus, while the chorus in the *orchēstra* responds in distraught lyric to her reports.

The sustained scene of eavesdropping, with its almost grotesque associations with listening at the keyhole, is quite without parallel in

surviving Greek tragedy; and it is powerfully suggestive. Not only
does it build up suspense towards the moment when Hippolytus will
burst out into the pure sunlight with the Nurse at his heels [601ff., see
9.7.1], it also captures symbolically Phaedra's reluctant and fatal
involvement with him. In Euripides' earlier *Hipp* play she had importuned him face to face, so that he had to cover his head with his cloak
to separate himself from this filthying shame:[7] but in this play there is
not one single line of direct dialogue between them. All communication is carried on indirectly [see further 6.7.3, 7.7.4]. So here, Phaedra
discovers Hippolytus' response, and hence her own fate, only by
overhearing, with the door as a barrier between herself and her
damnation. Yet even this half-heard, distanced quarrel is enough to
commit her to quick death. Before Hippolytus ever comes into her
presence she is already determined beyond reverse:

> I know only one way: to die at once –
> the single cure of all the ills about me. (599–600)

   I have already touched on the suggestion that in the last 20 lines of   [5.7.4]
Hipp (1442–61) the mortals are made to compare favourably with the
petty vindictiveness of the two goddesses [4.7.2]. The simple, noble
stage-actions contribute to the moving quality of this final episode.
Hippolytus has probably been lain down on a bier earlier [see 8.7.2]:
he calls on his father:

> Ah, darkness now descends upon my eyes.
> Hold me, my father, and set straight my corpse. (1444–5)

So the two form a close group, with Theseus probably kneeling by his
son and embracing him. At this point Hippolytus releases him from
all guilt for his death (1449ff.): this is not just a noble gesture, it meant
in Attic law that the killer was absolved from all further prosecution
and punishment.[8] Theseus tries to comfort Hippolytus, but there is
no help for it:

> My strength is spent. Yes, father, I am dead.
> Quick now cloak my face over. (1457–8)

So Theseus covers his head with a veil (in very different circumstances from other more notorious veilings – see 6.7.2); and then he
stands up. The separation of death is compulsory. Theseus turns to
go into the desolated palace, and Hippolytus companions presumably follow him with the corpse. As he goes, his last line – 'How
keenly, Kypris, shall I dwell on your malice' (1461) – recaptures the
contrast between god and man in the whole preceding tragedy. While
we should not forget with our intellect the warning, often voiced in
Euripides, that the immortals do not move on the same moral plane as

mortals and so are not subject to moral judgement in worldly terms, the fact remains that dramatically and emotionally the long-suffering men and women of *Hipp* have bettered the blessed goddesses. Euripides characteristically exploits the tension between the intuitive impulses aroused by the shaping of his drama and the ineluctable pressures of superhuman forces.

[5.8.1]   Recognition scenes naturally culminate in the heart-warming *embrace* of the long-separated kin, and in Greek tragedy this is usually the cue for a lyric duet which squeezes the last tear from this favourite episode. But before this satisfaction is allowed the recognition is often long delayed by incredulity, misunderstanding, the production of proof and so on. The plays where the embrace is most skilfully delayed and the longing for reunion most tantalizingly drawn out are probably Euripides' *Iphigenia (among the Taurians)* (467–901) and *Helen* (541–699), both nearly contemporoay with *Ion*. In *Ion* the sequence is first sketched, but purposely left in a low key, in the 'recognition scene' between Xuthus and Ion. When Xuthus first comes out of the oracle [517ff., see 4.8.1], he is over-eager to embrace his new-found son without further ado, and Ion not unnaturally repulses him [8.8.2]. It takes a laboured dialogue of half-lines (530–56) to persuade Ion of the plausibility of the oracle. At last he accedes, and they embrace (560). But there are no songs, no lingering endearments. Ion still has not found his mother (563ff.), and he is unprepared for departure into the secular world outside [585ff., see 4.8.2]. Also this is not, of course, a real recognition, as Xuthus is not Ion's real father, only his stepfather (Hermes prepared the audience for this in 69ff.). The real recognition will come later in a much more elaborate and exciting manner.

[5.8.2]   Creusa and Ion do not confront each other between 400 and 1261. In between, the instinctive fellow-feeling of their first meeting has been turned to deadly hate. The scenes from 1260 to 1511, which finally restore them to each other, display Euripides' theatrical virtuosity at its most brilliant [9.8.1]; and they are frequently enriched and inten-sified by the use of stage-actions. At the very beginning Creusa rushes on in flight (1250ff.): the Delphians have condemned her to be stoned and hurled from a precipice, because she attempted to kill the sacred boy within the sacred precinct (see 1217–26). As armed Delphians led by Ion approach, the chorus-leader urges her to take sanctuary at the altar of Apollo (1255–60); but she senses the paradox of such an act – how can she, who has denounced Apollo and attempted murder on his own ground, how can she now look for protection from him? Ion then faces her, apparently trapped, and denounces her before turning to his companions with the command to seize her (1261ff.). Then follow the lines:

Cr: I forbid you: do not put me to death
    for my sake and Apollo's, where we stand.
Ion: What can there be between you and Phoebus?
Cr: I dedicate my body to the god.
       [she runs to the altar]   (1282–5)

I should myself like to see the transmitted text so rearranged that it is at this moment, and not before, that Creusa suddenly decides to rush to the altar and so establish the physical contact with the sacred object which is essential to supplication [see 5.7.1].[9] But whatever the truth about the text, and whether Creusa goes to the altar at 1260 or at 1285, it is those thrilling words 'I dedicate my body to the god' which give the stage-action its dramatic impact. Long ago Creusa once gave her body to Apollo, or had it taken by him, with that mixture of shame, reluctance and awe so vividly evoked in her aria at 859–922, the core of the play [7.8.3]. During the course of this play she has rejected Apollo utterly and has turned to hate him. But now, reduced to utter helplessness, she makes an intuitive act of faith: she clasps his altar and puts herself, her body, entirely at the disposal of the god. This grasp of faith not only saves her life, it begins a spiritual reunion with Apollo which will be consummated at the very end of the play [4.8.3].

Some of the details of the scenes which follow will be discussed in later chapters: here I shall pick out the two significant embraces. Ion's indecision whether to violate sanctuary – the sanctuary which has been his whole life up till now – is interrupted by the entry of the Pythian priestess [1320, see 7.8.1] – Ion's 'dear mother, though you did not give me birth' (1324). Now that he is leaving Delphi she gives him up to the world and hands over the cradle and tokens which she has kept since she first found him (1357–62); and her last line is 'And so farewell. I kiss you, as a mother, goodbye' (1363).[10] Earlier in the play Apollo, Ion's supposed foster-father, gave the boy to his supposed real father: now Ion's real foster-mother gives him to his real mother. And her kiss of farewell preludes the embrace of reunion between mother and son.   [5.8.3]

All this while Creusa has clung to the altar, silent and almost unnoticed. Suddenly she leaves it (1401ff., quoted on p. 138). When she took sanctuary, Apollo was a last uncertain resort; but now she sees the cradle, a small light of hope rapidly spreading in the darkness of desperation. The scene of testing by tokens is brilliantly handled [6.8.3], as the moment approaches with sweet surety when they throw themselves into each other's arms. We are at last granted this and a fine lyric duet (1439–509 – Creusa dominates, Ion only speaks or chants). Though the hugs are a tear-jerking cliché they are also deeply worked into the emotional pattern of the play. Creusa exposed her baby almost as soon as it was born: she never gave it suck, never held it close. The anguish of that deprivation, never blunted by later childbearing, lives as keenly in her memory as Apollo's rapacious injury:

> If you had seen the baby stretching out,
> wanting the breast or just my cradling arms,
> there where it never was – I did it wrong. (961–3)[11]

The repair of that terrible long frustration is bliss almost greater than mortals can know:

> With tears, my child, were you brought into this world,
> and with sad cries were parted from your mother's arms.
> But now my breath is on your cheeks and it is bliss –
> I now know heavenly delight. (1458–61)

Ion, too, senses that he has lacked a mother's care and fostering

> Throughout the years when I should have lain in
> her arms imbibing joys of new-born life,
> I was deprived of my dear mother's love.
> She too was wretched, suffering the same
> as me, missing the joys of motherhood.
>
> (1375–9; cf. 319, 562ff., 1369ff.)

But now, 'Dear mother, fast within your arms, dead and yet not dead, I reappear' (1443–4). Some of the perennial strength of the recognition plot, where a lost baby is restored to its parents, lies in the way that all the years of love that have been lost are concentrated in the moment of reunion. *Ion* contributed more, perhaps, than any other play to this favourite ingredient of European comedy: and perhaps the sweetmeat is nowhere more exquisitely flavoured than in *Ion*.

[5.9.1]   The entry immediately after the choral entry-song is often reserved for a kind of set-piece for the most powerful human character. But in *Ba* it is not Pentheus who enters at this point: it is the blind seer Tiresias, who is soon joined by old Cadmus (178ff.). They are decked out as bacchants [176–7, etc., see 6.9.1]; and they seem to themselves to be rejuvenated (188–90, etc.), though it is likely that in performance they should still go about with the difficult movements of very old men. Consider, for example,

> *Cad*: Are the old to lead the old like children?
> *Tir*: The god will lead us both without trouble.
> *Cad*: Are we alone in Thebes to dance to Bacchus?
> *Tir*: We two are sane and all the others mad.

Cad: We wait too long. Take hold of my hand here.
Tir: There, take it and so make us hand in hand. (193–8)

All this verges, no doubt, on the grotesque – and it is surely meant to. But scholars have found it hard to gauge the tone of the episode and to explain why Euripides should demean the reverend elders in this way.[12]

The explanations lie, I think, in the interaction of this treatment of the old men with Pentheus, who enters soon after (212ff.). Firstly, they have accepted Dionysus, and they have done so of their own volition (unlike the women who have been sent mad). Though their justifications of acceptance are odd – Tiresias delivers a string of sophistic rationalizations (266ff.), Cadmus chauvinistically claims honour for the family (330ff.; cf. 181) – none the less the point is that they do *accept* the outward tokens of Dionysus' cult, and they do not attempt to resist. We must beware of the interference of Christian notions of conversion: what is demanded of Thebes is not necessarily conversion through a mystical religious experience, it is a willing acceptance of the cult. Cadmus and Tiresias seem to show that there are many ways of accepting Dionysus, so long as he is not rejected. Secondly, the old men are the first evidence actually *seen* by Pentheus of the arrival of Dionysus in Thebes. When he arrives he has only heard of the new phenomenon (see 215ff.). He has heard that the citizens' wives have taken to the mountains and that this is the work of a newly arrived exotic foreigner. The Athenians were obsessed with the legitimacy of the children of citizens and with the promiscuity of unguarded wives, and so Pentheus' first response of outraged indignation is perfectly respectable – so long as that is all the evidence he has. The sight of the two most venerable men in the city decked out in this indecorous way is something extraordinary – 'But here's another wonder . . . I see . . .' (248–9). But while a wiser man would think again, Pentheus shows all the characteristics of the young tyrant: he is impetuous, self-confident, suspicious, and he never doubts that his own judgement is to be equated with the best interests of the city. He is also quick to resort to force, and always has with him a group of armed henchmen ready to be dispatched on violent missions. Here he sends some to destroy Tiresias' place of augury (346ff.) and others to arrest the stranger before his stoning (352ff.). He does not consider for a moment the implications of Cadmus' and Tiresias' behaviour nor of their explanations; he assumes without a second thought that his first impressions are final. This is, in fact, the first of a whole series of signs of the reality of Dionysus' godhead which Pentheus will ignore, and the first of a series of violent responses which will end in his own destruction [see 9.9.1].

[5.9.2]   The cat-and-mouse scene in which Dionysus toys with the doomed
and humiliated Pentheus (913–76) is one of the most macabre in
Greek tragedy. Part of its disturbing effect comes from the detailed
use of stage-action. Pentheus, in 'drag', minces and preens himself
effeminately, and Dionysus fusses round him like some assiduous
handmaid; and in the dialogue at 925–44 the stage action deals with
each item of the transvestism (the details are prepared for in 830ff.).
First Pentheus poses with a feminine stance (925–7). Some curls of his
luxuriant wig have fallen from his headband because he has been
shaking his head like a bacchant: Dionysus sets this in order (928–34):

> *Dion*: Hold your head up straight.
> *Penth*: There, you set it right: I am in your hands. (933–4)

Dionysus then tells him that his girdle is loose and the pleats of his
linen dress are not hanging properly; Pentheus looks over each
shoulder and lifts back his heel to check that the folds are now right
(935–8). Finally he asks Dionysus how he should carry his thyrsus,
and obeys his instruction to raise it in time with his step (941–4). What
is it that is so sinister about all these fussy trivialities? Partly it is the
pleasure the god takes in humouring his victim's degradation, partly
it is the pointlessness of such concerns to a man doomed to death,
partly there may be the sense that, as for a sacrificial victim, everything must be just right: but it must also in large part rest in the
diametrical contrast between this Pentheus and his earlier 'proper'
self. Dionysus' power over him is not only total, it takes a perversely
appropriate form. The masculine aggressive persecutor of the bacchants has become a simpering ninny, and a bacchant, *par excellence*,
down to the last curl. The political male with all his force has become
the trivial, helpless effeminate, obsessed over her appearance. And
yet there is something of the same thoroughness and obsessiveness
about Pentheus here as in the earlier scenes. This transformation by
opposites along the same pole is one of the things which make this
scene so unsettling and fascinating [see further 8.9.1].

6 Objects and tokens

And she did gratify his amorous works
with that recognizance and pledge of love
which I first gave her: I saw it in his hand:
it was a handkerchief, an antique token
my father gave my mother. (Shakespeare, Othello)

It implies no doctrine of property and worldly goods to observe that objects are important: they can define and substantiate people's roles, their standing, their way of life. And some objects gather, especially through the art of a playwright, special associations so that they betoken much more than themselves. A wedding ring, a lock of hair, a jester's skull, a hollow crown, a handkerchief spotted with strawberries. And in a society which is bound about by roles and ceremonies, like that of the Greeks, symbols of status, gifts, keepsakes, heirlooms, works of art have an especially prominent place as miniature repositories of huge associations. This is already part of Homer's vivid particularity, and the tragedians develop the use of significant props still further. The tragedian isolates a brief sequence of crucial, catastrophic events; and in such circumstances, fraught with change and destruction, special objects are likely to be brought out of safe keeping, to be used, destroyed, worn, and handed on to others. Props and costumes are a particularly straightforward means for the dramatist to put his meaning into tangible, overt form. As with all stage business the Greek tragedians are sparing in their use of stage-properties, but this very economy throws more emphasis on their employment.

It might seem that costume should have a separate chapter to itself. But, while the lavishness of the costumes was perhaps the chief element in the visual grandeur of the tragic stage, the specific use of clothing as a significant part of the play's meaning is fairly straightforward, perhaps because the size of the theatre precludes detail. It is, as a rule, simply a matter of contrast: Greek and Barbarian, costly and poor, finery and mourning. The instances I discuss are, in fact, mostly distinct items which can be taken off and given special attention – wreaths, armour, veils and so forth.

[6.1.1]   When Clytemnestra comes to the door to meet Agamemnon on his return from Troy [*Agam* 855, see 4.1.2], she greets him with ambiguous and deceitful reassurances. These are not addressed directly to him, however, but deviously through a challege to the chorus (855–905). Only at the very end of her speech does she turn on her husband personally:

> But now, dear heart, step from
> your chariot; yet do not set upon
> the soil, my lord, that foot which trampled Troy.
> My women, hurry, do as you've been told:
> bestrew the ground he treads with coverlets;
> and make a pathway spread with purple here,
> so may justice bring him home beyond his hopes. (905–11)

So a voluminous cloth (or cloths) of purple or dark red (on the colour see pp. 81–2) is laid out, stretching all the way from the chariot right to the very threshold. Agamemnon resists the suggestion that he should tread on it, an act which he regards as excessively exalted and fitter for gods than men (914–30), but in a line by line contest (931–41) Clytemnestra persuades him to do it.

> Very well then. Someone quickly undo
> my shoes, the vassal covering of my feet. . . . (944–5)

As his shoes are taken off, he draws attention to Cassandra [950–5; 7.1.3]; and then with his last words, he steps off his chariot and on to the cloth –

> And seeing I have been thus beaten down
> in deference to you, I go into
> my palace halls trampling a purple path. (956–7)

It seems fair to reconstruct that he slowly walks the length of the rich pathway to the door in silence during the next fifteen lines (958–72), lines in which Clytemnestra assures him, in oblique and ornate language, of the wealth of the house and of his vital place in it. 'There is the sea. And who may dry it up? . . .' As he goes the maids probably gather up the cloth behind him. And, finally, as he passes indoors, Clytemnestra prays in a final couplet of quite another tone,

> Zeus, Zeus, fulfiller, now fulfil my prayers;
> do as you are determined to fulfil. (973–4)

and then she follows him inside.

Can we do better than the scholar (A. W. Verrall) who protested 'the tapestry is a mere detail, introduced chiefly for spectacular effect'? Anyone who has read *Agam*, let alone seen it, must sense that the path of cloth is imbued with dark significance. When Agamemnon sets foot on it something sinister and portentous is happening, and it somehow leads towards his death. The overt issue of the clash with Clytemnestra is, after all, over *how* he will go into the palace: will he tread on the ground or on the coverlets? Nearly fifty lines separate the spreading of the cloth from the moment it is first stepped on; and this interval persistently forces us to ask what this extraordinary object can mean.

Most discussion of recent decades has concentrated on the significance of this scene for the revelation of Agamemnon's psychology. It has even been claimed to show that he is a tired gentleman who bows before the wishes of ladies; but the usual analysis is that Clytemnestra contrives to bring out Agamemnon's subconscious desire to rival the gods and so to expose his suppressed 'fatal flaw' – hybristic pride. So far as I can see this sort of psychology simply is not there: in order to extrapolate it one has to read between the lines. And this sort of interlinear 'reading' presupposes an audience which is on the look out for such phenomena as subconscious desires. I cannot see that *Agam* is much concerned with such things; but rather than rule this approach out of court I shall simply try to point to some of the themes and issues which demonstrably *are* there and leave it open whether there may be psychological substrata beneath them.

The other approach to the scene which has received most attention is at least there for all to see, though it has been overemphasized: its religious significance. (The study of pagan pre-Christian literature has tended to a guilty obsession with the history of the numinous.) However, it is true that Agamemnon's first reponse to his wife's invitation (914ff.) is that the act is more suited to gods, and that it would be a fearful thing for a mortal to do since it might invite divine resentment. Clytemnestra undermines this scruple in the stichomythia dialogue, but as his shoes are removed Agamemnon dwells on it once more:

> And as I walk upon this sea-wrought purple,
> I pray no distant eye of divine envy

> may strike me, for it is no light matter
> to ruin underfoot the stuff of the house
> and spoil this rich and valuable fabric. (946–9)

So the action is one to invite divine envy (*phthonos*):[1] but does it in fact provoke it? Perhaps Agamemnon's cautious prayer successfully averted it? None the less, we are, I think, meant to regard his act as impious; not so much because this is central to the scene itself – it is not – but because it takes its place in a larger pattern of imagery. Images of kicking and of trampling underfoot are insistently associated with unrighteousness in the choral songs of *Agam* and of the trilogy as a whole – see especially *Agam*, 369ff., 381ff.; *Cho*, 639ff.; *Eum*, 538ff. Agamemnon's sin here should not in itself be overemphasized, however; for among all his sins and among all the rationales which are given for his death elsewhere in the play this one does not figure again. The impiety which we witness here may be seen to stand for the other factors which condemn Agamemnon, but it is in itself comparatively trivial: it is representative rather then literal and particular. This religious misdemeanour can hardly be the only point of the scene: it is not, in my view, even its chief significance.

What is the point of the cloth itself, the fine fabric which spreads so fascinatingly from chariot to door, and draws the eye irresistibly to it? The features which are stressed are these: it is woven stuff, highly decorated (*poikila*) and easily damaged, it is costly and is part of the treasure of the household, and it has been dyed by being dipped in the expensive purple dye derived from shellfish, *porphyra*. The stress on the costliness of the cloth fits in obviously with the reiterated theme of the dangers of excessive wealth (see especially *Agam*, 374ff., 776ff., 1008ff.): overmuch wealth is liable to disaster, and the wastage of the precious cloth is a sign of the vulnerability of the prosperity of Agamemnon. Furthermore it is the wealth of his own house which he damages by this trampling: see lines 948–9 quoted in the previous paragraph, and note the reiterated 'house' words during Clytemnestra's justification of the waste in 958ff.[2] This destructive action typifies the way that the royal house harms itself, above all by kindred murder.[3]

Two other ways in which the cloth is worked into the thematic patterns of the trilogy are not, perhaps, so clear at the time that it lies before our eyes, but become clear in *retrospect*. It is later, that is to say, that the vivid reminiscence of the purple path gradually accumulates its full complex of significances. Firstly, it would be interesting to know whether the elaborate decoration of the fabric was at all web-like; for the language which is used of the net-cloth in which Clytemnestra trapped Agamemnon is unmistakably reminiscent of the cloth on which he walked. It is 'an inescapable encircling net, like for fish, a deadly wealth of cloth' (1382–3), a 'spider woven web' (1492), and 'the woven garments of the Furies' (1580). It is even more vividly brought to mind when in *Cho* Orestes holds up Clytemnestra's trap for all to see:

> I call this cloak
> to witness how Aegisthus' sword has dyed it.
> The oozing stain of blood combined with time
> has ruined its decorative dye-work. (*Cho*, 1010–13)

It is unlikely that the same stage-property was used throughout both for the coverlets and for the trap; but even so the associations between them are clear. In terms of the echoing metaphors the fabric which Agamemnon steps on is equated with that in which he is caught and killed; and these are the same as the garments in which Iphigenia was wrapped when she was slaughtered (*Agam*, 231ff., see below), and the same as the inescapable net which was cast over Troy (357ff.; cf. 822f.). When we see Agamemnon walk the delicate cloth, which is then gathered up behind him, the associations may not have yet come into focus, but as the trilogy progresses the recollection becomes sharply defined in its full setting.

Secondly, what is the colour of the cloth? Difficult though the idea is to come to terms with, the Greek colour vocabulary was differently arranged from our own, and seems to have been basically in terms of light and dark, bright and dull. The dye of *porphyra* gave its name to a colour adjective in the dark range of brown-red-purple. It is an epithet appropriate to blood; and the colour of the cloth in *Agam* was surely uncomfortably like that of blood. In that case the sight of the cloth will inevitably have stirred thoughts of a pathway of blood leading up to the house or of a stream of blood flowing out of it. The butcher of Iphigenia and the leader of the mass slaughter at Troy returns to his own house of blood. But these vague associations are, I think, directed into a more particular train of thought. The language used of the sacrifice of Iphigenia at *Agam*, 227ff. is particularly elusive, but the chorus sing of her 'pouring her yellow dye-stuffs to the ground' (239). Dyed cloth pouring to the ground, once it is associated with blood pouring to the ground, sets off a series of images of blood on the ground, which continue to their eventual embodiment and resolution in *Eum* [see 4.3.1]. The accumulating ideas first emerge into clear expression in the disquiet of the chorus in their song immediately after the scene with the purple cloth:

> For once a man's dark death-blood has spilt
> on the ground, who could fetch it back again
> by incantation? No one. . . . (1019–21)

On his return to the palace Agamemnon comes back to the soil where kindred blood is spilt: he cannot walk on plain ground that is unstained by it. This notion is implicit in the dyed cloth, and it soon finds explicit expression.

I have left till last what I find the dominant – and most obvious – significance of Agamemnon's action. The whole scene is put in terms of a *battle* between the man and the woman, a battle which Clytemnestra wins. This is particularly clear in lines 940–3:

> *Ag*: It is not womanly to long for battle.
> *Clyt*: Even defeat becomes the prosperous.
> *Ag*: Do you value this victory so highly?
> *Clyt*: Give in. You still reign if you yield by choice.

Cassandra looks back on the scene in these terms (1231ff., especially 1237 'as though at the turning-point of a battle'); and so does Clytemnestra herself at 1372ff. The struggle in *Cho* is also put in terms of victory and defeat, and the theme of evil victory is carried through until it is superseded by Athena's victory over retribution in *Eum*. Agamemnon returns as the mighty conqueror: yet at the moment Clytemnestra enters victory deserts him [4.1.2], and on her chosen terrain of the purple cloth we see him conquered. Notice also the delicate weapon with which Clytemnestra defeats him: persuasion (*peithō*). Troy was brought low by the *peithō* of Paris (*Agam*, 385ff.), *peithō* fights for Orestes (*Cho*, 726ff.); but in the end Athena's constructive *peithō* prevails on the Furies to stay at Athens [*Eum*, 829ff., 885ff., 970ff., see 9.3.2]. We are always told that battles and bloodshed could not be presented on the Greek stage: but Aeschylus' theatrical inventiveness and far-reaching imagery overcame that inhibition with inimitable daring and ease. We witness the woman's victory in a manner far more vivid than any amount of iron and blood could convey.

In conclusion, the significance of the purple cloth is not simple and obvious: this unusual scene is *complex and puzzling* in a way that is (appropriately) unusual in Greek tragedy. Some meanings are more prominent than others; some are explicit, some implicit; some literal, some symbolic; some are invoked at the time, others emerge into focus only in retrospect. The confirmation that the scene is meant to be difficult and complicated is the following choral song at 975ff., where the old men are all but lost in a darkening sea of confusion and foreboding: 'Why, why does this persistent dread flutter obstructively before my prophetic soul?' (975–7). But all these elements combine to mould one certitude, for the audience as for the otherwise bewildered chorus: Agamemnon is as good as dead. As he tramples the precious fabric we know we are seeing him for the last time in a vivid prevision of his death [see further 9.9.1].

The tiny lock of Orestes' hair in *Cho*, while it cannot compare with [6.2.1] the momentous and complex importance of the purple cloth, is far from being merely a circumstantial detail, but has a formative place in the opening scenes of the play. In Greece, as in many other societies, the hair was cut in connection with certain important social rituals: entry to adulthood, mourning, for example, and, perhaps, on claim-ing paternal heritage.[4] Unfortunately, textual damage has left us with only fragments of the prologue, but we do have the lines in which Orestes dedicates two locks: 'I dedicate one lock to the river Inachus as a recompense for nurture; this second as a token of my mourning . . .' (6–7). He and Pylades hide on the approach of Electra and the chorus, who are wearing black and carrying libations (hence the play's title). The libations of wine have been sent by Clytemnestra to be poured on Agamemnon's tomb; but Electra and the chorus turn these against her, and pray to Agamemnon that Orestes may come home. The lock of hair appears to be the first hint of an answer to their prayers since it is at the very moment that the libations are completed that Electra sees it (164–5). Electra must surely have picked the lock up as she considers who could have dedicated hair so like her own and yet not her own (165–94). She even wishes that it might be animate so that it might tell her whether it is friend or foe (195–200).

Her musings over the lock end in a confusion of fearful hope:

> I call upon the gods, who know full well
> amid what storms, like sailors, I am whirled.
> But if I'm safely rescued, then, who knows,
> a massy stock may grow from tiny seed. (201–4)

The strands of hair are like seeds from which Orestes might grow, and, at that very moment,[5] as an answer to her prayer, Orestes comes out of hiding and reveals himself:

> Pray on, pray to go on with such success,
> and tell the gods your prayers have been fulfilled. (212–13)

Although she so hopes for Orestes, Electra will not acknowledge him at first; but he makes her fit the lock to the exact place on his head which he cut it from (229–30) – and this along with a piece of cloth made by Electra effects the recognition. So the children of Agamem-non, 'the orphan children of the eagle father, king of birds, who died among the squirming coils of the vile snake' (247–9), are united, before the great invocation which dominates the first half of the play [7.2.1]. So at first the brother and sister are separated, though their link through the dead is established by their separate prayers to

Hermes (1ff., 124ff.). The lock is the tangible token which brings them together, first in wish and then in reality: though from the head of Orestes, it might as well have been from Electra's (see 172, 176). It constitutes a solid proof of grief for the dishonoured memory of Agamemnon: it is the seed of their reunion, and the demanding memory of Agamemnon is the ghostly yet fertile ground in which it grows.

[6.3.1]   Still at Delphi Apollo tells Orestes that he must be pursued to Athens, and that there he should 'take refuge at Athena's ancient statue and clasp it' (*Eum*, 80). Athenians all knew the old wooden image of Athena, which was housed in a temple on the Acropolis (fifty years later the building we know as the Erechtheum was constructed for it). The stage-object which represented the image may have been inconspicuously in sight from the beginning of the play, or it may have been brought on at the change of scene at 234/5; in any case, Orestes on entry (235ff.) addresses Athena, and approaches her statue (242). Evidently he sat or knelt and put his arms round it for the Furies find him 'clasped around the statue of the immortal goddess' (259). He is still there 'cowering' (326) during the 'binding chant', and when Athena arrives she still finds 'this stranger sitting in refuge at my statue' (409; cf. 439–41). After that, however, there is no further reference to it. For the trial the scene shifts from the Acropolis to the neighbouring hill of the Areopagus, and the statue, if still there, is once more disregarded.

The ancient image of Athena provides the inviolable refuge for Orestes from the Furies. It is important for the first scenes at Athens that he must stay still cowering by the image while the Furies perform their 'binding spell' (306ff.) around him and all but overwhelm him.[6] But the statue does not only provide a secure still-point in the stage-picture, it is also the presence by proxy of Athena herself. Even her inanimate presence is able to keep the two sides from brute contact, even though it can do nothing to bring them into communication [7.3.3]. Athena's arrival (443) brings on the arbitrator who will break the stalemate; and before that her solid image provides some sort of promise for a future solution. It is worth noting that the choral song at 490ff., unlike the previous 'binding spell', is not centred on Orestes: it is, rather, concerned with much wider moral and social issues which foreshadow the final resolution. Orestes is (probably) still on stage, but he is no longer at the statue, and no longer in the *orchēstra* and implicated in the choreography. This suggests that Athena has already broken the charmed circle of the blood vendetta, now that her presence has replaced her image.

[6.3.2]   The Furies look like nothing earthly. The Pythia is at a loss to describe them; the nearest she can get is that they are like and not like

Gorgons, or the Harpies in pictures (*Eum*, 46ff.). They are female, in black, wingless, their eyes stream pus, and they are twined about with snakes, probably on their heads (see *Cho*, 1048–50, 1058; *Eum*, 46–59). Obviously Aeschylus had great confidence in his mask-maker. But while in *Eum* the Erinyes become the Eumenides and undergo a change of aspect from horrific vampires to beneficent guardians of fertility, it is, none the less, important that they do not change their appearance. The theory was once current that they changed their masks: this is not only impracticable, it is contradicted by Athena's lines 'From these fearful visages I foresee great benefit for these my citizens' (990–1). Nor do they change their costume. It is true that at 1028 someone apparently puts on 'purple-dyed garments' (which obviously take up and put to rights the purple cloth of *Agam*); but even if we assume, despite textual trouble, that it is the Furies who don these garments, they do not put them on *instead* of their black: the Greek word *endytois* in 1028 makes it clear that they are put on as well as their basic clothing. The point is that, although the Furies here become beneficent settlers in the city, they remain reminders of that element of dread and awe which a law-abiding city needs. This requirement is spelt out by the Furies themselves in their song at 508ff., it is confirmed by Athena in her foundation speech at 690ff., and she ratifies it in her anapaestic contributions to the lyric dialogue at 916ff.:

> Clearly, conclusively they rule in human affairs;
> to some they bring glad song, to others
> a life darkened by tears. (952–5)

Many forces conspire to ensure the death of Ajax: the anger of [6.4.1] Athena, the shifts of time and fortune, the meanness of his allies, his own determination. But there is also a material object which has an active, almost malign, part in his ending – his sword, which was once Hector's sword. It is debatable when it was first seen by the audience. It is usually supposed that during his first appearance (91–117), while he is still mad, Ajax was holding a whip (see 110, 242), but there is much more stress on the sword, with which he has wreaked such bloody havoc among the cattle (10, 26, 30, 55f., 97, etc.), and so it may be that the gory sword was seen in his hand at this stage.[7] It is also uncertain whether he has it with him during the scene 348–595; there is nothing in the text which certainly shows it was visible. So up until the 'deception speech', whether it was seen or not, the sword, though often mentioned, is simply the instrument with which he shed so much useless blood, and nothing more. But when he enters at 646ff. he has it with him; and he soon explains, with the balanced ambiguity that characterizes this whole speech, what it is he intends to do with it:

> I shall go find an unfrequented place;
> there shall I hide this hateful sword of mine,
> and dig a hole for it where none will see.
> Let night and Hades keep it down below.
> Since I accepted it from Hector's hand,
> an enemy gift, I've had no good from Greeks.
> The proverb's true: the gifts of enemies
> are no true gifts and bring no benefit. (657–65)

So at 692 he departs carrying the sword, the instrument with which the dead Hector will at last kill Ajax. It has an apt place in Ajax's scheme.

Eventually the stage is cleared for Ajax alone [4.4.3, 8.4.1]. The first thing that he does on entry is to fix the hilt of the sword in the earth so that its point sticks upward: we cannot tell exactly how this was staged, but surely the waiting blade was visible to the audience. His last, lone speech begins:

> There stands the butcher most incisively.
> This sword was Hector's gift, most loathed of all
> the men I know, most hateful in my sight:
> and now it's fixed in hostile Trojan soil,
> new sharpened by the iron-gnawing whetstone.
> And I myself have carefully fixed it
> to be kindly disposed and kill me quick. (815–22)[8]

Then he makes a brief prayer to Zeus: that the news of his death shall reach Teucer,

> . . . so he may be the first to take me up,
> when I have fallen round this bloody sword;
> and so no enemy may see me first
> and I be thrown out for the dogs and vultures. (827–30)

Next he preys to Hermes, who conducts the newly dead to Hades,

> to put me well to sleep, with one swift leap,
> without a struggle, transfixed through the ribs
> by this blade. (832–4)

These, then, are the opening lines of the death speech, one of the most direct and moving passages in Greek tragedy. At the end (865), without any hesitation, he leaps. His prayer to Hermes is, it seems, answered at once: thus far, at least, the sword is 'kindly disposed' (the word *eunoustaton* in 822 would normally be used of people, since its core is *nous*, 'mind'). The prayer to Zeus is the concern of the remaining third of the play.

The decisive raising of the corpse of Ajax comes at the very end of

I

2

3

4

5

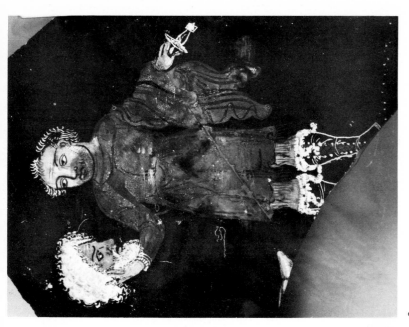

8

7

10

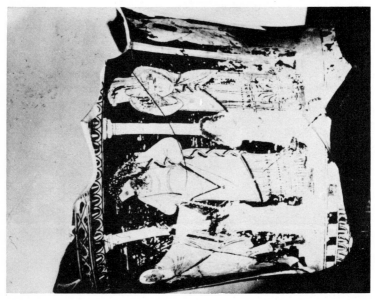

9

11

12

1. The theatre at Epidaurus, one of the great sites of Greece, was built as an architectural unity in the mid-fourth century B.C. Like all other Greek theatres it is modelled on the layout developed at the Theatre of Dionysus at Athens. This photograph may be compared with the conjectural ground-plan on p. 10.

2. Over 20,000 spectators are said to have squeezed into Epidaurus to hear Callas sing *Medea*; the theatre at Athens is reckoned to have held some 14,000. The company of such a large audience is indivisible from the experience of Greek tragedy. (Modern performances do not, as a rule, attempt to be authentic in matters of lighting, masks, etc.)

3. These six dancers were painted in Athens in about 490 B.C. (earlier than any tragedy to survive). This fascinating vase, now in Basel, was first published in 1967. The chorus, costumed as young soldiers, are not certainly from a tragedy, but their similar faces and hairstyles suggest masks. The other figure (standing behind the altar, not—as the artist makes it seem—sitting on it) is probably supposed to be an actor. This, unlike almost all later painting inspired by tragedy, appears to represent actual performance.

4. It is a pity that this mysterious painting (Athens, about 460 B.C.) is so fragmentary, since the *aulos*-player and the costume are clear evidence that it is based on tragedy. Some orientals (note the caps and trousers) are busy around a pyre of burning logs: the shoulders and bottom half of the face of a regal figure (Croesus?) are visible above the pyre.

5. These two chorusmen getting into their costume were painted in Athens in about 430 B.C., and supply good evidence for the masks and buskins of the period.

6. The 'Pronomos' vase, painted in Athens in about 400 B.C. (now in Naples) is the best preserved and most detailed evidence for the Greek theatrical outfit. It is named from the famous *aulos*-player seated in the centre. He is shown with the troupe for a satyr play; but the costumes and masks of the three main actors seem to be indistinguishable from those of tragedy.

7. The vase is close in style and date (c. 400) to the 'Pronomos' vase and confirms its evidence for tragic costume. It is based on Euripides' *Andromeda*, produced in 412

B.C., about the same time as *Ion*. The princess Andromeda is left fastened to a rock to appease a sea monster (Perseus—on the right—will rescue her). The painting as a whole is clearly not copied from an actual scene in the theatre.

8. This actor was painted in southern Italy some half a century later, about 350 B.C.; but his mask is still relatively naturalistic and his buskins, though ornate, are not thick-soled. It is uncertain whether his monochrome costume is meant to be royal purple or merely an undergarment. The special interest of this vase is the actor's seedy appearance, ill-shaven and balding: all the player-king has to do is to put on the mask and he becomes a noble hero.

9. This vase was painted in Sicily in the later fourth century B.C., and was dug up there in 1969. Despite poor quality and condition its special interest is that it is not only one of the rare paintings inspired by Sophocles, but even seems to be based on an actual performance of *Oedipus the King* (around lines 1000–1050). Jocasta (right) has now seen the truth, while the old Corinthian (left) tells Oedipus about his past. (The two daughters were added by the painter for emotional effect.)

10. This fine painting (now in Boston) of the murder of Agamemnon shows such a fascination with the bizarre robe-net thrown over the king in the bath that when it was first published in 1966 it was argued that it must be inspired by Aeschylus. But the painting is probably too early (about 470 B.C.) and, in contrast to Aeschylus, it is Aegisthus not Clytemnestra who deals the death blows. The net-robe must have intrigued an earlier narrator, probably the lyric poet Stesichorus.

11. This cup was painted about 470 B.C. by one of the great masters, known as the Brygos painter. Ajax lies dead, and Tecmessa covers his corpse over (compare Sophocles *Ajax* 915 ff.). Again the painting is too early to be inspired by the tragedy we know; but we see the tragic potential in the earlier visual tradition.

12. This painting of the death of Pentheus by the great artist Euphronios has no direct connection with Euripides' *Bacchai*, which was produced a whole century later. But the tragic tension between the Bacchants' elation and the physical horror of the murder seems already captured here.

the play [4.4.4]. But the sword is drawn from his corpse long before that, as he hoped in his prayer to Zeus (quoted above). Teucer's lament (992ff.) has reached a low pitch of hopelessness, as the future looks unrelievably bleak:

> What shall I do? How shall I wrench you from
> this bitter, gleaming spike, on which you died.
> You see how Hector dead was to kill you?
> Consider well the fates of these two men.
> Hector was fastened from the chariot rail
> with the belt that Ajax gave him, and was
> carded on the stones until he died:
> and Ajax had this as a gift from Hector,
> and so was killed by him in his last fall.
> Surely a Fury bronzesmith forged this sword,
> Hades was cruel craftsman of that belt. (1024–35)

But the action of drawing the sword from Ajax is the turning-point away from the low ebb of despair: it is the first stage of Zeus' answer to Ajax's prayer and it marks for Teucer the beginning of a new assertion. Teucer adds to his grim irony some lines of more universal reflection:

> I reckon for myself that all such things
> must be contrived for mortals by the gods. (1036–7)

This is not just 'a rather trite observation', as a recent editor (W. B. Stanford) put it, it is the truth which underlies the final scenes of this play. There is a far from coincidental *appropriateness* in the way that Ajax dies – strong, constant and alone – and there is an appropriateness in the instrument. And it is not all ironic malignancy: for it is also appropriate that Ajax should be buried, that his honour should be restored, and his dependants saved [9.4.2]. The gods see to such things. The 'butcher', the gift of Hector, proves in some ways 'kindly disposed', and plays its ambivalent part in this pattern.

In this context we might also consider the use that Sophocles makes [6.4.2] of the locale of the Trojan plain in *Ajax*, the landscape so powerfully laid down by Homer in the *Iliad*. Though it is not so intimately invoked as in *Phil* [4.6.3], it has its place, nevertheless, like the sword, in the shift from hostility and shame towards some sort of saving grace. The besiegers of Troy have spent the best ten years of their lives by the shore of the Troad, and in the final lines of his great lyric lament Ajax in his isolation calls on the place itself:

> O you sea-surged paths, shore caves, and coastal thickets,
> long, long, too long have you kept me by Troy.
> But no longer, not alive at least. . . . (412–16)

He treats the river Scamander, which irrigates the Trojan plain, as a kind of impartial observer who will witness his dishonour, despite the fact that he is the greatest Greek who has ever come to Troy (418–27). He feels some affinity with the place, and it is away from the encampment along the unfrequented shore that he goes to kill himself. 'I shall go to the bathing places in the meadows by the sea . . .' (654–5). These wooded grasslands are the setting of Ajax's suicide and of all the last part of the play. This is the enemy land in which he fixes his sword (819, quoted above); but this is also the place which he addresses with his very last words:

> . . . you springs and rivers and the Trojan plain,
> I say farewell, my generous sustainers.
> This is the last word Ajax speaks to you;
> the rest I tell to those below in Hades. (862–5)

And the land is not unreceptive: this is, after all, the soil in which he is to be buried, and where he shall have his 'ever-famous tomb' (1165–6). The tomb at Troy represents the restoration of his due honour: the 'enemy' soil does not reject his corpse, but, like the hateful sword, plays its part in his reinstatement.

[6.5.1]   There is no stage-property in *OT* which has a sustained meaning comparable with that of the sword of Ajax; and I shall simply pick out two or three which contribute in their place. At the very beginning, for instance, a crowd, probably consisting of old and young people, comes and sits before Oedipus' doors: they carry branches bound with bands of cloth (3; cf. 19f.), the sign of the suppliant. It is the gods they supplicate, but the visual picture, as Oedipus stands before them, inevitably suggests that it is him they pray to. The old priest of Zeus puts this delicately:

> I and these boys sit here as suppliants,
> not holding you as equal with the gods,
> but picking you as first of men in the
> events of life and dealings with the gods. (31–4)

Oedipus is not a god, but he is especially favoured, and among mortals he is the nearest to a god. This all contributes to the picture which is built up of him as the most blessed, most powerful and highest of men: all to be reversed to the opposite extreme before the tragedy is done.

[6.5.2]   Even more ironic use is made of the cultic paraphernalia of suppliancy later, in the scene when Jocasta comes out (911ff.) to approach the various gods 'carrying wreaths and offerings' (912–13). First she turns to Apollo, whose altar is by the palace (919–23); and immediately, as though in answer to her supplication, the messenger from

Corinth enters [cf. 4.5.1]. His news – that Polybus of Corinth is dead – seems to be excellent; but he then goes on to divulge more informa- tion which serves to bring Oedipus much nearer the truth. The act which began so hopefully for Jocasta ends with her exit to death [7.5.4, 9.5.2]. It was Jocasta who in the previous act tried to under- mine the authority of oracles from Apollo and of prophecy in general (705ff., 851ff.), and it is she who, when she hears the Corinthian's news, immediately responds 'All you prophecies from heaven, where are you now?' (946–7; cf. 973, 977ff.). Yet it is Jocasta who, as soon as she is in distress, goes through the motions of supplication to Apollo: so it is appropriate that the character who brings disaster much closer should arrive as an answer to her contradictory ritual. The chorus has just sung that *if* oracles are not fulfilled, then religion is dead (863–910): the reassurance is as prompt as the ritual is futile.

A word on Oedipus' mask in the final scene. The actor must have [6.5.3] changed his mask to one with dark eye-sockets with streams of blood running down from them. The messenger reports in gory detail how Oedipus jabs out his own eyes (1268ff.); and he is, as often, imme- diately followed by the revelation of the results of the events he has just been narrating (what German scholars have labelled an *Ecce- szene*). The sight of blood has a horrible fascination: it is yet more repellent and more fascinating when one has been told all about its shedding. The great variety of emotional range in the final scenes of *OT* (1297–523) is inaugurated by Sophocles' exploitation of the down- right physical shock of Oedipus' bloody, empty eyes. When he is revealed there is a pause before he speaks, and during this the chorus responds to the dreadful sight (1297–306):

> Poor wretch, I cannot even bear to look at you;
> although there's much I want to ask,
> and much to hear, and much to stare at –
> how you make me shudder! (1303–6)

Phil involves a stage property which is, perhaps, the most integ- [6.6.1] rally incorporated of all material objects in the Greek tragedy we have: the bow of Heracles. This calls for a selective survey of the whole play, since the significance of the bow develops and deepens in the light of what is said and done in connection with it. In the opening scenes it is introduced under three aspects. First, it is ordained that Troy shall only fall to his bow (68–9, 113, 197–200) – that is why Odysseus and Neoptolemus are on Lemnos at all. Also, since its arrows unerr- ingly hit the mark, it is Philoctetes' unconquerable defence against his enemies (75–8, 104–7) – that is why Neoptolemus must use deceit, and why Odysseus must not be seen. Third, as Neoptolemus and the chorus see, once they use their imagination enough to sympathize with Philoctetes [4.6.1], it is the castaway's means of life (162–8).

When Philoctetes enters he has the bow with him, of course. But no direct attention is drawn to it: throughout the whole long deception scene (219–538) Neoptolemus studiously avoids showing any curiosity about it. It is mentioned just twice: first when Philoctetes introduces himself – 'I am the man – you may have heard of this – I am the inheritor of the bow of Heracles' (261–2); and soon after he mentions it as his means of getting food (287–90). Often the audience must glance at the great arc apprehensively in the knowledge that this is really the object of the plot. But they must wait. The 'merchant' (539–627) does not mention the bow either: in his careful version of the prophecy of Helenus it is only Philoctetes, not the bow, which is needed at Troy. It is not until the very end of the act that it becomes the centre of attention, and even then Neoptolemus takes care to approach the subject obliquely. Philoctetes says that before they go he must collect some things together, including any arrows that may be scattered around (647–53). This dialogue follows:

> Ne: Is this the famous bow you have with you?
> Phil: Yes, this is it that I am holding.
> Ne: And may I look at it in close detail,
> and hold it, and revere it as divine?
> Phil: You may, my child, and have anything else
> within my power which may be for your good.
> Ne: I certainly long to – I am longing,
> if it is right – if not, then never mind.
> Phil: Your speech is pious, child; it is alright.
> For you, and you alone, have let me see
> the sun, and my homeland and my old father
> and my dear ones; and have set me above
> my enemies, who had me on the ground.
> Rest assured, it's yours to handle it
> and to return, and boast that you alone
> of men have touched it, in return for your
> goodness. It was, you see, because of a
> good deed that I myself received it first. (654–70)[9]

This gives the bow a new dimension, a moral significance: it is an object of special *trust*, and it may be handled only by an outstanding benefactor of the owner – someone who stands to Philoctetes as he did to the greatest of all heroes, Heracles, when he was the only man who would light his pyre. That Neoptolemus should be thus privileged is a measure of the success of his deceit throughout the preceding act – too much a success for comfort.

All this carefully prepares the ground for the next scene, when the bow does indeed pass to Neoptolemus' hands, and unforeseeably soon. When Philoctetes is halted by his wound [730ff., see 5.6.1] the appropriate course of action is obvious: he will hand the bow over to Neoptolemus' safekeeping until he should recover:

> Phil: . . . but if they come meanwhile, then by the gods
> I charge you do not give it up to them
> by any means willingly or not. If you do
> you kill yourself and me, your suppliant.
> Ne: No. Rest assured. None shall be given it
> but you and me. Give; and may all be well.
> Phil: Take it, my son. And pray the jealous gods
> it may not prove as troublesome to you
> as to me and to its previous lord. (769–78)

So it changes hands, the dangerous token of great heroes. But now that Neoptolemus actually holds it, he is only too conscious that he has obtained it in a way unworthy of its past. Philoctetes unwittingly reminds him of this as his agony increases:

> O noble child, take me and immolate me. . . .
> Burn me. Be noble as once I was when
> I did that very thing for Heracles:
> this bow was my reward, which you keep safe. (799, 801–3)

In the face of his pity for Philoctetes' suffering and of his own unworthiness to be classed with the almost extinct race of great heroes, which included Heracles and his own father, Achilles, Neoptolemus is almost at a loss for words [804ff., see 7.6.4]. It must now begin to become clear beyond doubt to the audience that his sense of right and wrong has begun to get the better of the Odyssean principles of profit and ambition: the deceitful words which have brought him this far are no longer available. The bow in his hands shames them to silence.

Once Philoctetes is unconscious, the chorus, speaking with the voice of Odysseus, urge him to make off with the bow and desert Philoctetes; but he resists [833–64, see 7.6.1]. Confronted once more with the open-hearted qualities of Philoctetes on his reawakening, Neoptolemus confesses the whole deceit [895ff., see 8.6.2]. But his reversion to his true nobility is not yet quite complete: that calls for action as well as words. He still holds the bow, the conqueror of Troy, and deadly threat to Philoctetes' enemies:

> Phil: I am destroyed, betrayed. What have you done,
> friend? Give me back my bow immediately.

Ne: I cannot. Duty and advantage both
   make me defer to my authorities. (923–6)

This pusillanimous yet firm reply provokes one of the most powerful of all Sophoclean speeches (927–62). (It is too long to quote in full here, but some passages are quoted on pp. 50 and 114.) Notice especially how Philoctetes interweaves with the plea that the bow is his only means of life (931–3, 953–60) the moral point that the son of Achilles has deprived him of a sacred object of trust by the use of fraud (928–30, 940–50). Odysseus might be able to resist such pressure; but a true man could not, and Neoptolemus decides to give the bow back, come what may. But before he can actually do it Odysseus intervenes and takes immediate control [974ff., see 8.6.1]. Odysseus will not even let Neoptolemus speak (981–2) but applies his relentless will, while the young man stands by silently holding the bow. Philoctetes is helpless: 'O hands, how you have fallen prey to this man here for lack of your familiar bowstring' (1004–5). With taunts that he himself will wield the bow at Troy (1058–65) Odysseus takes off Neoptolemus, who still has it in his hands, and Philoctetes is left behind [4.6.2].

During the consequent lyric dialogue Philoctetes laments his bow, because deprived of it he is doomed to die of starvation (1081ff., quoted on p. 50). But in close association with this, as in his speech at 927ff., he feels no less keenly that the bow has fallen into unworthy hands, the hands of his worst enemy, the man least worthy to inherit an object of trust from the heroic generation of Heracles. Odysseus is the antithesis of that nobility:

> To think that he sits by the grey surf,
> mocking me, and wielding in his hand the source
> of my poor life, which no one else has handled.
> O my bow, forced from my own hands,
> if you have any feeling, how you must look on me with pity –
> I shall never use the gift of Heracles, never again.
> But with this change of hands you shall be steered
> by a man of many twists, and you shall see low tricks,
> and see my detested enemy
> and watch the countless rising evils
> that he has devised against me. (1123–39)

But he is mistaken. Neoptolemus has not relinquished the bow, and when he returns [4.6.2] he makes it clear that he intends to return it to its rightful owner after all [8.6.1]. But Philoctetes will no longer listen to his compromising words: 'This is how you spoke when you were stealing my bow – plausible, but underneath it ruinous'

(1271–2). Only an action will restore trust between them once more. When Philoctetes begins to curse him for his falsity (1281ff.), Neoptolemus quickly sets about the necessary deed:

Ne: Curse no more: but take this bow from my hand.
Phil: What? Are you tricking me a second time?
Ne: I swear not, by the sanctity of Zeus.
Phil: Your words are wonderful, if they are true.
Ne: I'll turn them into deeds. Hold out your hand,
and take control of your own bow again. (1286–92)

Again Odysseus tries to intervene; but this time he is too late, and he would, in any case, have been ineffectual [8.6.1]. Now that he has his bow again Philoctetes quickly draws an arrow on Odysseus (1299), and he would have killed him as he fled, but for Neoptolemus' physical intervention [1300ff., see 9.6.1].

Now that a true relationship has been restored between them by means of the sacred symbol of trust Neoptolemus can in all honesty try to persuade Philoctetes to come to Troy, and he tells him of the cure and the glory promised to him if he goes (1314ff.). But his enemies at Troy have proved themselves, through their representative Odysseus, every bit as hateful and unworthy as he always claimed. In the end Neoptolemus agrees that the bow should not go to Troy, but that it should be used instead against the Greeks themselves (1402ff.). There is now only one being who could send the bow to Troy, its true owner, Heracles [see 8.6.2]. Three times in his speech 'from the machine' Heracles stresses that the bow is his (1427, 1432, 1439f.): Philoctetes has it in trust from him, and in return he must dedicate his spoils from the campaign to Heracles' pyre (1431–3). So, in the end, the glory of the sack of Troy is to go to the great generation of past heroes – to Achilles through his son, and to Heracles through his bow, symbol of the old values of noble integrity.

Statues of deities are used as props now and then throughout [6.7.1] Greek tragedy, though seldom with such direct attention and obvious symbolic value as in *Hipp* [on *Eum* see 6.3.1]. Before the palace on one side is a statue of Artemis, on the other Aphrodite.[10] Hippolytus is carrying a garland when he first enters with his companions [4.7.1]; and after they have sung their hymn to Artemis (58ff.), he dedicates it to her, evoking vividly the inviolate meadow where he gathered it (73–81). He places it on the head of the statue at 82–3 – 'Accept, my goddess, from my reverent hand this garland for your gilded hair . . .' – it is a token of his special initimacy with her (84–7). Hippolytus is now probably moving forward to go inside when an old servant intervenes to try to redress his imprudent religious partiality (88ff.). The old man actually points to the statue of Aphrodite to make his lesson that she is no less a goddess, whose image calls, no less, for attention – 'Cypris – she also is set up here by your doors' (101). But Hippolytus replies 'I am pure, and greet her only from a distance' (102); and he goes inside with what amounts to a taunt 'as for your Cypris – I say goodbye for good' (113). The old servant is left on and prays to the image of Aphrodite that she may forgive such youthful extremism (114–20). The statue is impassive; but the audience already knows that Cypris does not forgive.

[6.7.2]   The garland presumably stays on the statue of Artemis for the rest of the play. There is one point where the audience is bound to glance back at it and to reconsider its meaning. When Theseus enters at 790 he is returning from an unspecified but successful state mission and he wears the conventional garland. When he hears of Phaedra's death he casts it to the ground: 'Why do I keep this garland of woven leaves upon my head, when my mission has ended in misfortune?' (806–7). As we see the sacred wreath on the ground we are bound to fear that the token of Theseus' public piety will be no more help to him than the garland which still adorns the statue of Artemis, token of Hippolytus' private devotion, is a help to him.

[6.7.3]   When the ailing Phaedra is first brought on stage there is a long scene of anapaestic chant between her and the Nurse (176–266). At first Phaedra lies uneasily on her sickbed, her head covered by the 'fine-spun veil' which the chorus has heard 'glooms her golden hair' (134); this will be fixed by a tiara-like ornament which holds her hair in place. Her very first words are:

> Raise up my body. Hold my head.
> I cannot knit the joints of my limbs.
> Hold my shapely wrists, my maids.
> This grip on my head is burdensome.
> Undo it. Let loose my hair over my shoulders. (198–202)

With the release of the hair-grip and the lifting of her veil Phaedra's longing is released, and finds voice in a series of passionate wishes to be hunting and racing in the fields and the mountains (208–31). She probably stands up and may even almost dance as her desire to be with Hippolytus finds this barely concealed expression (though to the Nurse, of course, it seems mere madness). Eventually the fit subsides, and Phaedra sinks back exhausted.

> Nurse, cover my head once more;
> I am ashamed of what I have voiced.
> Cover me, I say; tears spring to my eyes,
> and my look is turned to shame. (243–6)

She then lies quiet, her head covered, until she rises once more to

break her silence, disastrously [310, see 7.7.3]. Thus Phaedra's tur-
bulent passion is reflected by the stage business: as her determination
on honourable death is cracked by the strength of her desire for
Hippolytus, she rises and casts aside the decorous restraints about
her eyes and hair. The expression of her passion is as yet indirect, but
its irresistible impulse is vividly conveyed.

The veil, which hides Phaedra's shame, is probably a deliberate
contrast to Euripides' earlier play *Hippolytus 'veiled'* [see 5.7.3], where
it was Hippolytus alone who resisted her passion. At the analogous
juncture in this play to the veiling scene in the earlier play Hippolytus
only turns his face away from Theseus (946–7), and away from the
silent corpse of Phaedra – there is no mention of a veil. Hippolytus'
face will be covered only in the finality of death [see 5.7.4].

Phaedra does not reveal in her final speeches (715–31) exactly how   [6.7.4]
it is she hopes to save her childrens' good name and to teach Hippolytus a lesson; and we cannot say whether, when her corpse was
revealed (811ff.), the letter hanging from her wrist was noticeable. At
any rate, it is not until 856ff. that attention is drawn to the folded
waxed tablets, probably no larger than a pocket-book. Theseus breaks
the seal and reads, while the chorus compensates in emotional lyric
for the immobility of his mask (866ff.).[11] Theseus' indignation over-
flows into lyric:

> It cries, cries out hurt, this letter.
> How shall I escape this weight of woe? I am broken, lost.
> Alas, the dirge I have read,
> which has found a voice in this script. (877–80)

His fatal curse on Hippolytus soon follows (887ff.). The tablet is an
unusually small and naturalistic prop for Greek tragedy; but its
impersonal, indirect and immutable message is typical of the lack of
proper communication in *Hipp* [cf. 7.7.3, 7.7.4]. Phaedra never con-
verses with Hippolytus or Theseus; the chorus and Hippolytus are
debarred from telling Theseus the whole truth. The unmodifiable
message of the letter is given the authority of a live – and unimpeach-
able – witness. Hippolytus' only answer to it (1057–9) is blocked by his
oath of silence (1060–3); and he has no witnesses [7.7.4]. Thus so small
and impersonal a messenger sets in motion large and tragic consequences.

Virtuoso arias sung by actors are a favourite showpiece in   [6.8.1]
Euripides' later plays. Often these monodies are accompanied by
novel and picturesque choreography, and in the best examples this
lyric action is closely tied in with the development of the play. When
Ion first enters he has an anapaestic recitative which delicately evokes
the early morning radiance of Delphi (82–101) and then goes on to

programme the three elements of his coming song: he has a broom of new-cut laurel to sweep the temple forecourt, a golden pitcher of water to scatter on the dust, and a bow to scare the birds off the sacred monuments (102–11). In the aria proper a strophic pair with the cult refrain of the paean covers the sweeping (112–43), and the ensuing astrophic part divides between the scattering of water (144–53), and the threatening of the various birds (154–83). But the lyric does much more than accompany the picturesque choreography, it puts these tasks in the context of Ion's sacred servitude: it is at one and the same time a work-song and a hymn. There is fresh innocence about Ion's aria, which makes this scene, often scorned for triviality by the book-ish, one of the most memorable parts of the play in performance. It ends:

> But in the tasks laid upon me I slave for Phoebus;
> and I shall never cease to minister to those who have
> sustained me. (181–3; cf. 124, 128ff., 151ff.)

Ion's initial innocence and unworldliness, which must be lost during the play [4.8.2], are conveyed with fine sensibility by Euripides' deft blending of levels. It is hard not to see this play, which proves in the end a glorification of Athens' past and a vindication of divine providence, as also a lament for the vulnerability of naive religious devotion.

[6.8.2]   Though we may feel uncomfortable over the chauvinism and credulous religiosity of the Attic legends and cults which surround *Ion*, it is essential for a full appreciation to realize Creusa's pedigree. She is the only surviving child of King Erechtheus and the royal line goes on through her. In Attic law there are complex provisions for the marriage of an heiress (*epiklēros*); for the inheritance does not belong to her, it is in trust for her children.[12] Creusa is the *epiklēros* of the heritage of Erechtheus; and on one level the play is about his threatened extinction and eventual renewal ('the house once more has a hearth, the land has kings; Erechtheus is rejuvenated', 1464–5). Erechtheus' story is repeatedly alluded to, and filled in early on by Hermes at 20ff. and by Creusa at 265ff.[13] His father was Erichthonius who was himself born from the earth; Athena had adopted Erichthonius and gave him for safe-keeping to the daughters of Cecrops, the half-snake first king of Athens; and she also gave two snakes to guard him (snakes are, of course, generally associated with autochthony and chthonic cult). Cecrops adopted him as king in turn; and in recollection of his infancy all descendants of Erichthonius used as babies to wear a gold necklace in the form of a snake. But in the next generation Erechtheus had sacrificed his daughters at a time when Athens was in mortal danger, and he had himself been swallowed up in the earth.[14] Creusa alone survived the sacrifice because she had been a new-born baby (see *Ion*, 279f.).

But all this legendary rigmarole takes on a new and more concrete significance as the play progresses, especially at those places where it is translated into tangible objects. Thus, as Creusa and the old servant search for a plot against Ion, Creusa suddenly embarks on a long legendary excursus about Athena's victory over the Gorgon and her gifts to Erichthonius (987ff.). What all this leads up to is that the Queen actually has on her wrist at this moment an heirloom, a gold bracelet that Athena originally gave to the infant Erichthonius. It has two chambers: one contains a healing elixir, the other deadly poison from the Gorgon's snakes – and this poison they will use to dispose of Ion. At 1029ff. Creusa hands this over – 'You know what to do. Receive from my wrist Athena's gold-work, this ancient piece of craftsmanship' (1029–30): a tangible link is made between the exotic-ism of fable and the present murderous reality of the tragedy. For the heritage of primaeval local heroes is at stake amid this fierce emotion; and such families have unusual, fabulous things at their disposal – an aspect dwelt on in the choral song which follows (1048ff.). The even more fantastical panacea remains unused, a transparent emblem of the unforeseen happy-ending.

More miraculous objects are put to exciting use in the recognition [6.8.3] scene. The Pythia gives to Ion (1337ff.) a round wicker-work cradle, with a lid bound down with sacred bands of wool (evidently like that in which Athena gave Erichthonius to the daughters of Cecrops – see 271–3). Possibly its cylindrical shape was unusual and especially associated with Erechtheian cult, for the curious word *antipēx*, which does not occur elsewhere, is used of it five times in *Ion* (19, 40, 1338, 1380, 1391).[15] That there is something miraculous about the cradle is clear from the way that its wicker-work has not deteriorated at all with the passage of time (see 1391–4). The cradle is recognized by Creusa (1395ff.); and she stakes her life or death on her ability to describe the tokens which are inside it (1412ff.). The objects are described and taken out one by one; and, sure enough, they are not without special significance both on a personal and on a legendary level. First (1417–25), there is a piece of cloth which Creusa wove as a girl. That is usual enough: but it is decorated with a snaky gorgon's head – source of the poison and the panacea (see above). Next (1426–32), there is the golden snake necklace, the special sign of descendants of Erich-thonius, singled out by Hermes back at 24–6. This is the symbol of the kingship; but it is probably also of identical design to the poison bracelet of the earlier scene [6.8.2], which had orginally been put on the baby Erichthonius. Ion is to be restored not only to his mother and to the royal house, but also to Athens – 'the house once more has a hearth, the land has kings' (1464). This is betokened by the third object (1432–6), a garland of olive leaves, still as fresh as the day it was taken from the sacred tree on the Acropolis. Athena had given this, the first olive, to Athens as the stock of its future prosperity.[16] These objects lead up the embrace of mother and son [5.8.3]: but at the same time they surround all the emotion of the reunion with an aura of legendary splendour. One of Euripides' achievements in *Ion* is, it seems to me, the inseparable blend of intense passion, human and immediate, with the distancing of patriotic fable. The stage-props by having both a personal and a fabulous significance are crucial to the working of this delicate mixture.

[6.9.1]   The Bacchic paraphernalia of fawnskin, flowing hair, ivy wreath and thyrsus (a rod with a bunch of ivy on it) are everywhere in *Ba*. Dionysus himself has them, so does the chorus, Agaue, Cadmus and Tiresias. They come to stand for the acceptance of the new cult – their absence for its rejection. Thus Tiresias urges Pentheus 'accept the god into this land: pour libations, be a bacchant, put a garland on your head' (312–13). Cadmus translates this into a small more concrete decision when he tells Pentheus:

> Come here and let me garland your head too
> with ivy; join us, give the god due honour. (341–2)

He holds out the wreath towards him; and Pentheus' reply is characteristically virulent, taking its metaphor from contagious disease:

> Keep your hands off me; go play the bacchant,
> don't try to wipe off your foolery on me. (343–4)

In the next act, the first confrontation with Dionysus, Pentheus' aggressiveness against these external symbols become more positive:

> *Pen*: First I shall cut off your fancy locks.
> *Dion*: My hair's sacred: I grow it for the god.
> *Pen*: Then hand this thyrsus of yours here to me.
> *Dion*: Take it yourself: for it belongs to the god. (493–6)

It has been suggested that Pentheus actually cut the stranger's hair and took away his thyrsus. But such a crudely blasphemous action would surely be given more explicit commentary in the words: rather, the impression is reinforced that the acceptance or rejection of the god can be made through these material emblems. This implication is then exploited to the full in the humiliation of Pentheus (912ff.), where his long hair and thyrsus are used tellingly to create the peculiar atmosphere of that scene [5.9.2].

[6.9.2]   Later in *Ba* we see one of the most memorably significant stage-properties in all Greek tragedy: that is the head of Pentheus – probably represented simply by the mask which the actor had worn, now daubed with blood. It is far more than merely a gratuitous touch of horror. But first it is necessary to work out the basic stage-directions involved.

The messenger prepares for Agaue's entry (1139ff.): she has treated the head as the spoil of a successful hunt, has stuck it on the end of her thyrsus, and is returning home in triumph. This introduces the institutional framework which is used – parodied almost – in the act which follows. After a successful day's hunting there should be a revel (*kōmos*, see 1167, 1172) with the quarry's head as a trophy, and a feast where everyone is to congratulate the best hunter.[17] Thus Agaue boasts that she struck the first blow (1179ff.), she invites the guests (1184ff.); the chorus congratulates her (1180, 1193ff.), and suggests that she should display her trophy to the citizens (1200f.). Agaue calls on the citizens to look, and even demands a ladder so that she can fix the head to the eaves of the palace (1202–15). It is probably at this stage that she takes it off the thyrsus. Before this macabre idea can be carried through, Cadmus returns with the dismembered corpse of Pentheus now reassembled on a bier (1216ff.). Agaue greets him triumphantly:

> Father, the proudest boast is yours to make. . . .
> As you can see, I'm bringing in my arms
> this prize, a trophy to hang in your house.
> Take it yourself, dear father, in your hands.
> Take pride in my good hunting – and invite
> your friends to celebrate – yes, you are blessed.
> (1233, 1238–42)[18]

But the gruesome fantasy of the hunting-*kōmos* has now been taken far enough: the head must now be put to a new purpose. In what has been called the 'psychotherapy scene' (1259ff.), Cadmus recovers his daughter from madness and brings her back to her right senses; and the focus of this slow, terrifying dialogue is the disembodied head:

Cadm: What head is this you're carrying in your arms?
　Ag: A lion's – or so my fellow-hunters said.
Cadm: Look properly. That is no great hardship.
　Ag: Ah! What's this I see? What am I carrying?
Cadm: Now study it, and see the truth more clearly.
　Ag: I see the worst thing I could ever see!
Cadm: Does it still look in the least like a lion?
　Ag: No, not at all. I hold the head of Pentheus. (1277–84)

Finally it is almost certain that in the lines which are missing after 1300 Agaue put the head on the bier with the rest of the corpse, and lamented it appropriately. The object which has held our gaze in reluctant fascination for 140 lines is at last laid to rest.[19]

The point of all this business with Pentheus' head is that it is an ambivalent object which sums up a central ambivalence in the play. It may be – and is – viewed in two ways. On the one hand the head may be seen through the eyes of Dionysus and of his followers, the chorus and Agaue while she is still possessed: for them it is the trophy of a great hunt, a triumph. Pentheus was a dangerous wild beast, preying on the bacchants (this imagery is recurrent, and obviously reverses the hunting imagery which Pentheus himself used of his persecution of the bacchants – 226ff., 434ff., etc.). Now the ravager has been hunted to the death; this is cause for great rejoicing, and the spoils should be displayed to all the citizens. The audience should not – and cannot – resist seeing the events of the tragedy partly under this aspect: but inevitably they will feel the other aspect much more keenly. That is the viewpoint of the royal house of Thebes, of Cadmus, and of Agaue *after* she has recovered her senses. Seen with their eyes the head means utter disaster – the pollution of kin-murder, exile, the end of the royal line. Pentheus was the great hope of the family; see 1308–10, quoted on p. 56 (this motif was probably pursued in the lost laments after 1300 and 1329). The person who experiences the ambivalence of the significance of Pentheus' head most cruelly is, of course, Agaue. For her it means first the proof of god-given elation and power; and then for ever after the brutal murder of her own son.

In fact, the dismembered head epitomizes what the play is, in one sense, about: the duality of Dionysus. He is, as he himself puts it in a highly stressed context 'a true-born god, most terrible – most gentle to mankind' (860–1).

7 Tableaux, noises and silences

First of all Aeschylus would bring on a character
Sit him down and veil his face . . .
Then the chorus would tie a string of endless odes –
not a sound from the mysterious figure . . .
Then after all this verbiage, when the play was half over,
he'd speak a dozen galumphing words . . .
incomprehensible to the audience. . . . (Aristophanes, Frogs)

This chapter is something of a miscellany. Noises and silences might seem to make a pair; but in terms of theatrical technique they are very different, since one is usually momentary and the other prolonged. Tableaux have something in common with both, since like a silence they petrify an emotional state in expressive immobility, and like a noise they begin with an instantaneously notable impact.

By tableaux I mean (rather loosely) those places where there is not only a lack of dramatic movement, but also some or all of the visual constituents of a scene are held still for a longer or shorter time in a combination which captures or epitomizes a particular state of affairs. This kind of 'freezing' will sometimes come about when a sudden interruption catches the characters on stage 'red-handed', so to speak, so that they hold the pose they had reached at the crucial moment. But the most common circumstances involve a deliberately arranged set-piece, for example at the beginning of a play or at some ritual event, or at the Greek theatre's special type of revelation-scene – the *ekkyklema* (see p. 12). And there are other less conventional ways in which the dramatist may sum up a stage in the sequence of the play so as to create a pictorial impression which will remain as a kind of after-image.

'Noises' in Greek tragedy bring to mind chiefly off-stage noises, and these are as a rule the sounds of violent deeds going on inside the background-building. There is nothing in the theatre so sustained as, for example, the knocking at the gate that continues through some 40 lines of *Macbeth*, and which links scenes 2 and 3 of Act II;[1] nor is there anything so weird and unexplained as 'suddenly there is a sound in the distance, as it were from the sky – the sound of a breaking harp-string, mournfully dying away', a sort of melancholy music of the spheres in *The Cherry Orchard*, Act II. Still, there are some telling sounds and off-stage cries in Greek tragedy; and I have also considered some important interjections and non-verbal noises uttered by characters on stage.

Silence can, at times, say more than words. Great events and tragic emotions may cut a person off from the ordinary possibilities of communication: crushing grief, defiance, fear, implacable vindictiveness, ineffable joy. Round about the individual who is isolated from the fundamental contact of words, the other characters are thrown into confusion and anxiety. In the tragedians' workshop silence is a basic tool for conveying a crisis in human relationships, provided it is used sparingly. Shakespeare's mastery is outstanding in this – one thinks of Macduff, Pericles, Coriolanus and so on. Aeschylus was famous for some of his silences, and in the *Frogs* Aristophanes makes great play in these in contrast to Euripides' garrulity. None the less Sophocles and Euripides did not fail to learn from Aeschylus in this as in everything, and among the surviving tragedies their silences are no less notable.

[7.1.1]   Agamemnon returns victorious from Troy on a chariot, and accompanied, no doubt, by a retinue of spear-carriers. While later productions have visually overloaded this scene (chariot loads of treasure and so on), it forms an impressive tableau. As the procession enters the chorus chants a welcome (783ff.), and the scene will have come to a halt long enough to be taken in and reflected on before Agamemnon speaks (810). The surface meaning is obvious: the king, awaited for ten arduous years, returns at last, the light at the end of the long darkness (cf. 22ff., 264ff., 522f.); and he is triumphant, the victor in the greatest war of the heroic age:

> Now, my king, city-sacker of Troy,
> offspring of Atreus,
> how am I to address you . . . ? (783–5)

Yet the superficial glory of the picture is tarnished, clouded with a host of dark associations. The play has already been permeated with disquiet and foreboding: Iphigenia and the departure of the army, the loss of Menelaus, the resentful people of Argos, the house and its watchdog, the whole war for one promiscuous woman. The last song before Agamemnon's entry is full of irony; it ends:

> Justice . . . who has no reverence
> for wealth and power with the counterfeit of praise,
> steers everything to its finish. (779–81)

And the tableau of the triumphant return is not only flawed by trains of thought linking with previous themes, there is also something wrong with what we actually see. In the chariot with Agamemnon is a woman who wears the trappings of a prophetess. It may be obvious to the audience from her costume that she is a Trojan, it may even be assumed that she is Cassandra. But no specific attention is drawn to her yet; she remains as a peculiar, unexplained part of the total picture, an anomaly, a source of disquiet [see further 7.1.3].

Although we see the last of Agamemnon as soon as 974, we do not [7.1.2] hear his last until 1343–5, when his two death calls sound out from the palace. We have long known and even longer feared that he is to be murdered by Clytemnestra, and are by now almost reconciled to the idea: none the less his cries beneath the fatal strokes come as a shock. The understanding of moral themes is turned to gash and blood. And perhaps these loud, dying shouts are not, as is often said, an expected formality in theatrical terms. Death cries from the palace are so familiar from later tragedy that they are almost a joke; but in 458 B.C. the *skēnē* building was probably still a novelty, and Agamemnon's cries may have been one of the first times the audience had ever experienced this device. It would be – and should be for us – as though the palace building had suddenly spoken. Agamemnon is part of the house, and his slaughter is the newel of its troubles. 'The house itself, could it but get a voice, would speak out all too clear.'

In contrast, the short incoherent cry of Aegisthus at *Cho* 869 is entirely expected and almost satisfying. He goes briskly to his death [9.2.1], and there is only a brief choral chant of suspense before the awaited cry is duly heard. It *is* little more than a formality. The death in *Cho* which is set against that of Agamemnon is Clytemnestra's, not the perfunctory snuffing out of the man-woman Aegisthus.

Cassandra is silent on stage for nearly 300 lines before she utters a [7.1.3] sound. For most of this time attention is fully occupied on other things, and she still remains only in the corner of our eye, so to speak [7.1.1] . From 783 to 949 she is not even mentioned. Even after Agamemnon has drawn attention to her in 950–5 she is allowed to recede into the shadows again during the following choral song, an unfocused mystery. Up to this point her silence has not been remarked as such, it is simply part of her unknowness. But then Clytemnestra comes out specifically to fetch her, too, into the 'sacrifice'

(1035ff.): Cassandra makes no response except perhaps some wild gesticulations. Her lack of speech becomes the active sign of her peculiarity. Clytemnestra does not, for the first time, have full intelligence of the situation; she finds the silence so bewildering that she thinks Cassandra may not even understand Greek (1050f.). As the chorus puts it:

> The stranger seems to need an interpreter.
> She's like some newly captured animal. (1062–3)

But once Clytemnestra has gone away frustrated [see 9.1.1] and Cassandra is left alone with the sympathetic chorus, she breaks her long silence, at first in strange cries, then in song and finally in speech. Most of her part is couched in strange riddles and metaphors – enigmas which have none the less a terrible clarity – but within her scene as a whole there is a movement from vague disquiet to fully comprehended knowledge. This is explicitly marked in Cassandra's words as she shifts from lyric to speech:

> My prophesy no longer shall glance from
> behind a veil, like a new married bride,
> but shall rush like a fresh breeze to the sunrise,
> and like a wave shall surge into the light
> a far greater calamity. No more
> shall I teach you in riddles. (1178–83)

The silence has its place within this enlightening movement. It makes Cassandra at first part of that overwhelming, benighted foreboding which is so powerfully invoked in the choral song 975–1033 [see 9.1.1] and which casts its shadow over the opening of her scene. Yet by the end of the scene some sort of pattern and insight will have emerged. We shall know about Cassandra herself and Troy, about the house of Atreus, the curse, the impending murders and the return of Orestes: the apparently snarled threads of the play are shown by Cassandra to form some design. So the mysterious foreign woman who remained so long silent turns out to be the one who tells most and who is least confusing. And this stream from silence to explanation has its place within a great sweeping current of the whole trilogy, from ignorance and obscurity towards clarity and understanding.

[7.2.1]   Soon after the reunion in *Cho* the focus of visual attention narrows on the tomb of Agamemnon. From 315 until 478 there is a complex and monumental lyric structure, sung by Orestes, Electra and the chorus, which is usually known as the 'great *kommos*'.[2] This *kommos* is at one and the same time a long-postponed funeral lament for Agamemnon and an invocation of his ghostly power to help in the revenge. This is continued in the following speeches and is finally brought to a close at 510ff., after some 200 lines. What is the stage picture throughout all this? Near the opening Electra sings 'Your tomb has received us as suppliants and as exiles also' (336–7); this suggests that they are actually touching or standing on the tomb. Near the end she cries:

> You see these fledgelings sitting by your tomb;
> pity the cry of the female and the male. (501–2)

So it seems that all this time Electra and Orestes have been grouped at the tomb – which it is hard to envisage as anywhere other than in the *orchēstrā* itself – while the passionate threnetic choreography of the chorus goes on around them. That is to say that the music and movements of this huge scene revolved around a fixed tableau-like grouping. This would provide an expressive centre to this magnificent and intricate set-piece. The disinherited orphans of the eagle cling to the eyrie (cf. 256–9), source of their sorrow and of their strength, while the choral movement and elaborate song build up into a presence almost tangible the vengeful help of the mutilated king.

A noise that was very rarely heard in the Greek tragic theatre was [7.2.2] that of knocking at the door, as at *Cho* 653ff. Orestes had planned that he and Pylades, disguised as travellers, would put on a Phocian dialect (563ff.): this he does not literally do, but it is worth noting that his opening words have a distinctly everyday ring about them: 'Hey slave, slave I say! Do you hear my knocking at the gate? Who's there? Hey slave, slave I say! Is anyone at home?' (653–4). This kind of language and action is an extremely common occurrence in Greek comedy, but not in tragedy. It looks as though it was considered too mundane and undignified for the tragic stage. This points to a difference between Orestes' approach to murder and Clytemnestra's [see further 8.1.1/8.2.1]. Her plot against Agamemnon worked through exotic, startling, oblique words and actions: Orestes' plot against her works through the domestic and everyday round, direct and real. There is a hint here of that tension between the mundane world and high tragedy which is so finely used in Shakespeare's 'Porter of Hell Gate'.

Pylades in *Cho* is a strange half-character, as indeed he tends to [7.2.3] be in the later Orestes' plays also. He follows in Orestes' footsteps, a shadowy figure behind his shoulder, seldom referred to, always there. Yet in the *Oresteia* he has no part to play after the murder: it seems as though he is primarily there in order to speak his three crucial lines at 900–2. Long before that we have become accustomed to his silent presence, and his silence does not of itself have any particular significance. We take him to be simply one of those characters who are found now and then in Greek tragedy, who say nothing, and merely form a pair with some more important figure. It is not his silence but the *breaking* of it which gives him his dramatic point. When Orestes is faced with his mother who points to the breast which suckled him and which he must mangle [see 5.2.2], he turns to an outside authority for judgement: 'Pylades, what shall I do? Should I stand in awe of killing my own mother?' (899). Orestes' resolution stands in the balance, to be tipped by the words of Pylades, the silent:

> Then what about the Delphi-given oracles?
> And what about your solemn promises?
> Hold anyone your foe before the gods. (900–2)

The intervention is decisive. And then Pylades is discarded, and after the murder no more is seen or heard of him. In *Eum* Apollo takes over his own part himself.

[7.3.1]   It was difficult to set up an effective trial scene on the Greek tragic stage since there were normally only three actors to provide the participants (prosecutor, defendant, presiding officer, jury, witnesses). In *Eum* Aeschylus manages this by the bold resort of making the chorus itself the prosecutors and by bringing on a group of extras as the jury. We cannot hope to know exactly how the scene was arranged on stage, but it is fair to suppose that there were three separate groups. In the centre would be Athena and her chosen citizens, the jurors; on one side would be the chorus and on the other Orestes with his 'witness and advocate' (576–9), Apollo. This positioning will have been quickly and unobtrusively taken up during the opening lines 566–73.[3] The grouping will have remained until it is finally broken up by the voting and resultant acquittal [cf. 5.3.2, 4.3.2]; there is then a completely new situation presented by a quite different stage configuration [see 9.3.2]. The tableau sets out the parties at the trial and is thus a formal necessity; but it may be rather more than that, for the trial is the aetiological foundation 'charter' of the Areopagus for all time, as Athena makes clear in her 'statute' speech (681ff. – the opening lines are quoted on p. 63). The stage-blocking carries, that is to say, all the awe and weight of an archetype.

[7.3.2]   The trial opens, it seems, with a trumpet clarion which presumably sounded after 569 (see 567–9). But earlier in *Eum* we hear some of the most extraordinary sounds ever to startle the Greek tragic theatre; these are the animal noises made by the sleeping Furies as the dream of Clytemnestra rouses them to action (117–30). Between her first and second speeches Clytemnestra delivers a series of couplets interspersed by noises from the chorus. The stage-instructions which have been transmitted with the text ('moaning . . . howling') were probably added, not by Aeschylus, but by a commentator in antiquity, but

the words show that he was along the right lines: 'Well may you moan
. . .' (118), 'You howl, but you sleep on . . .' (124). Finally the chorus
cries out more clearly 'Catch, catch, catch, catch, look out!' (130); and
Clytemnestra responds:

> You are hunting a dream prey and you bay
> like dogs that never can forget the kill. (131–2)

(Apparently they dream simultaneously of the pursuit of Orestes and
of Clytemnestra's rousing them.) It is usually held that the Furies,
lying asleep, have been revealed to the audience back at 64; but in my
view there are good reasons for thinking that they were not seen in
Aeschylus' production before they awake for their first song at 140ff.
Their entry would, surely, be far more effective if it is held back as
long as possible [cf. 8.3.1]. That would mean that the noises in 117ff.
would issue from an unseen source inside the *skēnē*, the Pythian
shrine. We not only hear about the Furies, but also hear them directly,
before we eventually see them. All that we hear contributes to a
picture of repulsive bestiality which is horridly confirmed by their
masks and costumes when they are eventually revealed. When we
first hear the Furies it seems that they are so remote from the world of
civilization that they cannot even speak except in bloodcurdling
noises: this impression will turn out to be very wrong. These wild
howls will turn before the trilogy is done to songs, full of grace and
benevolence.

During the trial Orestes hands over his defence to Apollo at 614 [7.3.3]
and then has nothing further to say until the counting of the votes
begins 130 lines later. His agonized cry 'O Phoebus Apollo, which
way will the issue go?' (744) sharply brings attention back to him
before the verdict that will dismiss him from the trilogy which has
now moved on to more far-reaching issues [cf. 4.3.2, 9.3.2]. But it is
not his silence which is of dramatic weight here, it is only the ending
of it: earlier Orestes has a briefer silence which is singled out in its own
right. He clings to the ancient statue and has called on Athena to
come and save her suppliant (287–98); but the Furies reject any hope
of salvation and try to taunt him into a response (299ff.). But he
remains silent:

> Not deign to answer? You spit at my words,
> do you, my victim fattened up for me?
> Yes, you shall feast me live, not at the altar.
> So listen to my binding hymn about you. (303–6)

The point is that all Orestes' hope is pinned on Athena; without her
he is saved from the Furies' power only by her image [see 6.3.1], and
there is nothing that he can do or say to help himself. On the other

hand there is nothing that the Furies can do, except to repeat their hideous travesty of a sacrificial hymn, and to continue their endless, homeless toils. There is stalemate. And Orestes' refusal to enter on a dialogue, bound in any case to be uncommunicating, captures the sterility of the conflict. There is not yet anything worth saying; it will take the institution of a trial to provide a means of fighting the issue out in words.

[7.4.1]   There is a tableau-like nightmare element in Ajax's appearance (91–117). He stands madly exultant in the doorway while he talks to Athena, and Odysseus made magically invisible to Ajax cowers on one side. But in the next act there is a more sustained and yet more elaborately posed tableau (384–595), where Ajax is revealed among the slaughtered cattle. There all the signs of an *ekkuklēma* scene here (see p. 12), including the introductory signal:

> See, I open the doors. Now you may look
> upon his deeds, the man, and his condition. (346–7)

This gory *nature morte* captures with shocking, unalleviated direct-ness the extent of Ajax's disaster. He sits there enmired with dishon-our and despair; he cannot move without touching his disgrace. Troy has never seen his like and yet, as he sings at the very end of his lament, 'now I am thus prostrate in dishonour' (426–7). This is the welter from which Ajax must rise up and regain his stature. During this scene he does not, it seems, stand up; but before it is through he has decided on his course of action and begun to implement it [see 5.4.1]. He will go off to kill himself; but that is to rise only in order to fall. When he finally rises it is to be lifted on the shoulders of his funeral procession [cf. 4.4.4].

[7.4.2]   Towards the end there is another tableau which is carefully posed and held still for a long time, for over 200 lines in fact. Tecmessa enters with her son (1168ff.) after Teucer's brawl with Menelaus, and he arranges them carefully by the body of Ajax.

> Boy, come here, and grasp in supplication
> the father who begot you; sit here as
> a suppliant, and hold fast in your hand
> a lock of my hair and hers and your own –
> a suppliant's treasure. (1171–5)

[For the cutting of the hair see 5.4.2.] For all the rest of the play the boy sits there and Tecmessa kneels or stands beside him. Sophocles carefully arranges the scene before Teucer leaves (1184), so that it may form a background to the choral song at 1185ff. The whole safety of his dependants still rests on Ajax and he is for them a kind of sacred object; they take asylum at the lifeless hulk and defy any man who dares to risk sacrilege.[4] They protect the corpse (see 1180), and he in return protects them. Ajax proves big enough, even in death, to save them. So the tableau is not moved an inch until its efficacy is proved.

Three times in *Ajax* the same cry of despair – *iō moi moi* (ah me, ah me!) – is heard from behind the scenes before the entry of a character. [7.4.3] This cry echoes in the ear of the audience, pointing the course of the desolation of Ajax and his dependants. First it sounds from Ajax himself within his tent (333, 336), before he is revealed amidst the carnage [7.4.1 above]. Next it is heard when Tecmessa first discovers the body of Ajax (891, reiterated in the antistrophic stanza at 937); she is seen a moment later at 894.[5] For Tecmessa this is the fulfilment of her worst fears, she can see no hope. Finally, we hear Teucer also before he is first seen (974). He also is in despair; though even in the first rush of grief he thinks of Ajax's son (983ff.). Teucer is the man whose return was so keenly awaited in the first part of the play (342f., 562ff., 687ff., 826ff.; cf. 920–2): he is the lynchpin of Ajax's scheme. After his initial hopelessness, he will rise to the occasion. So, thrice in the see-saw movement of this play (see Athena at 131f.) a low point is marked by this off-stage knell.

There are no outstanding dramatic silences in *Ajax*, but it may be worth noting two places where Tecmessa stands silent for a long time. [7.4.4] Ajax tells her that silence is a woman's part (293; cf. 369, 579f., 587ff.). During the entire 'deception' speech she stands at his side. At first he speaks of her only in the third person (652f.), and at the end he gives her a final instruction:

> And you, woman, go and pray the gods
> they may fulfill the things my heart desires. (685–6)

She goes without a word. She does not understand what Ajax really means by this speech, and it would be out of place for anyone else to speak [see 8.4.1]. Secondly, she is a silent element in the supplication tableau at the end (see above). She is played by a mute actor, but there is, in any case, no place for her to speak at this stage. It is her part to act by not moving, to stand firm by Ajax. Contrast this positive silence with her passivity during Ajax's 'deception' speech.

OT begins with a tableau. A crowd (probably the old priest and a group of boys, but the text of 16–19 is disputed) sit as suppliants at the [7.5.1] altars before the palace of Oedipus. They must have entered, of course, but it looks as though, as in several other tragedies (e.g., Aesch. *Agam*), the entry happens before the play begins, so to speak. The audience realizes that it is to neglect the gathering and to imagine that the opening tableau has been in place for some time before the play begins. Oedipus then enters:

> My children, new issue from old Cadmus,
> what does this gathering mean, as you sit here
> with suppliant branches garlanded with wool? (1–3)

He looms above the suppliants, fatherly, dominant, wise – the nearest thing among men to a god (see 31ff., quoted on p. 88). The picture is to some extent reproduced when Oedipus next enters after the first song (216). The song has taken the form of a long intense prayer for salvation to the various gods. The chorus is perhaps still held in an attitude of prayer when Oedipus enters:

> You pray. And you may get help and relief
> from all these ills, if you will pay heed to
> the things I say to medicine the plague. (216–18)

He certainly seems the best hope for the Thebans in answer to their prayers. In the following proclamation of excommunication on the murderer (219–75) Oedipus is at his highest. His words are authoritative, definitive, overpowering. This is the height from which, through the exercise of those very qualities which have made him great, Oedipus must fall.

[7.5.2]   Once more Oedipus will present himself formally at the doors of his palace to all the people of Thebes. The messenger prepares for the sight (possibly on the *ekkyklēma*):

> He is weak and has none to guide his steps;
> for his disorder is too great to bear.
> Yet he will show you; the doors are opening;
> now shall you see a sight at which even
> one who is revolted still must feel compassion. (1292–6)

So Oedipus is now seen, fallen, polluted, blind, bloody [see 6.5.3]. Yet in the depths of his despair and self-loathing, is he in some way greater than he was earlier in the play, more worthy of awe and admiration? For at the beginning he was mighty in his temporal power and his ignorance: now he faces the world with the knowledge gained by his own insistent searching.

[7.5.3]   Eyesight and ignorance, blindness and insight – these important themes in *OT* are first established firmly in the Teiresias scene (cf. 300ff., 348f., 370–3, 388f., 412–14, 454). Sophocles is also master of the ways of putting blindness in theatrical terms, a skill which he uses with extraordinary effectiveness in *Oedipus at Colonus*. As well as the blind man's dependence on others to lead him and see for him, Sophocles makes telling use of the heightened senses of touch and of hearing. So when he brings Oedipus' daughters on stage at *OT* 1468ff. he has them weep out loud, and he makes the audience hear

them with Oedipus' ears. To the others this may be a mere formality,
but for Oedipus the sound of sorrow is also the knowledge that there
is some comfort in his world of darkness:

> Above all let me touch them with my hands
> and so unburden my great misery.
> Do it, my lord.
> My noble kinsman, do. Could I but feel them
> then I might think them mine, as when I saw.
> But what is this?
> You gods, can I hear two girls somewhere near
> weeping? Has Creon taken pity then
> and sent my dearest daughters here to me?
> Can I be right? (1466–75)

Even those without eyes might weep at this.

Jocasta is usually ready to speak. At one point, in an attempt to   [7.5.4]
reassure Oedipus, she reveals two fatal pieces of the picture of the
past [707ff., see 9.5.1]. But when she sees the truth she refuses to tell
it. At 1054ff. Oedipus turns to her for information, but she only begs
him to stop asking questions [cf. 4.5.5]. When he persists, she speaks
her last:

> It's out! unhappy man! That's all I have
> to say to you, and nothing ever more.   [exit]
> Chorus: Why, Oedipus, should she have rushed away
> in violent grief? I am afraid that from
> this silence will break out some storm of ill. (1071–5)

Two queens elsewhere in Sophocles depart to suicide: Eurydice at
Antigone 1244 and Deianeira at *Trachiniae* 813. But they both turn and
go in complete silence; the 'silence' of Jocasta here must be her refusal
to answer Oedipus' questions. She can not, will not, speak what she
knows. She has already said too much.

Yet a different, even more disturbing silence of Jocasta will be
alluded to later. When the chorus laments the truth about Oedipus
they sing:

> One and the same generous haven
> harboured you as a baby
> and as your landfall in the husband bed.
> How, oh how, could your father's furrows have borne you,
> wretch, have suffered you so long in silence? (1208–13)

How was it Jocasta's very womb did not scream aloud in protest?

The event which cauterized Neoptolemus' deceit by inflaming his   [7.6.1] pity and shame is Philoctetes' agony at the recurrence of his wound (730ff.). The scene includes several moments when the characters are fixed in physical attitudes which epitomize their distress. For example, after the bow has changed hands [776, see 6.6.1], Philoctetes asks Neoptolemus for his promise to stay with him while he is unconscious:

> Ph: Give me your hand in promise. Ne: I swear to stay.
> Ph: There, now, take me there! Ne: Where do you mean? Ph: Up. . . .
> Ne: Is this some new fit? Why stare at the sky?
> Ph: Let me go, go. Ne: Go where? Ph: Let go, I say.
> Ne: I will not. Ph: You will kill me by your grip.
> Ne: All right; you are returning to your senses.
> Ph: O earth, take me, I am at point of death.
> This illness will not let me stay upright. (813–20)

Neoptolemus stands firm grasping Philoctetes' hand, while the sufferer is contorted by some terrible fit. It is not clear exactly what is happening here, and perhaps the staging would have made things clearer. But it may be important that this is the first time that the two have physically touched (they did not, apparently, at 485, 733, 761ff., 776); for it seems to be Neoptolemus' hand which brings on the frenzy. Giving the hand is an important gesture in this play: giving the hand as a guarantee (as here), giving a hand to help [5.6.1, 8.6.2], or handing over the bow [6.6.1, 8.6.1]. So this first clasping of hands is stressed and prolonged. 'Let me go' means 'let me die', but it is also as though the contamination of his deceit aggravates Philoctetes' anguish. This is admittedly an obscure passage, but the human relationships are confused and distorted and the stage postures seem to reflect this.

[7.6.2]   As Philoctetes lies oblivious there is another statuesque tableau full of conflicting tensions at 833–64. The bow is won and the chorus urges Neoptolemus to make off with it; but Odysseus has lost his influence on him and he stands firm. 'To leave a task unfinished through lying would be a disgrace, no call for boasting' (842). The chorus' Odyssean response – 'No, no, my child, the god will see to all this . . . ' – is valid: now that they have the bow, Philoctetes is powerless. Although Neoptolemus' lines 839–42 foreshadow the full revelation of the prophecy at 1326ff. they remain unelaborated here, since the conflict here is to be seen in human terms. What Neoptolemus' immobile stance by the prostrate figure of the sufferer conveys is the conflict between Odysseus and his own better nature, his Achillean nature. His torn fixity embodies both the conflict and, because he does not move, the incipient victory of the Achillean side. Not long after at 895 another suspended physical movement will mark the next stage in the battle [see 8.6.2].

Philoctetes is heard approaching throughout the last strophic pair   [7.6.3] of the first song [201-18, see 4.6.1]. The sounds are not written in the text, and we have to imagine them from what the chorus sings (with the help of the inhuman cries transcribed during 732-90) 'Though distant, I can detect the cry of a man worn down by pain' (207-8), and so forth. The cries which they hear in this wilderness are made by a man; yet they are incoherent, terrible. Greatly though we may pity and admire Philoctetes, we must not forget that these cries of his were intolerable. They would be impossible to live with. The howls, with the stench of the wound, disrupted all secular and religious activity: that was why he was abandoned on Lemnos in the first place. The foul noise and stink are repeatedly stressed – see 8-11, 481-3, 520, 693-5, 872-6, 889-91, 1031-4. The sound of Philoctetes' approach, heard in the theatre, serves as some reminder that Philoctetes' wound affects others as well as himself.

Neoptolemus' silences in *Phil* are the most telling in all Sophocles.   [7.6.4] It is by means of *words*, the abrogation of silence, that he has to deceive Philoctetes [see 86-120 and 4.6.1]; and his silences mark the progress of his moral dilemma. When Philoctetes first enters Neoptolemus can hardly bring himself to speak. This is shown by the way that Philoctetes has to urge him to answer (see 230f., 238), and the way that Neoptolemus replies abruptly and briefly (232f., 239-41). But once he begins to lie, he warms to his task and meets with total success. A measure of his success is the way he behaves when Philoctetes pleads that he may go with him to Greece (468ff.). Philoctetes pauses for a response after 479, 483 and in the middle of 486. Neoptolemus remains silent, pretending to be undecided; and it is only after a lyric plea from the chorus (507-18) that, with a feigned show of hesitation, he agrees.

These silences are all sham. But when Philoctetes is in the throes of his agony Neoptolemus is silent under the stress of genuine emotional conflict. As Philoctetes pleads with him, he cannot speak:

> [*silence*] What do you say my child? [*silence*]
> What do you say? Nothing? [*silence*] Where do you stand?
> *Ne*: I have long been in pain at your distress. (804-6)

(Literally 'in pain groaning at your distress' – the paradox of silent, mental groaning to match Philoctetes' physical groaning.) It is this pain, the pain of attempting to be a pitiless liar, that makes Neoptolemus abandon the deceit [see 8.6.2]. But once he has gone that far, he is faced with another, more demanding test, when he is asked to return the bow [924 ff., see 6.6.1]. Again and again in the course of this great speech Philoctetes turns to Neoptolemus and waits for some response;

> . . . Are you not
> ashamed to look at me, your suppliant? [*silence*]
> You've robbed me of my bow and of my life.
> Give it back, I beg, give it back, I entreat you, child. [*silence*]
> By your fathers' gods, do not take my life.[6] [*silence*]
> Alas! He will not speak to me again;
> he looks away – for he will never give.
> I call on you, you bays . . .
> > . . . What am I to do?
> Give it back. Even now become yourself. [*silence*]
> What do you say? Silence? [*silence*] Then I am done for.
> O cave with two mouths . . . . (929–36, 949–52)

He ends:

> My curse . . . no, first I must see one more time
> if you will change your mind: if not, die damned. (961–2)

Still Neoptolemus is silent, and the chorus has to prompt him –

> What shall we do? It is now up to you
> whether we sail or give way to his pleas. (963–4)

All along Philoctetes has taken Neoptolemus' silence to mean that he is intractable: but in fact, it marks another turning-point in his internal conflict. This is plainly but movingly put in the couplet with which he breaks his silence:

> I have been overwhelmed by fierce pity
> for this poor man – not just now, long ago. (965–6)

Palai ('long ago') is the same word as in 806 quoted above and in the phrase 'this has long been hurting me' in 906 and 913: Neoptolemus' pity and shame constitute a sustained, aching pain. He is now close to returning the bow, and only the intervention of Odysseus stops him [8.6.1]. Neoptolemus is silent again for the entire scene 974–1080, except for the last few lines of it. But no attention is drawn to it; it simply marks his subjection to Odysseus. Odysseus speaks for him. But we have seen how Neoptolemus' better nature can overcome the Odyssean voice within him.

[7.7.1]
> Open the doors, servants, undo the bolts,
> so I may see the bitter spectacle,
> my wife, who dying has done me to death. (*Hipp*, 808–10)

Theseus' lines are almost formulaic as the cue for the *ekkyklēma*. What is revealed is the corpse of Phaedra; and the chorus sings a brief lament (811–16), while Theseus stands frozen at the sight before embarking on his dirge (817ff.). The chorus has just told Theseus a lie (804–5); the corpse as yet only tells the truth. But once Phaedra's letter has been opened the body remains there as silent, false proof of the lie [cf. 1022–4, 1057f. and 6.7.3]. Throughout the scene between Theseus and Hippolytus Phaedra is there, unrelenting, unaltering, accusing. As Theseus says:

> Why should I wrangle, when her corpse is here,
> most unmistakable of witnesses? (971–2)

Hippolytus had looked forward to witnessing a cross-examination of Phaedra by Theseus [661-3, see 9.7.1]. This would have been a tense scene; but Phaedra makes sure it never materializes. On the contrary, it is Hippolytus who has to confront Theseus, and it is Phaedra who is the damning witness.

Theseus enters at 790 on return from a sacred mission; but it is also [7.7.2] in response to a call for help. This call is, in Greek, a *boē* (790); the help is *boētheia* or *boēdromia* (cf. 776f. 'Help, help [*boēdromeite*], anyone near by the palace; my mistress, Theseus' wife, is hanging'). The cry for help sounds from inside at 776–7, it is more urgently elaborated at 780f.; and at 786f. we hear the call that she is dead. Thus, the calls from within which conventionally accompany the catastrophe are also used as a link to the entry of Theseus [see 9.7.1].

The *boē*, which is often used in tragedy, is also important in practice and in law, for as well as being a call for help it was a call for witnesses to the injustice. It is for witnesses that Theseus calls at 884–6:

> Hear me, citizens.
> Hippolytus has dared defile my bed
> by force, flouting the awful eye of Zeus.

But it is not some neutral citizens who answer this call, it is Hippolytus himself: 'I heard your call, father, and have hurried here' (902–3).[7] His dutiful response to the co-operative institution of the *boē* is full of irony in the circumstances. He runs on eager to help Theseus and to witness any injustice done to his father: in the event it is he who is to be witnessed against, and he will be driven off to his death.

'The choice between speech and silence is the situation which [7.7.3] places the four principal characters in significant relationship and makes an artistic unity of the play', thus Bernard Knox in one of the best essays on *Hipp*. Certainly the play is hung round a nexus of silence, of reticence and of non-communication. The most dramatic is

that of Phaedra in her first scene with the Nurse. When she is first
brought on she is ailing, and it is quite a long time before she is even
heard for the first time (176–98). After she has been carried away by
her passion, she sinks back once more, is veiled, and again lies silent
[see 6.7.2]. The Nurse desperately tries to get Phaedra to speak again
(288ff.), but she neither moves nor utters a sound:

> . . . speak out. . . . [*silence*]
> Why silent then? Do not keep silence, child,
> but contradict me if I was mistaken,
> or else confirm me if I spoke the truth. [*silence*]
> Say something; look at me. [*silence*] O misery,
> we are taking all these pains for no return;
> we are no nearer than before. (296–302)

At last, however, an incidental mention of the name 'Hippolytus'
(310) draws a cry of distress (*oimoi*) from Phaedra. She throws off her
veil and rises to her feet; and now that she has at last been drawn into
dialogue the Nurse presses on relentlessly until the truth is out [cf.
5.7.1]. Phaedra's only hope of secrecy lay in silence; once she breaks it
she is lost.

When she has heard the truth, it is the Nurse's turn to be at a loss for
words, though not for long (362–432). When she speaks again it is to
urge her defence of lust and to sow her insinuations about potions.
Phaedra pleads

> O dreadful words! Stop up your mouth. No more.
> Don't let out any more of this vile talk. (498–9)

But it is too late.

[7.7.4]　Phaedra's silence would have been better unbroken. But in the
great scene between Theseus and Hippolytus there are proud silences
which only compound the mistakes and misunderstandings. Hippolytus tries by questions to make Theseus look into the real reasons
for Phaedra's suicide, but his horror and disgust are so great that he
cannot bring himself to respond:

> What happened to her? How did she die? [*silence*]
> Father, I want to know; tell me. [*silence*] Silent?
> In times of trouble silence is no use. (909–11)

Before long Hippolytus is silent with shock and shame in the face of
Theseus' denunciation of him (see 946ff.). But his fatal silence is due
to his pious respect for the oath of secrecy which he made to the Nurse
before she importuned him (see 611f., 656–8). When Theseus is
adamant in his condemnation, Hippolytus is tempted to break the
oath:

> Gods, why should I not speak out, seeing that
> my reverence for you is ruining me?
> But no: I still should not convince my man,
> and I should confound for nothing my sworn oath. (1060–3)

This merely serves to aggravate Theseus' rage – 'Your sanctimoni-
ousness is death to me!' (1064). Hippolytus is trapped in a conspiracy
of silence. The chorus has been sworn to secrecy by Phaedra (710–14),
Phaedra herself is silent in death [7.7.1], the letter is silent [6.7.3].
Hippolytus appeals to the very palace:

> House, house, if only you could speak out loud
> and witness whether I'm an evil man. (1074–5, cf. 792f.)

When the Pythia enters at *Ion* 1320 both Creusa and Ion are frozen [7.8.1]
at a crisis of inactivity. Creusa simply clings to the altar [5.8.3]; Ion is
torn between his conviction that the god could not protect the evil and
his respect for the plain fact of supplication at asylum. Although the
Pythia's first words are 'Stop, my child' it is unlikely that Ion had
actually embarked on action; he is still trapped by indecision. The
play has at this point sunk to a deadlock of hatred, despair and
misunderstanding: it is this that the Pythia breaks. Her entry is
designedly unprepared for, unmotivated, coincidental so to speak.
Though it may also be seen as the intervention of Apollo – 'he found
ways to rescue you' (1565).

The Pythia is almost a proxy *deus ex machina* for Apollo, and in this [7.8.2]
she foreshadows Athena at the end. Just before that final epiphany
we have the last of a whole succession of almost-committed acts
which have run right through the play [see 8.8.1]. The reunion of
Creusa and Ion is complete, but there remains the inconsistency
between Creusa's claim that Apollo was the father of Ion and the
oracle to Xuthus (1536ff.). Creusa's reaffirmation of faith in Apollo
enables her to see the truth of the situation (1539–45); but this does not
satisfy Ion (compare the way Creusa had wanted to press the oracle
about her own case at 330–91):

> I cannot turn about so carelessly.
> No, I shall go inside and ask Apollo:
> 'Am I son of a mortal or of you?' (1546–8)
>   [*he approaches the shrine*]

At this moment Athena appears, probably on the roof of the temple
(the sun reflecting from her shield? – see 1549f.). So Ion is caught even
as he approaches the temple, venially guilty of an act of doubt, the last
act of doubt in the play.

There is a slight and delicately handled dramatic silence at *Ion* [7.8.3]

582–4, which introduces Ion's reservations about going to Athens [4.8.2]. But much more important for the development of the play are the silences which are *not* kept and which upset Apollo's original plan for Ion. Xuthus' last words as he leaves the play are a threat to the chorus:

> You handmaids, I command you to keep quiet:
> if you tell my wife anything, you die. (666–7)

The chorus is often bound to secrecy in Greek tragedy when it is essential to the plot (as in *Hipp*); but here, rather, the convention is introduced in order to be broken. The maids are faithful to the sole surviving child of Erechtheus, not to her imported husband; and when Creusa asks them what was the outcome of Xuthus' consultation of the oracle, they cannot bring themselves to conceal it:

> Cho: What shall we do? The penalty is death
> Cr: What tune is this? And what is it you fear?
> Cho: To speak or to stay quiet? What shall we do?
> Cr: Speak, since you have some news which touches me.
> Cho: Yes, we must tell – even if we die for it.
> My queen, it's not for you to cradle children
> in your arms, or ever put them to the breast. (756–62)

So the truth – the false truth – is out.

After her first desolate reaction (763–99) Creusa lapses into silence, while the old servant (mouthpiece of Erechtheus) fired with loyal indignation and hatred, tries to goad her into desperate action (803–56). But it is *Apollo*, not Xuthus, whom Creusa wants to punish. When she breaks her silence it is with recitative, and her words are breathtakingly dangerous:

> How can I keep silent, o my soul?
> How to lighten my dark ravishment,
> how to rid me of my shame?
> Is there restraint to hold me any more?
> What point in keeping up the virtuous struggle?
> Has not my husband proved a traitor?
> Am I not deprived of home, deprived of issue,
> my hopes all faded?
> I had hoped to make all well
> by keeping silent my first union,
> keeping silent my lamentful childbed
> – but I could not.
> No, by the starry seat of Zeus,
> no, by the goddess of my native citadel,

pure queen of the watery lake Tritonis,
no longer shall I hide the secret of that bed.
So shall I find relief in overflowing my full breast. (859–75)

With this prelude Creusa braces herself to deliver her monody,
881–922, in my eyes one of the masterpieces of Greek lyric poetry. The
song purports to be a denunciation of Apollo, full of loathing; but it is
at the same time a hymn of praise. It is a parody of a hymn which
cannot help being a genuine hymn as well. Euripides strains syntax,
vocabulary and the formulae of the hymn to their limits to convey this
passionate extreme of ambivalence. For all these years, while there
has been a spark of hope, Creusa has concealed and dwelt on her
shameful secret. But now there is no point, no saving grace: so here at
Delphi, before his temple and among the famous sculptures and
paintings, Creusa publishes her indictment of Apollo. Her royal spirit
can contain it no longer. And so the calculations of Apollo, set out by
Hermes at 69–73, are knocked askew. First the chorus could not keep
quiet and now Creusa: murder, sacrilege and disaster very nearly
ensue. This is no ordinary silence which is broken here, it is a silence
of nearly *twenty years*. Creusa at last releases in her great aria the
tensions which have so long been her private preoccupation.

Gods do not often take part in Greek tragedy as characters; their   [7.9.1]
direct contributions are usually restricted to prologues and to distanced epiphanies. Dionysus' unusual part in *Ba* is prepared for by
the prologue, where he speaks as a typical prologue-god, but also
explains his disguise as a human, a disguise he already has on [cf.
4.9.1].[8] None the less there is still the occasional epiphanic element
about his role later in the play. This is particularly evident in the scene
usually known as the 'palace miracles' at lines 576ff. The previous
choral ode (519ff.) had turned into a kletic hymn, that is a hymn which
calls on the god to come and reveal himself. At the end of it, as though
in answer, the voice of Dionysus himself, not of his disguise, sings
out from the palace. During a scene of increasing devotional excitement the divine voice from within continues and the chorus sing and
dance in frenzy as an earthquake strikes the palace, lightning fires it,
and a flame springs up in the extinguished pyre of Semele (I doubt
there was any attempt to represent these lightning effects, and I very
much doubt the earthquake was conveyed in any way less effective
than the choreography and the words themselves). Finally, in terror,
the bacchants fling themselves to the ground:

Cast your trembling bodies to the ground, maenads,
down. For our master, son of Zeus, is come
against this house, upturning everything. (600–3)

The music stops, the devotees lie prostrate: this is the moment for an
epiphany above the palace. Instead, 'the stranger', the holy man,
walks calmly out of the door. Something of the agitation lingers on in
the trochaic scene which follows (604–41); but by the time Pentheus
re-enters (642), Dionysus wears the same amused impassivity as
before. The tableau moment at 603 is, in a way, an anti-climax; but it
conveys most impressively Dionysus' blend of brute power and
gentle humour. Pentheus has no eye for it, and the humour will have
to become brutal.

[7.9.2]   At the end of the play Dionysus did appear above the palace in the
manner of the conventional 'god from the machine'. Nearly all this is
lost in the missing lines, 60 or more, after 1329, and we cannot,
unfortunately, recover the tone and impact of his epiphany. We
cannot know, for instance, whether Cadmus and Agaue embarked on
some course of action which Dionysus had to prevent, a situation
which commonly occurs at this juncture. But we can be pretty sure
that Dionysus was now without his disguise, unconcealed, stark and
merciless. To judge from what we have, he cast off all the elaborations
of his earlier assumed character, and revealed himself as unmitigated
power:

> Cadm: . . . but you have gone too far.
> Dion: Yes; you humiliated me, a god.
> Cadm: But gods should not descend to human passions.
> Dion: My father Zeus has sealed this long ago. (1346–9)

There can be no reply to this.

[7.9.3]   I have just discussed [7.9.1] the scene in which the voice of
Dionysus was heard inside the palace calling for its destruction
(576–603). It is a curiously thrilling and eerie sequence: nowhere else
in Greek tragedy is a god heard calling from off-stage, let alone
accompanied by thunder and lightning.[9] But I want, finally, to look at
a noise made by Dionysus in a very different mood.

It is, perhaps, cheating to include interjections in this chapter; but
interjections, meaningful non-verbal utterances, are interesting,
though often difficult to interpret for those outside their 'vernacular'
culture. With a language like Greek one simply has to look at the
various contexts in which the interjection occurs and try to elicit a
common factor. What, then, are we to make of Dionysus' 'ah' ($\bar{a}$) at
810? Is it an 'ah' of surprise, or protest, or confidentiality, or readjustment? I find it impossible to pin down any single emotion or
tone: all one can say is that the delivery must capture the tension of a
turning-point which means death for Pentheus. Up until this point
Dionysus has left Pentheus' fate conditional but with 809 – 'Ho

there, bring out my armour. And stop talking you' – he casts away his
last chance [see 9.9.1]. Then:

> Dion: Ah –
>> Would you like to see them huddled in the hills?
> Pen: Yes, yes! I'd give the world in gold for that. (810–12)

With his question Dionysus touches a chord in Pentheus which
instantly begins to bewitch him and from now on Pentheus has no
control over his fate [cf. 8.9.1]. (Contrast the scene in which Cadmus
leads Agaue *out* of madness [6.9.2]. In performance this should be
obvious in a change of atmosphere – in some ways a relief that the
suspense is over and the sentence passed, in some ways pity for
Pentheus, in some ways fear of Dionysus' latent power. The 'ah'
means death; and yet it epitomizes Dionysus in this play that this
terrible moment should be conveyed coolly, enigmatically, monosyl-
labically.

8 Mirror scenes

> 'Everything in this world', continued my father (filling a fresh
> pipe) – 'everything in this world, my dear brother Toby, has
> two handles . . . .' (Sterne, Tristram Shandy)

Mirror reflection, echo, doublet, parallelism, correspondence, pair-
ing – it is a basic possibility for the artist that separate different events
may be seen to be also similar. So a pattern begins to emerge.
Whether or not it is true that the human mind has a binary basis of
operation, whether or not the Greek mind had a special tendency to
order the world in terms of polarity and analogy,[1] it is the case that the
Greek tragedians often set up pairs of scenes, and almost invariably
set up the similarities in order to bring out the differences. While the
similarities may rest primarily in contextual or verbal parallelism
there is as often as not a visual dimension to the mirror effect; the
double exposure of the stage picture reinforces the patterning.

Again the particular spareness of Greek tragedy lends itself to such
devices. The components are few and large, the invitation to find
pairings easy to convey. Also the tendency to a central catastrophic
reversal (*peripeteia* in Aristotle's terminology) encourages arrangement by doublets on either side of the fulcrum. Of course, there are
plentiful examples of this technique in other schools of drama, but, on
the whole, their richness and complexity of incident obliges their
correspondences to be less tellingly obvious than in Greek tragedy.
One Shakespearean example. In II.v. of *Romeo and Juliet* the nurse

teases Juliet by holding back her news of an assignation with Romeo; in III.ii she does not clearly convey to Juliet the news of Tybalt's murder. The distinct similarity in the scenes brings out the way that Juliet's life is blighted by the event which turns the play from a comedy to a tragedy. Later the parallelism of Juliet's taking the false 'poison' (IV.iii) and Romeo's taking his true one (V.iii) subserves the same downward movement. The doubling is undeniable; but it is only a slight factor among many.

A point to bear in mind is that it is only with the second element of a pair of scenes that they become a pair. The audience cannot know that any particular situation is going to be significantly repeated. When the mirror reflection materializes, and not before, the doublet can be appreciated and its suggestiveness explored. This may, in its turn, involve some sort of reconsideration and even revaluation of the earlier element. But, as always, the theatrical technique must be taken in its sequence and full context.

There is a complex of correspondences between *Agam* and *Cho*, [8.1.1/8.2.1] arising out of the basic repetitiveness of the sets of murders. One or two of the visual mirrorings are so marked that even the most bookish scholars have recognized them. (On the other hand, it would be a mistake to press the parallelisms too rigidly and to follow one scholar who, applying the pseudo-analogy from metrics to strophe and antistrophe, tried to trace precise and consistent correspondence throughout both plays – and thus neglected some of the doublets which are there.) The mirror scenes are individual within the complex, and of shifting significance; and by being single and well-marked they are, in fact, much more effective as drama than any unaccentuated regularity would be. Here I shall single out four main examples.

In both plays the royal male, father and son, returns home after a long absence; each has come a long way, and each stops before the door of his palace. Once, however, the audience of *Cho* 653ff. has recognized the parallel between the two scenes it is the differences which come into full play. Agamemnon returned as the conquering hero, dominant, speaking proudly and openly to his subjects; Orestes returns surreptitiously in disguise, speaking with the guarded civility of a stranger. Agamemnon is on a chariot which enters to the accompaniment of a choral greeting [7.1.1]: Orestes is on foot, carrying his pack on his back like a trader (cf. 560, 675), and he has to go and knock on the door himself [7.2.2]. Yet the play before the entry of Agamemnon has cast over him a cloud of moral suspicion and vulnerability, while Orestes brings with him a righteous optimism, that has not yet been seriously tarnished.

At this point (*Agam* 810/*Cho* 652) the correspondence is still chiefly one of situation. The visual mirroring becomes clearer and fully evocative, however, when Clytemnestra comes out at *Cho* 668 as she had done to face Agamemnon at *Agam* 855. She is still queen, she still stands in the palace doorway to supervise the entry of the man. The differences which are brought out by the similarities have now shifted. In *Agam* Clytemnestra was the deceiver, now she is the deceived; Agamemnon resisted Clytemnestra and failed, now Orestes is subservient and he is succeeding. When Agamemnon is met by Clytemnestra it means defeat [see 4.1.2]; for Orestes it is the first step to victory [cf. 4.2.1]. Also in *Agam* Clytemnestra meets the king with brilliant and disturbing language and with the purple cloth: in *Cho* she meets Orestes with everyday courtesy, and takes him inside within a domestic setting:

> Take this gentleman to the men's guest-quarters,
> and his attendant fellow-traveller.[2]
> Let them have whatever our house can offer. (712–14)

So Clytemnestra still appears to control the palace door; but, just as she has lost her strength of rhetoric and deceit, she has really lost her power over the house.

[8.1.2/8.2.2]   However, it is not the exit of Orestes at *Cho* 718 which mirrors the exit of Agamemnon at *Agam* 972 so much as his later exit, the exit to the murder at 930 – for in *Cho* there are, of course, two confrontations and not one. The hint of repetition at 718 returns with more force and clarity in the later scene. Once more a man and a woman argue about going into the palace, and once more what is at stake is mortal victory and defeat. For the stage movement of the exit means death for one of the two at the other's hand [cf. 6.1.1, 4.2.1]. Again the dispute takes the form of a line-by-line dialogue between the two actors (a rare technique in Aeschylus, where dialogue between the chorus and an actor is the norm). Clytemnestra, like Agamemnon, eventually gives way, and at the end of the scene the victim is accompanied by the slaughterer into the house. But the significance of the mirror scene is now more disturbing than the earlier scenes, for the similarities of the situations blend with and stain the differences. There are differences: in *Cho* the situation is open and honest unlike the lavish and con- torted ambiguities in *Agam*. Orestes bluntly perseveres with a task which distresses him, unlike Clytemnestra who gloatingly indulged her calculated murderousness. Orestes recognizes the moral duality of his situation; he does not deny that a mother as well as a father may invoke wrathful hounds of vengeance (924f.). And his last words as he takes her in are 'You killed one you should not have killed: now suffer what you should not suffer' (930 – a single line in Greek!). And this is where the similarities come into view again. The parties have changed, a new generation is involved, yet the deed is the same. We are now too near the actual shedding of blood to turn a blind eye to the repetitiveness of the situation. Killing is killing, kin is kin. This begins to prepare us for the turn of events in the last part of the play.

Lastly, and most strikingly, there is the visual correspondence of [8.1.3/8.2.3] the two murder tableaux. The abrupt revelation of the *fait accompli* at *Agam* 1372, to affront an outside world of doubt and indecision, must be one of the most memorable moments of the play [cf. 4.1.3]. Clytemnestra stands there by the corpses of Agamemnon and Cassandra (spattered with gore?, cf. 1389ff., 1428?). There is no flinching, no prevarication:

> I stand, where I struck, by my handiwork.
> Thus I did it, I don't deny the deed. . . .
> This is Agamemnon, yes my husband,
> this corpse, the handiwork of my right arm,
> a craftsman true and just. And that is that. (1379–80, 1404–6)

(For Cassandra see 1440–7.) It is clear, moreover, that Agamemnon's corpse was seen actually lying in the silver bath, still enveloped in the lethal cloth which Clytemnestra so glories in at 1381ff. The chorus laments:

> To lie in this spider-woven web
> expiring there in foul death.
> Ah woe is me, to lie in this mean servile bed,
> by deadly trickery brought low,[3]
> by a two-edged blade wielded by a woman. (1492–6)

This may seem to verge on the grotesque, but the point is that Agamemon's death is as unworthy and shameful and humiliating as it possibly could be. It is not certain how the scene in *Agam* was staged,[4] but however it was done, there can be no doubt that the tableau at *Cho* 973ff. was staged in exactly the same way. Once more the murderer stands, blood on his hands (1055, etc.), by the corpses of a man and a woman, lovers (976ff., cf. *Agam* 1443ff.). Once more the murderer stands up for the deed. And, above all, there once more is the robe-net which was wrapped round Agamemnon – now, like other things in *Cho*, brought out into the open. Orestes has it held up for all to see (the similarity to the scene where Shakespeare's Antony holds up Caesar's mantle is remarkable):

> You who witness this sad affair, once more
> look on this trap, bonds for my poor father. . . . (980–1)

'Once more' (*aute*) surely refers back to *Agam* – the chink in the dramatic illusion is not noticed as such.

Whatever the differences, the similarities are too pressing, too close: the mind goes straight back to *Agam*. The blood feud is repeating itself, it is self-perpetuating. Despite the optimism which has run through *Cho*, especially in the last choral song at 935ff., this new realization of repetitiveness is quickly reflected in the ambivalence of the chorus' first reaction:

> For him who is still here suffering also begins to bloom . . . .
> One ordeal here today: another is still to come tomorrow.
> (1009, 1020)

Clytemnestra had gradually come to see the proven truth of the maxim 'the doer shall suffer' [*Agam* 1560ff., see 9.1.2]. Orestes much more quickly realizes the unfinality of his deed – 'I am pained at what has been done and suffered and my whole house: no one could envy this victory which brings pollution' (1016–17). This soon takes on a more direct form with his encroaching frenzy and his vision of the gathering Furies (1021ff.).

Yet there are still differences. Above all, Orestes has the express sanction of Apollo, and hence of Zeus. And this is brought out by a new – and therefore intrusive – visual element in the tableau in *Cho*. In one hand Orestes probably holds his sword (see *Eum*, 42), which marks him as like Clytemnestra: but in the other he has a suppliant's branch and wreath:

> And that is why you see me here, equipped
> with this branch bound with wool. I shall appeal
> to Apollo's sanctuary, a suppliant. . . . (1034–6)

Now we can see why Orestes ends the play, as he began it, still a homeless wanderer [see 4.2.2]. Clytemnestra ended *Agam* by going into the palace and taking over Agamemnon's power and possessions: Orestes sees that his difficulties are not finished with the achievement of the murder, indeed they have only just begun. The bloody hand and sword attract the Furies and drive Orestes from Argos. The suppliant's branch will take him to Delphi; and Delphi will refer him to Athens, where the chain of the vendetta will in the end find resolution. In a mirror scene any difference will stand out in the repeated surroundings; so in *Cho* the branch and wreath draw the eye as a signpost to the future.

[8.3.1]   The mirror-scene I have picked out from *Eum* does not, like those in *Cho*, span the gap between plays and between generations; rather, it gains its effect from its very closeness. If I am right, against the usual view, that the chorus of Furies is not seen until it enters to sing its 'entry song' (*parodos*) at 143ff. [cf. 7.3.2],[5] then we should ask how it made its entry from the Pythian shrine (the *skēnē*). First note that the

Furies wake up one by one – 'Wake up; and you wake her; and I wake you . . .' (140) – and next that their opening pair of stanzas is split into short syntactical units, which could easily be distributed among individuals or small groups. This suggests that the Furies did not enter in a block formation, as most choruses did as they came up the *eisodos*, but that they emerged from the door one by one or in small disordered groups. This would make an effective revelation after the horrific reports and sounds [7.3.2] which have led up to this moment. The pouring out of the entry and the 'disarranged' choreography of their song would make the most of their black, inhuman costumes and their masks with their snake-hair and eyes dripping blood and pus (see *Cho*, 1048–50, 1058; *Eum*, 46ff.). It so happens that there is a story in the ancient *Life of Aeschylus*: 'Some say that in his presentation of *Eumenides* Aeschylus brought on the chorus in a scatter (*sporadēn*), and so alarmed the people that children fainted and women aborted.' While we should not for a moment credit this anecdote, since much of the ancient biography of early poets was merely sensational fiction, it is, nonetheless, evidence that at some point in the stage-history of *Eum* the chorus was brought on *sporadēn*; and this may well be the way Aeschylus himself handled it.

The horror of the swarming first entry of the chorus is not discarded, but is, I suggest, re-aroused on their re-entry at Athens at 244ff. It is not likely that this re-entry was made in formation; surely they once again came on in scattered groups which will have been reflected in the 'disordered' choreography of the astrophic lyric 254ff. They are, after all, hounds following a trail of blood which they have tracked over land and sea [4.3.1]. This time they come on from a side *eisodos* and not from the *skēne* doors; but all the same the scenic reduplication is obvious. The audience rarely saw choral entries out of formation (up to three other instances survive) – and in this play they see it twice. The point is that the Furies' pursuit of Orestes is relentless; they dog him wherever on earth he may go. This is conveyed the more vividly and inescapably if the re-entry visually mirrors their earlier blood-chilling entry, which in turn resumes in the flesh their first invisible invasion back in *Cho* ('they come in swarms', *Cho*, 1057). All this could not contrast more tellingly with the ordered solemnity of the Eumenides' final procession to the security of a new home at the end of the trilogy [see 4.3.4].

Ajax is made round two great speeches, the so-called 'deception' [8.4.1] speech at 646–92 and the death speech at 815–65. Both times Ajax, with his sword [6.4.1], holds the stage; the first time Tecmessa and the chorus are in the background, the second time he is completely alone. But while there is some hint of a mirror scene which might be made clearer in performance, the thing which makes the two speeches a pair is, above all, their formal positioning. The first speech is all that comes in between two choral songs (596–645, 693–718); so it is an entire act to itself, and no-one else speaks during the act. This struc-tural technique, while it has some analogy in Aeschylus, is unique in later tragedy. It has the effect of framing the speech as a monolithic unit and of singling it out as a prominent set-piece. The second set-piece is even more strongly isolated and spotlighted, obviously enough; for Sophocles goes to the unusual lengths of sending the chorus off and of changing the scene in order that the speech, like its speaker, may stand entirely by itself.

The death speech shows Ajax at his greatest – brave, forthright, determined. Now, during the performance of the deception speech the audience cannot know that they will soon hear this contrasting companion speech; but does the second speech call in turn for some reconsideration of the earlier one? But before attempting any answer we must look at the deception speech without foreknowledge of its sequel. This speech is one of the great problems of Sophocles, and anything anyone says about it is bound to be controversial; neverthe-less I shall start by ruling out some of the explanations which have been proffered. Some say, for instance, that Ajax has gone mad again; but there is no explicit sign of this and it would have no point in the play as a whole: the speech is eminently sane and cannot be so facilely discounted. Others claim that he really has changed his mind about committing suicide. But again this would be totally inconsequential; also it does not do justice to the ambiguities in the speech, particularly towards the end, which indicate that Ajax is still set on death. Nor can we, I think, accept a more plausible and widely accepted account (well-formulated by both Reinhardt and Knox) that, while Ajax recognizes the validity of his observations for the rest of the world, he excepts himself from their application. Not only does this go against our intuitive reponse that Ajax should be committed to the insights he so sublimely expresses; but he also repeatedly applies what he is saying to himself with connectives like 'I too . . .' or 'I therefore . . .' (see 650, 661, 666, 677). The speech is destroyed if these are twisted to be ironic. Above all at 684ff. he does not say 'but in these matters all will be well for *others*, but I . . .', he says, 'but in these matters all will be well [sc. for me], but you, wife, . . . and companions'. Whatever it is that Ajax is saying about time and change in this speech, it must apply to *himself*.

The usual question critics ask is 'Does Ajax mean to deceive his wife and friends by this speech?' I am not sure how far this arises: the question is, rather, 'Does Sophocles mean to deceive his audience?' It is certainly the case that Tecmessa and the chorus are, as a matter of fact, misled, because the speech may be taken to mean that Ajax has

changed his mind and decided to live. The chorus is inspired to sing a
wild song of relief and joy (693ff.); and Tecmessa says later

> For now I see my husband has deceived me,
> rejected from my old favour with him. (807–8)

Their mistake is a source of tension and pathos, and is also necessary
for Sophocles' shaping of the play. Ajax must die alone and there
must be time for Teucer to find him and gather his determination
before the other Greeks learn of his death. But does the *audience* share
their misprision? Surely not. The whole scene from 333 to 595, especially 430ff. puts it beyond all doubt that Ajax is going to kill himself
[cf. 5.4.1]. Any spectator who wavers in this conclusion is warned by
the absence of any direct declaration to the contrary and by the
sustained ambiguities of the speech; and he is finally confirmed by the
double meaning of the final lines 685–92 which clearly show his
determination to die. For the audience, unlike Tecmessa and the
chorus, it cannot be the *suicide* which is at issue. Allowing, then, that
whatever it is that Ajax is dwelling on it is not the issue of whether or
not he will kill himself, what is he talking about?

It is not, I suggest, by chance that this speech is the subject of such
disagreement and confusion among scholars: for Sophocles means it
to be a kind of conundrum, and he supplies no obvious or unequivocal solution, not yet. The clue is the concern with *time*, with the
long-term view of the world; for this is the preoccupation which has
been added to Ajax's concerns of before 595. It is established in the
first line ('Long time incalculable . . .') and is carried on throughout
the speech. Ajax is not talking about his immediate course of action -
that is irrevocably decided – he is talking about the longer future,
about all time. An alert member of the audience should at least get this
far in reading the puzzle.

Why not take the opening words of the speech at face value, always
remembering that Ajax had decided to die?

> Long time incalculable brings to flower
> what was obscure and perishes the blooms.
> Nothing is out of the question: strong oaths
> even and rigid wills are overturned.
> Thus I was marvellous tough not long ago,
> like tempered steel, but now my edge is softened
> by this woman. And pity will not let me
> bereave her and the boy among my foes. (646–53)

What I suggest is that Ajax's new appreciation of the action of time
gives him a new view of his death: he sees that it is the best thing for

the others as well as for himself. In the previous scenes he was only concerned about himself: now he pities his wife and child. This makes no difference to his decision to die, but enables him to see it in a different and deeper perspective. Even Ajax, the intractable, has learned to soften. He now sees that not only is he as inevitably subject to change as the seasons, as night and day (669ff.), but that the process may benefit both himself and those he pities. Far from excepting himself from these insights, he sees himself as a mighty exemplar of them – as he is. The lesson he draws is 'And so we must learn to be temperate' (677). This is not ironic. Ajax has learned to be 'temperate' by seeing that even he is subject to the changes of time. Furthermore he sees that the reversal will come both to him *after* his death and to those he leaves behind alive.

Let me at this point do what the audience cannot do: look at what lies later in the play and read it back into this speech. The point is that everything Ajax says here about the shiftiness of the world is confirmed, and it is true of himself *after his death*. His honour, the fate of his corpse and hence of his dependants, will be subject to the gods and will require the acquiescence of Agamemnon. He will depend on others. Odysseus, his enemy, will stand up for him and be acknowledged by Teucer as a friend. I am saying, in effect, that Ajax foresees in outline what will happen after his death; he foresees the last part of the play, so to speak. That is why he finishes:

> For I now take the path that I must tread.
> Do as I say, and shortly you will find
> perhaps that, though low now, I have been saved. (690–2)

I am *not* suggesting that this interpretation of the deception speech is clear at the time of its delivery. Though a shrewd spectator might well have an inkling, the speech becomes clear, rather, in the light of events and it falls into place in retrospect. Sophocles sets the puzzle – if this is not about the suicide what is it about? He gives the speech a prominent place in the articulation of the play and expresses it in such powerful poetry because he wants his audience to concentrate, to dwell on it and to recall it. And the crucial revaluation may come, as I hinted initially, with the death speech. From its very beginning Ajax is decided, and he sets about his death in the manner of a man who has known all along what he is doing. What does this single-mindedness tell us about his earlier insights into cosmic mutability? It is now, I suggest, when death is so imminent and inexorable, that the audience sees beyond doubt that Ajax must have been reflecting on the future, on the world he is about to leave behind. For he must, of course, stay the same if he is to benefit from change. This realization leads the audience right into the final third of the play which is thus given deep roots in what has passed earlier.

The 'deception' speech has prepared us to look for the effects of time and change, to look for the way they have enabled Ajax to pity his dear ones and the way they might lead to his salvation. 'You will find . . . I have been saved.' By becoming temperate (677, see above) Ajax has made his peace with the gods and that is why he is able to spend much of his death speech at 815ff. in prayer. We remember the words with which Athena closed the prologue (132–3): 'The gods love the temperate and hate the wicked.' At the time we supposed that by the 'wicked', she meant Ajax: now he is temperate we think again. The last third of the play will make it clear who are the 'wicked' in *Ajax*.

I do not deny that I am proposing highly unusual dramatic technique: that a whole crucial scene is deliberately left unclear and unresolved and that its full sense only emerges in retrospect. The nearest analogy may be the Agamemnon scene in Aeschylus [6.1.1]. Sophocles would be requiring flexibility and perspicacity from his audience, and he is running the risk of creating confusion and misunderstanding (and the disagreement among critics might be taken to show that his boldness does no succeed). But this does at least do justice to the balance between these two great central speeches.[6]

OT does not include, so far as I can see, any outstanding mirror [8.5.1] scene. There are many patterns and recurrences [see e.g., 4.5.1, 4.5.3, 6.5.2], but none is especially accentuated by visual doubling. This may be because the whole play hinges on Oedipus' discovery that he is the mirror-reverse of all he seemed to be: the most powerful, blessed and wise of men is found to be the most accursed, the outcast, the most ignorant [cf. 9.5.3]. The whole play is the reversal, and the movement is too sustained, perhaps, to allow any particular stage of the reversal to be thus highlighted. Perhaps the nearest thing to a mirror scene is Oedipus' appearance at 1297ff. as contrasted with his entries at lines 1 and 216 [see 7.5.1 and 7.5.2]. Oedipus once more stands in the palace doorway to make a formal appearance before his people. But the polarity lies in the whole situation, not in any particular visual reflection.

Philoctetes contains, on the other hand, a particularly prominent [8.6.1] and important mirror scene. It is a sad commentary on the neglect of the visual dimension of Greek tragedy that it has been overlooked until recently, for the detailed visual repetition is reinforced by verbal echo, and its significance is clearly signalled. At 974 Neoptolemus is on the point of giving back the bow. Philoctetes' speech at 927ff. has struck home [see 7.6.4]. Once he realizes this, Philoctetes presses his point:

You are not evil. But you seem to have come
here under evil influence. Give ill
to those it suits, sail on: leave my bow. (971–3)

(The truth of 971–2 was remarked by Neoptolemus himself at the
height of his deceit, see 387f.) At this Neoptolemus asks 'What am I to
do, men?' – the latest of a series of dilemmas which have reduced him
to this question cf. 757, 895 (quoted on p. 133), 908, 969. But he is
evidently on the point of action: Philoctetes stands with hand out-
stretched, Neoptolemus is either within arm's length or approaches
him holding out the bow. At this very crisis Odysseus intervenes

. . . *Od*: O Villain, what are you about?
      Get back and leave that bow to me, I say.
Phil: Who's that? Is it Odysseus' voice I hear?
  Od: Indeed, Odysseus! Here before your eyes!
Phil: Oh, I am sold, lost. So this is the man
      who caught me and deprived me of my bow.
  Od: Yes, me, no other – I acknowledge it.
Phil: Give it back, my son, hand me my bow. *Od*: No,
      he shall not do that, even if he wants to. (974–82)

This is a tense and crucial moment, and Sophocles accentuates it by
bold theatrical techniques. Not only does Odysseus enter in the
middle of a line, which is most unusual, he comes out of ambush
without warning. We can have had no idea he was eavesdropping on the scene. This is quite unlike the usually explicit plot-
ting of Greek tragedy. Moreover the staging is strange: Philoctetes
hears Odysseus before he sees him. Although ten years have passed, he recognizes Odysseus' voice immediately; through ten years
of solitary resentment that voice has echoed in his mind, and he
needs no face to know it. Probably Odysseus comes up behind him
at 974f. and Philoctetes is too lame to turn quickly; then at 977
Odysseus comes round in front of him. Anyway, Odysseus' last-
minute intervention is completely successful. He is brutal and effective, and Neoptolemus gives way in silence; he is still under Odysseus' control, or so it seems.

   This is the picture to bear in mind when we come to 1292. Neoptolemus is now determined to return the bow to Philoctetes; Odysseus has tried to stop him, but Neoptolemus rejected him as easily as
he had been overcome in the prologue (1222–60). Again Philoctetes
stands with his hand outstreched, and Neoptolemus reaches the bow
towards him:

   Ne: Hold out your hand and take your bow: it's yours.

> Od: [entering]: No, I forbid it, the gods be witness,
> in the name of the Atreidai and the Greeks.
> Phil: My child, whose voice is that? Is it Odysseus'
> voice I hear? Od: Yes, indeed, before your eyes.
> And I shall take you off to Troy by force,
> whether Achilles' son wants it or not. (1291-8)

Again the sudden ambush, again the approach from behind (however it was staged), again the sequence of hearing before seeing. The complex of verbal echoes is obvious. Philoctetes is just the same in both scenes: the differences have to do with Neoptolemus and Odysseus. Earlier Neoptolemus had not the courage of his convictions, but now he has: instead of retreating submissively, he fulfills his intention and hands over the bow. Philoctetes draws an arrow on Odysseus who only just escapes with his life [see 9.6.1]. Earlier Odysseus overcame by strong words and by the sheer force of his presence: but now Neoptolemus has stood up to him, and he is no match for two true men.

> You may be sure of this: the Greek leaders,
> their pseudo-envoys, are cowards before
> weapons, however bold they are with words. . . .
> And you have shown your family blood, my child.
> You are no bastard brat of Sisyphus,
> but true son of Achilles, held the best
> of men alive and now among the dead. (1305-7, 1310-13)

Thus Philoctetes bluntly and incontrovertibly draws the moral of the action: both Odysseus and Neoptolemus have shown themselves for what they really are.

The other mirror scene I shall point out in *Phil* is not so striking, nor, [8.6.2] perhaps, so important; but it does help to show how this complex play is meshed. Among the many frustrated exits [5.6.1] there are two occasions when Philoctetes and Neoptolemus set off together for the ship, both times ostensibly to sail for Greece, though the first departure is sham and the second genuine. The first time, Philoctetes has recovered from his fit and insists that Neoptolemus himself and no-one else should help him to his feet (877-92). Odysseus' plan is on the verge of success. Neoptolemus helps him up and supports him as they begin to go together (893-4). But the destination is false, the support is false, every step is false. Neoptolemus cries out in pain *'papai'* (cf. Philoctetes at 746, 754, 785f., 792f.) 'what on earth am I to do now?'

> Phil: What's the matter, my son? What do you say?
> Ne: I don't know what to say – I'm at a loss.

> *Phil*: What kind of loss? No, don't say that, my child.
> *Ne*: But that's what my distress has brought me to. (895–9)

So they stop, and Neoptolemus lets go of Philoctetes. They must turn their backs on falsehood and face the truth. The turning round in the stage movement marks a turning point in the direction of the drama.

Finally at 1402ff. Neoptolemus, denied any alternative by Philoctetes' stubbornness, agrees to take him home [see 5.6.1]. He has come to see so clearly the demands of personal sympathy and trust that he is about to abandon all the spoils of Troy and the promise of his glory there. It is clear that he supports Philoctetes once more ('lean on me as we step' 1403), and they begin to move off with the change of metre at 1402. Probably they stop at 1404 and then begin to move again with Neoptolemus' words at 1407, 'Make your farewell to the land, and come'. At this moment Heracles intervenes:

> No, not yet; first you must hear my words,
> son of Poias. It is the voice of Heracles
> you hear and his face you see.
> I have left heaven and come here for your sake,
> to tell you of Zeus' purposes
> and to halt the journey you are bent upon. . . . (1409–16)

They will still go – but to Troy, not to Greece. For the fact is, that, although Odysseus was a contemptible and false agent, it is still the will of Zeus (the 'all-subduing god' of 1467f.) that Troy should fall to Philoctetes' arrows. This is the truth, and, as at 895, Philoctetes and Neoptolemus must turn back and face it. But this time they are together, not alienated, and the truth is imposed on them from outside: earlier it lay within one of them and it broke them apart. Only after they have explored human trust and sympathy to its full depth does Zeus intervene. Only after the journey to Greece has begun, even though it means the rejection of political integration, of ambition, glory and even of the cure of Philoctetes' wound, only then does Zeus impose his contrary will. He allows the nobility of man full play, and then directs it with ease.

[8.7.1]   Hippolytus is not alone in his devotion to Artemis. Though his relationship with her is special, he has with him a group of youths who share in his hunting, racing and ascetic outdoor pursuits. They are with him on his first entry (see 54–6, quoted on p. 51), and they join him in his hymn to Artemis (61–71) – that is to say, they form a kind of secondary chorus. The whole scene is imbued with a radiant purity combined with youthful athleticism, and the chorus of companions fills out this 'genre picture'.

These companions (or some of them) will bring on the dying Hip-

polytus [see 8.7.2]; but the moment which most strikingly corre-
sponds and contrasts with the opening is the departure into exile at
1101. Theseus will not relent in his sentence of exile, and at 1089 he
leaves Hippolytus with no alternative but to depart at once. He takes
his farewell of the statue of Artemis (1092-3), the statue which he had
approached and crowned at the beginning [6.7.1], then of Troezen
and of Athens to which he can never return (1093–7); and finally he
calls on his companions to accompany him on his way:

> Come then, my close companions, make your
> farewells, and then escort me from this land.
> You'll never see a man more *virtuous*
> than me, whatever my father may think. (1098–101)

(Their fulfilment of this task is recounted in 1173ff.) I think that the
address to Artemis' statue will inevitably cast the spectator's inner
eye back to Hippolytus' first entry. He is still the same paragon of
youth among his companions; but now he has to turn his back on his
home and haunts. And this has come about through the very virtue
which he regards as the crown of his way of life: *sōphrosynē*, the word
whose adjective is translated as 'virtuous' in 1100 above. *Sōphrosynē* is
the key term in Hippolytus' address to Artemis at 73–87 (cf. 993ff.,
1363ff.); the noun and its cognates occur at least fifteen times through
the play. It was for the Greeks one of the greatest virtues, and implied
the purposeful control of appetites, 'the overcoming of the impulse to
immediate or short-term pleasure or gain'.[7] But a control over sexual
desire runs against the way of the world, and means a rejection of
Aphrodite: this is the contradiction in which Hippolytus is caught.
And it is this conflict which the slightest mirror reversal of these two
scenes brings out. The very untouchability of our first vision of
Hippolytus is what will take him into banishment from society and
worse.

By having Phaedra resist her lust instead of indulging it Euripides is   [8.7.2]
able to introduce some similarity between her and Hippolytus, the
agents of each other's tragedy. When Phaedra is first brought on stage
(170ff.) she is lying on a bed accompanied by her maids. To die in
silence by self-starvation is not easy, and Phaedra is in an agony of
physical as well as mental discomfort. She tosses about on her sickbed, unable to lie still (see 181ff., 203ff.). Forced to express her pain
somehow she rises and expresses in an anapaestic chant her longing
to be elsewhere, to be taken away from her present malaise out into
the wild places which Hippolytus frequents [208ff., see 6.7.3].

Now compare this with the scene where the bloody, broken Hippolytus makes his final entry. He is, it seems, supported by his
followers; and in chanted anapaests he laments, racked by pains,

telling his companions to bear him in different positions (see 1353, 1358ff.). Finally he tells them to lay him down, and he changes to singing metres as he calls on death to release him from his agony (1370–88). There is a distinct similarity in the way that both Phaedra and Hippolytus cannot rest in their anguish and call to their attendants to move them to a more comfortable position; also in the way they chant and sing of a relief from this agony. And, once the comparison is made, then there are other more telling similarities beneath the obvious differences between the two scenes. Both are mortally harmed. But Phaedra, though her symptoms are clear, will not reveal their cause. In their first song the chorus longs to know which god has so affected her (141ff.), but it is not until 352 that the truth is finally out: Cypris (see 359–61, 400f.). Comparably Hippolytus' symptoms are obvious; but the cause is put down to Theseus' curse and to Poseidon. Artemis names the true culprit:

> *Art*: Cypris, who stops at nothing, devised this.
> *Hipp*: I see now: she's the god who has destroyed me.
> *Art*: She resented your disdain and loathed your virtue (*sōphronounti*).
> *Hipp*: So one god has destroyed all three of us.
> *Art*: Yes, you, your father and his consort – three. (1400–4)

The play sees two corpses, and both are mourned by Theseus. For all the contrasts between Phaedra and Hippolytus they are both destroyed by Cypris, and Theseus is left forlorn. Euripides' arrangement of these two scenes helps to bring out the pattern.

[8.8.1]   The peculiar blend of the fabulous and the immediate in *Ion* is established right away in the prologue when Hermes recounts how on Apollo's instructions he whisked the cradle containing the baby Ion from Athens and put it down on the temple threshold at Delphi; and how the Pythia found it and assumed sacrilege 'She was keen to cast the child outside the sacred precinct; but pity overruled her savagery . . .' (46–7). And so she spared the boy and he grew up in the sanctuary. This is mere fable until one realizes with a shock that this very temple threshold is the setting of the play, where Ion is going to sweep and where Xuthus will meet him. It was on this very spot that the priestess took pity on the baby. (Later in the play she will try to explain her motive for that act, see 1349ff., 1360ff.)

This prepares the way for a succession of actions which are to be prevented on the temple threshold during the course of the play. The acts, which are all somehow impious or contrary to Apollo's will, are all stopped in one way or another. The first instance seems hardly serious, yet it sets the pattern. Ion in his opening song draws his bow against the birds [161f., cf. 6.8.1], but then he thinks better of it

(179–83). These are birds of augury, and Ion's threats to them are paradoxical since he tells them to fly off to other famous sanctuaries. Later one of these sacred birds will reveal the plot against him and will die in his stead (1196ff.). Ion again impulsively draws his bow at 524ff., when Xuthus has been over-enthusiastic in his advances to his new-found son [see further 8.8.2 below]. It is Xuthus' retort 'go on, kill me and then cremate me: for it is your father you are so keen to kill' (527) which makes Ion lower his shaft. Much later Ion will also hesitate before killing Creusa; he is on the verge of violating her asylum when the Pythia interrupts [1320ff., see 7.8.1]. It might be tempting for a director to have him draw his bow here too; but it is near certain that Euripides did not do this, not only because it is not signalled by the words, but also because Ion is acting as an agent of the Delphians who intend to stone Creusa. The next similarly prevented action comes at 1384ff., where Ion is on the point of dedicating his cradle to Apollo rather than discover he is a bastard 'But what am I doing? I am clashing with Apollo's providence . . .' (1385–6). Next, he does not kill Creusa when she leaves sanctuary (1402ff., see below); and, finally, he is about to go into the temple to question Apollo on his paternity when Athena appears [1546ff., see 7.8.2]. We can see in these places how the feeling world of passion and human dilemma is subtly and indivisibly mixed with the magical world where Apollo impels everyone to put everything to rights.

But among the errors and successes of *Ion* there is one pair which is particularly closely parallel: the false recognition scene with Xuthus, and the real one with Creusa [cf. 5.8.1, 5.8.3]. I shall pick out here one particularly delicate and telling correspondence. When Xuthus first comes out of the oracle the dialogue, in rapid trochaic metre, runs thus:

[8.8.2]

> X: Greetings, my child. Yes, that's a fitting opening to my speech.
>
> Ion: I thank you. And if you are in your right senses, then we are both well.
>
> X: Let me kiss your hand, and throw my arms about your body.
>
> Ion: *Are* you in your senses, sir? Or has some god struck you mad?
>
> X: Would I be in my senses if I let go my loved one once I'd found him?[8]
>
> Ion: Stop! Do not violate Apollo's garland with your grasping hand.
>
> X: I will touch. I am not confiscating; I am claiming my own.
>
> (517–23)

At this point Ion draws his bow, and the passage verges on the comic as Ion retreats and fends off the embraces which he evidently takes to be pederastic.[9] The unusual wording of the last line (523) stands out. The rare legal term *rhusiasdō*, which I have translated as 'confiscate' means strictly 'taking away the person or property of another as security for one's own legal claim'.[10] The procedure was evidently that the claimant had to lay his hand on the distrained property; and evidently the procedure for claiming lost property was the same. So Xuthus is saying that he is not seizing someone else's property, i.e. Apollo's, but that he is simply claiming his own long lost property (the verb is *heuriskō*, literally 'find'). This is a kind of joke on Xuthus' part, and as such is in keeping with the scene as a whole. But within the play as a whole it is an ironic joke against Xuthus, for the point is, in truth, that he *is* seizing Apollo's goods (Ion), not claiming his own.

Compare and contrast now the deadly earnest of the iambic dialogue when Creusa leaves the altar at 1401ff.

> *Cr*: I leave the altar even if it means death.
> *Ion*: Seize her. She leaves the sculptured altar, driven
> by madness from the god. Fasten her arms.
> *Cr*: Slaughter me, go on and sacrifice me; I shall cling
> to this cradle, its secrets, and to you.
> *Ion*: This is absurd. I am being confiscated (*rhusiasdomai*).[11]
> *Cr*: Not so. A loved one is claiming her own (*heuriskē*). (1401–7)

Again the parent claims the child and attempts to embrace (though Creusa, it seems, embraces the cradle as a token of Ion's person): again Ion protests and attributes the behaviour to divine madness. And again there is the odd legal terminology. But this time it is utterly appropriate: this time it *is* a case of claiming lost property and not of seizing by distraint. The whole movement of the play by which Apollo's compromise is eventually superseded by the whole truth is brought out vividly by the mirror-reversed correspondence. The emotional power of this scene is also greatly enhanced by its contrast with the frivolity and misprision of the earlier 'recognition'. And the way that the rather precious legal joke is repeated, now in all earnest, is typical of this strangely brilliant play.

[8.9.1]   When Dionysus is brought on as a prisoner at *Ba* 434ff. he is in bonds, at least round his hands; and the reluctant attendant tells how the stranger put up no resistance. Pentheus has him released (451f.); but towards the end of the scene he again resorts to chains –

> *Pen*: Seize him. He is insulting Thebes and me.
> *Dion*: I forbid you: I am sane, you are not.
> *Pen*: I have the whip hand, and I say bind him. (503–5)

– and the stranger is taken off to the stables to be imprisoned (509–18). Of course everyone knows that chains simply fall off Dionysus; but the staging conveys that the stranger appears to be in Pentheus' power. Certainly the chorus is taken in – see 547ff., 610ff. The stranger is, then, brought on and taken off in custody at the command of Pentheus.

After the central scene of judgement and reversal [576–861, see 9.9.1], the picture is turned the other way round. Dionysus comes first out of the palace and calls Pentheus after him (912–16); he follows in a sort of trance ('As you lead you look like a bull before me . . .' 920). The stranger is to lead Pentheus up to the bacchants on Cithaeron (see 819f., 840, 855). This arrangement is reiterated at 961ff., and after Dionysus' words 'Follow me; I will give you safe escort . . .' (965), the dialogue breaks into half-lines, as (probably) they begin on the fatal, sacrificial journey. Dionysus leads his victim off with his final chilling lines

> Agaue and you sisters of Agaue,
> stretch out your arms. I'm leading this young man
> to his big struggle now. And I shall win,
> and Bromios. The rest shall all be clear. (973–6)

No less than Dionysus in the earlier scene Pentheus is a prisoner in bonds; but the chains by which he is pulled are invisible, they are psychic chains. And no less then Dionysus earlier, Pentheus is led without resistance: it is essential that the god-driven sacrificial animal should go to the slaughter willingly. Hunter and quarry, active and passive, all is reversed [cf. 5.9.2]. The reversal in the stage roles of the leader and the led, the custodian and the prisoner, vividly presents the overturn in the balance of power, and the impotence of human force when a god is provoked.

9 Scenic sequence

The most important of the elements is the arrangement of the events. . . . (Aristotle, Poetics)

The ordering of material (*systasis tōn pragmatōn* as Aristotle called it) is central to the dramatist's art; the interaction of scenes through their sequence is the key to the effect of the play as a whole. Easily said, and very true – but what does it mean in practice? Consider a sequence from Euripides' *Phaethon*, a play from which we have only intriguing fragments. Phaethon is the son of Clymene and the Sun, though (as usual) he has a mortal 'stepfather', Merops. On his wedding day Clymene persuades Phaethon to go to the Sun and prove his paternity – with catastrophic consequences. At the start of one large fragment of Euripides' play the smouldering corpse of Phaethon lies on stage, lamented by his guilt-stricken mother. Suddenly she sees Merops approaching with a band of girls, and she and her maids just get off into the palace with the corpse before Merops arrives with the girls (a supplementary chorus) who have come to sing a wedding song for Phaethon. No sooner is this hymeneal over than a servant rushes out with the news that the palace is on fire; and the melancholy truth about Phaethon is soon out. The ironic juxtaposition of guilt and innocence, of macabre calamity and festive sweetness, overtaken in its turn by grief and recrimination, is obvious. It is not typical of Greek tragedy, however, and requires two unusual resources, an exit followed immediately by an independent entry (see p. 51), and a second supplementary chorus.

Generally speaking, the continuous presence of the chorus, the resultant continuity of time and unity of place, and the limitation to three actors all conspire to obstruct the rapid variation of scene sequence. Or, since this is a chicken-and-egg matter, the slow pace and sustained concentration of Greek tragedy are reflected in the technical restraints on rapidity and variety. A glancing comparison with almost any other school of drama makes the point. There is no possibility of scenic interweaving like the alternation of the Lear and Gloucester plots in the central parts of *King Lear*, or of the practicality of Rome with the hot blood of Egypt in *Antony and Cleopatra*, let alone the triple plaiting in *Henry IV Part I* of the royal court, the rebel court of the Percys, and the court of misrule in the tavern. Still less is there anything like the rapid cutting and juxtaposition of much of, for instance, Brecht – techniques made commonplace by the film.

Greek tragedy offers comparatively less variety, richness of texture, rapidity and complexity: even so the great three achieved a remarkable degree of structural variety and tension within their basic scenic framework. I gave a very basic account of that framework, which was far from inflexible, on pp. 19–21. This chapter attempts to show some of the ways in which the ordering of delivery, pace and movement in scenic sequence contributes to the overall meaning of Greek tragedy.

The Cassandra scene in *Agamemnon* is perhaps the most daring [9.1.1] stroke in a play which tries language and theatre to their limits. The act is firmly fixed within the tragedy, since Cassandra is a victim of Troy, of Apollo, of Agamemnon, and of Clytemnestra; and yet at the same time it stands outside the tragedy through Cassandra's freedom of vision, which ranges without restraint in time or language. So it comes about that the part which is delivered in the strangest and most enigmatic language is the one which says most about the underlying currents of the play and which sheds clearest light in a drama of doubt, distortion and partiality.

It helps to see this in its sequence with the preceding act. For Agamemnon's one and only act should, one would have thought, be the centrepiece of the play – and so it must seem while it is in progress. Yet it turns out to be in some ways only a prelude and frame for the longer Cassandra act. The actors are as far as possible kept separate: Cassandra is barely referred to in the former scene, Agamemnon has gone to his death before she moves or speaks.

All that Agamemnon has to do is to make his way from the chariot in the *orchēstra* across and in through the doors of the palace. The question is whether he will do this on the bare earth or on the pathway of cloth. Once he submits to tread Clytemnestra's way then his steps become a journey from victory to defeat, from triumph to disaster, to deception, to more wastage of the house, of more kindred blood, and a journey into an even more inextricable wealth of cloth [cf. 6.1.1]. It is an ignorant walking song into death.

This is the setting for the choral song at 975ff. It is a song dominated by dark foreboding, fear-ridden hopes, obscure premonition. All the old men can do is to descry in the sea of menace and bewilderment a few dark rocks: the departure of Aulis, the Erinyes, disease, excess of wealth, blood spilt irrevocably on the ground. And at the fringe of all this disquiet is the silent figure of Cassandra in the chariot [cf. 7.1.3].

As soon as the song is over and Clytemnestra comes out again with the line 'You too get inside, I mean you, Cassandra' (1035), attention centres on Cassandra; and with a shock the outline of her place in the pattern suddenly begins to appear. She, too, must make the journey from the chariot to the door, the very same route – a path no longer strewn with red cloth, but none the less a path to certain death. Cassandra is somehow going to parallel Agamemnon. Yet almost as quickly during 1035–67 the contrasts with Agamemnon emerge: not only will Cassandra not obey Clytemnestra, she will not even speak to her or make acknowledgement of her presence. When the queen goes back in (1068), we realize that Cassandra is not going to enter the palace, like Agamemnon, under Clytemnestra's control and on her terms: she will do it independently. Momentarily it seems as though Cassandra might go straight in, but she turns back [1087, see 5.1.1]. She then begins to sing and say things which show the chorus that she not only knows as much as they, but that she may well know much more. So the chorus – and the audience with them – are pulled round from the role of patronizers to that of the receivers of enlightenment.[1]

Agamemnon, man, king, conqueror, entered his own house as a broken slave: Cassandra is a woman and a slave, yet she will go into the alien house her own mistress. Their telling mirror reversal leads into another which runs still deeper. Agamemnon's journey to the door was made in a state of unknowingness, Cassandra's is a journey of knowledge and insight. By the time she eventually enters the palace she knows all about her imminent death, and much more. With the change from lyric to speech (cf. 1178ff., quoted on p. 104) she takes on a new authority and clarity, though still through visionary language. Her scope takes in Troy and Argos, the human and the divine, the distant past, recent past, the present, the near future and distant future; and she combines and makes coherent sense of them all. There is no room to question the validity of her insights. 'Woman most wretched, and yet most wise . . .' (1295): she wins not only our pity but also our belief and gratitude. For while Agamemnon only led us deeper into distortion and obscurity, Cassandra, while taking the same path from chariot to door, brings us out into a new enlighten- ment and perspective which will only be superseded at the very end of the trilogy.

Thus after Cassandra has gone, the chorus can chant a few act- dividing anapaests (1331–42) and make out far more of the setting of Agamemnon's fate than they could when they sang at length at 975ff. And now, at last, Agamemnon's death cries can make sense. They come as a shock maybe [cf. 7.1.2]; for the voice is like a voice from the distant past, and huge perspectives lie between us and the strange spectacle which represented his death nearly 400 lines earlier. Long, long ago Clytemnestra said 'the victims are standing by the central hearth ready for the sacrifice' (1056f.). It is as though all the vision given us by Cassandra has been conveyed in a suspended moment, the moment before Clytemnestra strikes. The great change is one of knowledge: now we have some clear idea why Agamemnon's death is inevitable.

Most accounts of *Agam* give the impression that the play is virtually [9.1.2] finished with the murder; yet this is far from the case. Though the final act may have the relaxed tension of aftermath, it is far from vacuous or conventional. Lines 1343–673 form, in effect, one long final act, divided from the Cassandra act by the few anapaests and the death cries at 1331ff. The major part of the act is taken up by the confrontation of Clytemnestra and the chorus (1372–576), in which the chorus always sings, often with repeated refrains, while Clytem- nestra at first speaks, and then (1462ff.) chants in shorter stretches of anapaests.

There is a direction to this monumental dialogue, though the movement is not a simple linear progression. Both parties start from a position of dogmatic assertion: both move towards a kind of com- promise which we can recognize, in the light of Cassandra and of the earlier choral songs, to be much nearer the truth. Thus, the old men begin at an extreme of condemnation and revulsion; but they come to recognize the place in the murder of Zeus, of the family curse, of Helen, Iphigeneia, of past guilt:

> Blame for blame –
> a hard struggle to decide.
> The spoiler is despoiled: the killer pays the price. (1560–2)

Clytemnestra, on the other hand, at first takes full responsibility – and credit – for the murder, and presumably intends to take over Agamemnon's wealth and power with Aegisthus (1431ff.). Yet she, too, comes to recognize the place of larger forces like the family doom.

She did not do the deed in her own person, it was 'the vengeful ghost of Atreus, primaeval, grim . . .' (1501). She even suggests that she will be content with only a small portion of the house's wealth if as a compromise the family *daimōn* will agree to leave her in peace (1568–76).

This is her last resort before the scene is interrupted by the sudden arrival of Aegisthus. We have not been led to expect this; and no other entry in Aeschylus, indeed scarcely any in surviving tragedy, comes so late in an act. Aegisthus rudely crushes any insight that was growing. Blustering self-righteousness deteriorates into crude abuse, and that turns to the threat of brute force against the old men of the chorus (1649ff.). Short-sighted lust, ambition and cowardice win the day. For this is not yet *Eumenides*, there is still *Choephoroi* to come.

[9.2.1]   The first half of *Choephoroi* consists almost entirely of one act (84–584) dominated by the monumental *kommos* at Agamemnon's tomb [cf. 7.2.1]. The second half, on the contrary, is the most quickly changing sequence of acts in all surviving tragedy.[2] It is worth first analysing its sequence and pace up until the murder. At either end come the two confrontations of Orestes and Clytemnestra. The first (652ff., 68 lines) is apparently mundane, but is fraught with deceit and suppression [cf. 8.2.1]: the second (870ff., 60 lines) is stark and open, concentrated solely on Orestes' will and Clytemnestra's defence [cf. 5.2.1, 8.2.2]. Only a few choral anapaests (719–29) divide the former scene from the nurse (730ff., 52 lines). And the second confrontation is preceded, with a division again made by a few anapaests (855–68), by the Aegisthus scene (838ff., only 16 lines). In between the nurse and Aegisthus is the one proper strophic act-dividing song of the whole sequence (783–837), a fine prayer for Orestes' vengeance. Thus, we have here a series of four exceptionally short acts, including even shorter appearances by individual characters: the nurse follows closely on the first Clytemnestra-Orestes scene and Aegisthus closely precedes the second. What is Aeschylus trying to do with these extraordinary techniques and their resultant structural symmetry?

At least part of the answer lies, I suggest, in the way that the two inner scenes reflect on Clytemnestra. In the first confrontation her behaviour seems irreproachable. She is presented as a courteous housekeeper and dutiful wife; and when she hears of Orestes' death, she reacts convincingly as a mother (691ff.). It is hard to detect any vindictive ambiguity here (indeed some editors have mistakenly wanted to attribute the lines to Electra); this seems to be, rather, the wiser, less assertive Clytemnestra of the end of *Agam* [see 9.1.2]. This Clytemnestra is hardly to be written off as an unnatural villainess, even though we are carried through this scene on the side of the righteous Orestes. But despite her claims by blood, Clytemnestra's domestication and motherliness is immediately undermined by the nurse, Kilissa, closely juxtaposed in the next act. It is not so much that she accuses Clytemnestra of sham grief (734–40) as that she reveals herself in a sense a truer mother to Orestes by her personal, physical sense of loss. For it was her, not the blood mother, who fed the baby Orestes, was woken in the night, changed and washed nappies. She challenges Clytemnestra's claims on the ground of mundane domesticity. No other slave in Greek tragedy is named, no other character (not even in Euripides) speaks of quite such menial chores as washing nappies. Her realistic detail reflects back on and detracts from Clytemnestra's claims as a mother.

Aegisthus reflects both back and forward. His brief act inevitably recalls the end of *Agam*, the philistine way in which he swept aside the struggle for perspective, his confident seizure of Agamemnon's power and wealth [cf. 9.1.2]. Moreover, Clytemnestra's adultery is the most obtrusive flaw in her moral case; her ulterior motive rankles with those who uphold Agamemnon's honour (almost as much as in *Hamlet*). Aegisthus barely pauses on the stage as he hurries to his death, and yet his appearance casts its discolouring light over the crucial scene which follows. Clytemnestra cannot and does not deny her adultery; and this is a serious element in her guilt which makes her defence impossible to sustain. In the former confrontation she may have seemed almost forgivable; but by the time that Aegisthus and the nurse have undermined her case she is seen as indefensible.

Yet it is in this second clash, when all is out in the open, that the ambivalence and unfinality of the murder comes to the fore. For all her guilt Clytemnestra is still Orestes' mother: she bore him, and she has thereby her curse (912) and her hounds (924). The adamantine bond of blood weighs equally with all the other factors put together. That is why the final struggle of mother and son is so powerful, and why it is not simply a colourless victory for right over wrong. It is also one reason why the votes will be equal in the trial at Athens.

The entry of Orestes at the beginning of *Cho* has close links with the [9.3.1] end of *Agam*. He is foreshadowed by Aegisthus who is also a son returning from exile to avenge an undeniable wrong done to his father ('now I am grown up Justice has brought me home again . . .' 1607). It is the very potential for a new generation of revenge-return that leads thoughts to Orestes in *Agam* 1646–8 and again at 1667–8. In some ways the two plays overlap.

The final exit of Orestes at the end of *Cho* (1062) interlocks even more closely with *Eum*. This exit is the beginning of the pursuit by the Furies which will be continued and presented on stage in the next play [cf. 4.3.1, and 8.3.1]. Moreover the rapid sequence of changing acts in the second half of *Cho* is carried over into a different, though no less extraordinary, concatenation of scenes in the opening quarter of *Eum*. There are three, or rather four, separate scenes even before the chorus enters. First the Pythia on her daily routine, and then after she has seen the horrors within [see 5.3.1]; then Apollo and Orestes; then the dream of Clytemnestra. After the Furies' entry song they are driven from Delphi; then Orestes is briefly by himself before the chorus re-enters. And yet we have still reached only line 244. Only now can the stalemate be fully established [cf. 6.3.1, 7.3.3]. The frequent alteration and independent articulation of these early scenes are managed only by means of the unusual techniques of the long four-part 'prologue' and by taking off and bringing back the chorus. What is it that Aeschylus is trying to convey by these exceptional means?

I suggest that he thus manages to give us different and independent angles on the whole conflict which will develop and which will face Athena at Athens. The Pythia gives us, so to speak, a neutral view, a view which can observe but cannot cope or solve. We then have the partial view of Apollo – that the Furies are monstrosities fit only to be tricked and abhorred. But this is followed by the other side in the shape of Clytemnestra. The clash of Apollo and the Furies (179–234) in some ways foreshadows the coming trial, except that the Furies are more set at this stage on pursuit than on making good their case (after all, it was these same Erinyes that Apollo had invoked on Agamemnon's behalf – see *Cho.* 283ff.). Orestes is then alone to set out the approach which he will make to Athena (235ff., cf. 276ff., 443ff.), before the Furies re-enter and begin to show their power to pin him down. Through this sequence the audience is able to witness and to take into account the different cases – all partially valid – which go to make up the tight knot which will face Athena on her arrival. Only thus will they be able to appreciate the vision and wisdom of her transcendent solution.

[9.3.2]   The *Oresteia* does not end with the acquittal of Orestes. What is the structural connection of the final act (778ff.) with the rest? On the traditional analysis (see p. 184 n. 11) the entire play from 566 onwards is the '*exodos*' (exit scene): this is ridiculous, not only because the term is inapplicable to a section which covers nearly half the play, but also because on any meaningful analysis a structural division must be recognized at 777/8 between the departure of Orestes (and Apollo) and the final settlement of the Furies at Athens. In fact this final act is even longer than the trial act; the exit of Orestes marks not the beginning of the end, but the beginning of a new beginning. It is true that there is no act-dividing song and that there is no new entry; the

separate acts are quite simply juxtaposed with no more formal indication of the juncture than the exit of Orestes and the change from
speech to song. None the less, though unique, the sequential technique is unmistakable and this scenic form should be a clue to what is
going on.

The Furies have been the prosecutors, and in their own eyes they
have lost the trial. On this verdict, they suppose, depend their very
functions and privileges in the universe. This is no place for an
act-dividing pause; the chorus is itself too closely involved in the
action. They move on at once to their response to the verdict: to blight
Athens, the only form of self-assertion which remains to them. The
trial is not the end. If the Furies cannot be given due honour in the
civilized world then the chain of vengeance threatens to continue on
into the future. To prevent this Athena must also make clear her new
offer as quickly as possible; so there is dialogue instead of pure choral
lyric. And there is no new entry precisely because there is no new
outside party to be brought into play: the outcome depends entirely
on Athena, her wisdom and her power to persuade – and Athena is
already there. The transition of the issue from Orestes to the city,
although long prepared for, is still a great wrench [cf. 4.3.2]. There is
no way to soften it, and Aeschylus takes advantage of this necessity in
order to realign his audience's attention and priorities by an unmitigated juxtaposition. The juxtaposition reflects both the continuity
and discontinuity of the final act in relation to the rest of the play and
trilogy.

It would be a mistake to try to isolate the section 778–891 as an
independent element which functions as a kind of act-dividing buf-
fer. It is in fact an integral part of the whole final act, 778–1047, a
structural unit with a clearly defined shape and direction. In the first
part (778–891) the chorus sings two pairs of stanzas which are repeated word for word in strophe and antistrophe; the repetitions are
not refrains, they are the song itself. In both pairs the Furies sing of
their dishonour and their incurable, poisonous rage, and the repetition marks the fixity and implacability of their sense of grievance.
Between each stanza, four times that is, Athena gently disputes their
view of the situation, and offers them a new home, new functions and
privileges. It is not until the dialogue 892–915 that her powers of
persuasion finally get through the barrier of reiterated resentment.
She is made to spell out her new dispensation once more, and this
proves to be the turning point. With the words

> I shall accept the settlement
> that Athena offers to share,
> and I shall not abuse the city . . . (916–17)

there begins a new lyric dialogue structure (916–1020) in which choral stanzas are interwoven with chanted anapaests from Athena. While Athena lays down the foundations of the new cult, the Furies, now Eumenides, far from repeating implacable threats, enlarge with fertile variety on the blessings that they will bring Athens. Once more, and the most important time in the *Oresteia*, a movement has been made from stubborn partiality and blindness to a new rewarding vision. And this time there is no distortion, no qualification, no interruption: the play flows on with a wealth of benediction to its final secure procession [cf 4.3.4].

> Follow us, you august goddesses,
> gracious and beneficent to our land,
> follow by the light of fiery torches
> rejoicing on your way.
> Raise the cry of joy in refrain to our song. (1040–3)

[9.4.1]   It is incredible, and yet typical, that the fact that *Ajax* is divided into two parts has so often been treated as though it were some accident or miscalculation, when Sophocles has constructed this division so carefully and deliberately, and when the relation between the two halves is so clearly one of his chief artistic concerns.

If one had to tie the divide to a particular moment then it would have to be the death of Ajax at 865; but it would be a mistake to be so precise. Ajax's last speech (815–65) is at once the last act of the first part and the first act of the latter part, something which becomes clear if we consider the structural sequence. At 814 the scene is suddenly and completely cleared [cf. 4.4.3]. Then Ajax enters alone with his sword, and it is at once clear that the scene has moved to the lonely places by the shore. His speech, while it is the climax and resolution of what has gone before [cf. 8.4.1], all looks forward – above all his prayer to Zeus on the fate of his corpse [824ff., cf. 6.4.1 where some of it is quoted]. The speech is, in a way, a second *prologue*, just as the re-entry of the chorus at 866ff. is a kind of second entry song (in Greek *epiparodos*). Between that and line 1226 there are no less than six entries of major named characters, and Sophocles thus gives the impression of a series of important people arriving and gathering at the scene of Ajax's death. This is achieved by some clever management of the three speaking actors and by some bold structural technique (especially bold if, as is often supposed, this is an early play).

Teucer enters after the '*epiparodos*' at 975, and thus opens a new act in the usual way. Tecmessa's re-entry (893), however, has already been worked into the preceding song; and her lament has also been incorporated by means of the device, not uncommon in later tragedy, of making the act-dividing song into a lyric dialogue. First there are some introductory lines (866–78) during which the chorus re-enters in two parts from opposite sides, searching for Ajax, rather as Odysseus tracked him at the very beginning [cf. 4.4.1, also compare Teucer at 994ff.]. There follows a long and complex lyric structure (879–973) which basically takes the form of a single strophic pair. Each pair has three parts; (a) 874–90 = 925–36, purely choral; (b) 891–914 = 937–60 lyric dialogue between the chorus and Tecmessa (enters at 891ff.); (c) 915–24 = 961–73, a spoken lament by Tecmessa.[3] By these means Tecmessa has found the corpse and entered and given her grief sufficient scope all within the structure of the act-dividing song. Now Teucer can enter, and now there is nothing objectionable in the way that he immediately sends Tecmessa off (985–9 – she does not speak again in the play): it is now Teucer's turn to hold the stage. His lament (992–1039) dwells firstly on the disasters that Ajax's death spells for him, himself; but his observations on the sword [cf. 6.4.1] lead him towards an insight into some larger shaping of events, and he is then prepared to face the inevitable threats of Ajax's enemies.

The arrivals of the chorus, Tecmessa, and Teucer bring friends first to the body of Ajax, as he had prayed in 826ff. ('so that some enemy might not descry me first'). The first of the enemies is Menelaus at 1040ff. He is the meanest and most petty of the heroes whose little world Ajax has abandoned. He is only too eager to kick a man who is down: to harm or dishonour a corpse was the kind of action which the Greeks (as opposed to moderns) really did call *hybris* (cf. 1092, 1151).[4] Menelaus' rhetoric is sly and low; and Teucer, who is no Ajax, is reduced to his level of argument. The scene ends with them bandying vulgar Aesopic tales (1142ff.). Menelaus goes off for reinforcements, but the act does not quite end there. In a curious, separated tailpiece (1163–84) Teucer arranges the suppliancy tableau with the boy and Tecmessa [cf. 7.4.2]. He then goes, and a choral act-dividing song follows.

In this song (1185–222) the chorus curse war, wish for an end to it, [9.4.2] and finish with a longing to escape back home to Attica. This is all a foil to the harsh reality: immediately Teucer returns (1223), just in time to intercept the approach of Agamemnon. Teucer's exit and return are in realistic terms unnecessary, but Sophocles' point seems to be to isolate the pathetic tableau which forms a background to the choral song, and to bring about the tense flurry of movement which opens the next act. Agamemnon is little better than his brother, and Teucer, though desperately courageous, again cannot lift himself above the low level of dispute. A kind of mean, carping deadlock is reached: what is needed is some sort of transcendent wisdom. That wisdom is provided by the last of this long series of entries, that of

Odysseus [1316ff., cf. 4.4.2]. Odysseus learned the lesson of the prologue, and he has something of the insight into time and change which is memorably expressed in Ajax's 'deception' speech:

> *Od*: He was my foe, yes, but he was still noble.
> *Ag*: What? Why such respect for an enemy corpse?
> *Od*: Because his worth far outdoes enmity.
> *Ag*: Men like you make man unreliable.
> *Od*: Many who are now friends will be reversed. (1355–9)

Ajax and Achilles (cf. 1340f.) may to some extent stand outside the shifts of the world, but those who wish to live must also let live. So, through Odysseus' insight, the play reaches its tragic 'happy ending'.

The last third of the play by no means balances the first two-thirds: the world without Ajax is a smaller meaner place. But, as the first part shows that he was too big for this world, so the rest shows how the world must adjust to his departure. Ajax was a great man, even in death, and the lesser world he leaves behind should acknowledge his stature. *Ajax* is not only the tragedy of the death of a hero, but also of the life of a heroic world. To explore this conjunction to the full, Sophocles composed a play in two parts.

[9.5.1]   The greater part of *OT*, up to Oedipus' discovery of the truth (1–1185), consists of five acts of increasing and then decreasing length. The longest, central act is that in which Oedipus is first with Creon and then with Jocasta (513–862). The length of the act is to some extent broken up by a divided strophic pair of lyric dialogue stanzas at 649–68 = 678–97, and these snatches of lyric also provide an overlapping transition between Jocasta, who enters just before the first (at 631ff.), and her brother, who goes immediately before the second (677). This transition in mid-act also marks an important change in the direction of the play. During the scene with Creon Oedipus still has no clues towards solving his problem – or none that he recognizes as such – and he vents his frustrated urge to progress in vain suspicion and irritation, as he had in the Tiresias scene. Jocasta, however, quickly gives this aimless energy a new direction when she unwittingly supplies a lead. At 707ff. in an attempt to discredit seers and oracles she mentions in passing that Laius was murdered 'at the junction of three tracks', and this takes Oedipus by way of his urgent interrogation to the near-certainty that he was the murderer of Laius, the damned victim of his own pronouncements [cf. 5.5.1]. In the course of the act Oedipus has moved from domineering confidence to distraught anxiety. The play comes close to a premature ending, an ending unfortunate enough, but nothing compared to the full truth. The denouement is held back merely by a lingering inconsistency in an eye-witness report (see 836ff.). This is small comfort, but it is

enough to restrain the final moves of a half-true ending, and to allow
the question of the killer of Laius to be replaced by the problem of
Oedipus' origins. Sophocles has split the quest into two stages, and
now leaves this first track unpursued until it eventually fits into place
in the larger fateful map, the chart of the truth.

Ever since Aristotle the plot construction of *OT* has, quite rightly,   [9.5.2]
been praised. But typical of Aristotle's discussion is the sentence 'In
the action there should be nothing contrary to reason; or if there is it
should be outside the play itself, as in Sophocles' *Oedipus*.' This
somewhat pedestrian and unfortunately influential concern with circumstantial probability (*eikos*) is not altogether obviously appropriate
to this plot which depends on several improbable coincidences. Just
as it was a coincidence that on leaving Delphi Oedipus should at a
lonely place meet Laius on his way to Delphi and that he should then
go on to Thebes, so it is coincidentally neat that Polybus should die
and the messenger from Corinth arrive at this particular juncture. It is
even more crucially coincidental that the messenger from Corinth
should be the very man who received the baby on Cithaeron, and that
the old man who was eye-witness to the murder should also be the
man who took the baby to Cithaeron (118ff., 756ff., 834ff., 1051ff.). In
mundane terms these are the most extraordinary, disastrous chances,
yet they all add up to a pattern – a pattern known all along to the gods
– which makes only too much sense. It could be argued that Sophocles means these 'improbabilities' to go unnoticed. But perhaps not.
Certainly we are meant to notice the way that the Corinthian arrives
in answer to the prayer of Jocasta [see 6.5.2]. The ultimate shaping of
events looks like mere random coincidence to man until he can look
back on it. Oedipus is right to see himself as the 'child of Fortune'
(1080, see below), but he is too quick to suppose Fortune is kind.

Once again, as with Jocasta and the 'three tracks', the Corinthian
supplies a new lead in a well-intentioned reassurance against
unpleasant oracles (989ff.). Oedipus' life has included a series of such
well-intentioned interventions which all lead towards disaster.
Oedipus presses on with increasing urgency until he reaches a state of
high elation. At the beginning of this act Jocasta describes how
Oedipus 'stirs his emotions to too high a pitch with all sorts of anxiety'
(914–15): but here he is at the end:

> Let the storm break for all I care, I still
> want to spy out my birth, however mean.
> She has a woman's pride, and it may be
> she is ashamed at my ignoble birth.
> I count myself the child of Fortune, Fortune
> the bountiful: and that is no disgrace.

> *She* was my mother, and the months, my brothers,
> have marked me out as humble and then great.
> That is my pedigree: nothing can ever
> change me or stop my finding out my birth. (1076–85)

And, with Oedipus still standing there on stage, there follows a wild, fanciful choral song about his divine origins on Cithaeron (1086–109). All this is ironically true, but in the worst possible sense. Only one short act (1110–85) is now needed. Nearly all the pieces of the puzzle are there, though muddled; a couple more, and everything will be clear. The old shepherd tries desperately to hold them back, but the innocent goodwill of the Corinthian (1132ff.), and Oedipus' violent determination [cf. 5.5.2] soon wring them out:

> It's out! It's out! Everything has come clear.
> Now, sunlight, may I look my last on you,
> as I have been exposed – unnatural
> in birth, in marriage, and in murder – all. (1182–5)

[9.5.3]   I shall return, finally, to the model of the riddle, introduced earlier in 4.5.2. This may seem frivolous since our first reaction is to associate riddles with children or winter evening amusement. But few adults do not appreciate a well-formulated riddle at any time. The ancient (and modern) Greeks, like many 'primitive' cultures, less drearily literal-minded than our own, have more respect for riddles, and for related enigmas like fables, dreams, curses or oracles.[5] Riddles, like metaphor, like poetry, relate in an intriguing way things which in brute life are unconnected or incongruous. The answer to a well-set riddle has an inevitable, almost magical, truthfulness to its premises – it works by a kind of irrational logic. It is this 'truth' which holds the fascination, along with the process of solution. For consider the sequence of events when someone is faced with a riddle. At first he is frustrated and irritated because he can see no pattern in its apparent nonsensicality; given some clues, he becomes involved, obsessive, eager for the moment when everything will fall into place; when he sees the answer (or is given it) then in a flash all is clear, obvious – 'Everything has come clear'. Afterwards he dwells on the way the riddle works and on his own stupidity in not seeing it. There is a fascination and delight both for the solver and for those who witness him going through this procedure, especially if they know the answer. The application of this to *OT* should be obvious.

It is often said that the question which Oedipus answers is 'Who am I?'. In one sense that has a specious profundity which suggests an existential search for identity: in fact the enigmas he solves are more numerous and more particular. Many of them are first posed by

Tiresias. For instance there is this complex: when is a father not a father, a wife not a wife, or who is a father and a son, a sister and a daughter and so on? These incest paradoxes have an enduring fascination; they are evoked in all the Oedipus tragedies, and in the last parts of *OT* are brutally explored, almost relished.[6] Some more conundrums: who sees and yet is blind, is wise yet ignorant, saviour and polluted, powerful and powerless, fortunate yet wretched, highest yet lowest? The answer to all these is a man who prospers yet has committed a great sin and does not know it, and then discovers it. One could well go on: who is an alien yet native, a king and a king-killer, a hunter and yet the quarry, curser and cursed? Oedipus sees all these together when all comes clear at line 1182. Although it is horrifying and pitiful, there is something intensely satisfying, thrillingly appropriate in the resolution of all these paradoxes in one great man. So many riddles to rest on the shoulders of one man, one answer – Oedipus.

At the same time the answer is, as with the riddle of the Sphinx, 'man'. It is the human condition to be subject to these paradoxes – we are all 'children of Fortune'. So in this other sense Oedipus did answer the question 'Who am I?'; in the sense of the traditional Greek warning 'Know thyself'. This means 'know you are human'; for every man, even Oedipus, is 'an insubstantial shadow', 'the shadow of smoke'.

Although he was very old, possibly over 90, when he composed [9.6.1] *Philoctetes*, Sophocles is here especially bold and novel in his structural techniques. After the prologue and first song there are only *three* acts: 219–675 (broken up by a divided lyric pair at 391ff. = 507ff.); 730–1217 (though this is virtually broken into two by the song while Philoctetes is unconscious at 827–64); 1221–470. In fact, the only fully conventional act-dividing song is that at 676–729. And yet the acts are highly fluid and varied, not only by the interspersed lyric elements but also by abrupt transitions, interventions, and new turns of event. Furthermore, these three acts are almost all taken up with the relationship of just two men, two men greatly contrasting yet with vital affinities, one stubborn and long-suffering, the other fresh and impressionable, both true-hearted and noble. Along with Heracles at the end and the 'merchant', who is in many ways a proxy for Odysseus, Odysseus himself makes up the unusually small – and all male – cast. Yet from so little Sophocles has wrought a play of extraordinary variety, complexity and activity.

This is why I have perhaps given *Phil*, and especially the central sequence 730–1217, more than its fair share of the other chapters; and I shall here look only briefly at the final scenes. The long lyric dialogue 1081–217 is preceded by the exit of Odysseus and Neoptolemus and followed by their re-entry and thus far functions as an act-dividing song. But it follows very closely on the preceding act and yet is finished very finally by an exit; and so, rather than dividing acts, it is an extended coda to the act before. The break at 1217/21, which stops and then restarts the play, is uniquely stark [see 4.6.2].

The next hundred lines contain a great deal of movement to and fro, and develop the situation rapidly and irreversibly. The bow soon changes hands and at 1293 Odysseus leaps out of ambush again [8.6.1]. The action now, when Philoctetes draws his bow, is exceptionally hasty. Odysseus runs for his life, and is probably off stage before line 1302f. ('Alas, why have you deprived me of killing my most hated enemy with my bow?'). Odysseus' appearance lasts less than 10 lines, and he speaks only five. The major characters of Greek tragedy seldom make appearances of less than 40 lines, and this is the briefest of all to survive. The rush and indignity of this intervention must show the final repudiation of Odysseus and all that he stands for. Now that a true bond has been at last established between Neoptolemus and Philoctetes, Odysseus has nothing to offer: his verbal bravado is useless and superseded (cf. 1305ff., quoted on p. 133). There have been critics who have stood up for Odysseus – he does have a certain plausibility and after all he has insisted on the outcome which the prophecy of Helenus sanctions and which Heracles finally ensures. But the whole point is that the end is nothing if the means are wrong. Philoctetes must come of his own free will (1332; cf. 612, 617); yet Odysseus would make him come willy-nilly by fair means or foul. Besides, the whole play, if I have seen it right, shows up Odysseus by contrast with Neoptolemus and Philoctetes. He is not such an obvious villain as a shallow knave like Menelaus in *Ajax* – he is much more insidious and so all the more dangerous.

Once Odysseus is out of the way, the play can proceed to its ending. We are allowed to see how far Philoctetes' stubbornness and Neoptolemus' new-found maturity of principle will go, before they are easily and gently deflected to Troy to find there glorious immortality. As Heracles tells Philoctetes 'Out of all your pains you shall, you may be sure, attain to a life of glory' (1421–2):

> But like a pair of lions, you each protect
> the other, he you and you him. (1436–7)

[9.7.1]   *Hippolytus* does not have a single central character, it has three (the Nurse makes a fourth, but she is dismissed from the play without consequence). This gives Euripides the opportunities for four combinations of direct confrontation between major characters. And yet he very deliberately eschews three of these: there is no face-to-face dialogue between Phaedra and Hippolytus nor between Phaedra and

Theseus, nor, *a fortiori*, between all three. In fact Phaedra is dead before Theseus ever comes on stage. That the play is despite this incontestably a finely constructed unity is due in part to the skill with which the transition is made from the first Phaedra half to the second Theseus half.

The huge second act (170–524) is devoted to Phaedra's love sickness (and the choral entry-song at 121ff. also leads up to this). The anapaestic opening (170–266) provides some variety, but the only major break in the impetus of the act is an isolated choral strophe at 362–72, which marks the point when the truth is out. In contrast to this massiveness the next much briefer act (565–731), in which the long wait for a meeting between Hippolytus and Phaedra is swiftly and unexpectedly concluded, is divided into three counterpoised sections. First there is the lyric dialogue (565-600) while Phaedra listens at the door [see 5.7.3]. The lyric intensity of Phaedra's decision to die is followed by the reasoned indignation of Hippolytus. The scene opens in the middle of his dialogue with the Nurse (a rare device in Greek tragedy), as he bursts outside to get into the fresh untainted air; but this soon gives way to his denunciation of women (616ff.). Throughout Hippolytus' invective *tour-de-force* Phaedra stands silent.[7] Every word is aimed at her, however unfairly, yet she is never once addressed. This is the only scene where both the step-mother and step-son are on stage together: there is no dialogue between them. Here above all Euripides shows the human attempt to do the right thing, to be noble, leading towards the ineluctable catastrophe. Hippolytus rushes off with the words:

> As long as Theseus is abroad, I'll stay
> away and say nothing. When he returns
> I shall come too, and see how you can face
> him eye to eye, you and your mistress here.
>   [*exit*]   (659–62)[8]

The last two words are the only reference to Phaedra. These lines anticipate a second half to the play which will never in fact materialize: Phaedra will make sure that it is Hippolytus who will have to face Theseus' accusing eye.

The sequal to the exit of Hippolytus uses some very unusual dramatic technique. Phaedra laments her disaster in a brief lyric (669–79) which is antistrophic to the choral strophe back at 362–72 (see above). This is doubly unique in surviving tragedy: not only does an actor sing the stanza which responds to the choral strophe, but they are also divided by a full choral act-dividing song (viz. 525ff.) The effect of this is to make a startling connection between Phaedra's despair now she is near to death and the insistent attempts of the chorus and the

Nurse to wheedle the truth out of her in the previous act. After this initial lyric outburst Phaedra does not take long to damn the Nurse and to determine on an end that will both save her name and teach Hippolytus a lesson (682–731).

Phaedra's exit to death concludes the first half of the play. Theseus' entry at 790 begins the second. The first strophic pair of the intervening choral song (732ff.) take us off to the translucent world of exotic legend; the second pair (752ff.) bring us back to the harsh reality of this particular legend – across the sea from Crete, into the palace, to the rafters of Phaedra's room, to the white neck in the noose. The cries for help from inside the palace at 776ff. are by then expected and inevitable. It is those very cries which bring Theseus [see 7.7.2], and they thus bring out both the continuity and discontinuity between the two parts of the play. At this late stage a new major character enters, a character who is totally ignorant of all that has transpired up to this point. He has only two items of evidence with which to piece together the tragedy so far; and these he quickly summons on stage. One is the corpse of Phaedra and her mutely clamorous letter [see 6.7.4, 7.7.1], and the other is Hippolytus who enters in response to his father's call for witnesses [see 7.7.2]. These two exhibits are at once too little and too much: the rest follows helplessly.

[9.8.1]   I have attempted at some length to show why I take *Ion* to be a major tragedy; and all I shall do here is to look at some of the techniques of variation which Euripides uses in order to make its 370-line long final act (1250–622) reflect the vicissitudes and excitement of its matter. In a sense the final act may be said to begin with the entry of the messenger back at 1106, since his speech paints the backcloth to all that follows and since it is divided from Creusa's entry, not by a full choral song, but only a brief astrophic lyric (1229–43). Still, this little song allows for an emotional readjustment from the brilliant virtuosity of the messenger's tale to the visible immediacy of Creusa's danger; and so it is, in effect, a tense little act-dividing song.

The act proper begins in excited trochaics (1250–60), but changes to iambics with the more awesome threat of Ion's denunciation (1261–81). After that, when Creusa has taken sanctuary [see 5.8.2], the delivery changes again to the peculiarly tense, darting movement of a regular one-line stichomythia (1283ff.).[9] The impasse is diverted by the entry of the Pythia [1320, see 7.8.1]. While the priestess takes her farewell of Ion (1320–63), Creusa stays completely neglected at the altar, and she remains there unnoticed during Ion's disturbed, almost lost, monologue (1369–94). But then she suddenly leaves sanctuary [1395ff., 8.8.2], and we return to stichomythia for the gathering pleasure of the recognition of the tokens [see 6.8.3]. As the longed-for embrace approaches [see 5.8.3] the regularity of the lines breaks up (1427ff.), and then lyric duet takes over for the bliss of reunion (1445–511). Back in spoken metre Ion and Creusa dwell on these strange events (1512–38), and Ion's doubts about Apollo's oracle gradually increase until his lack of faith has to be set right by the epiphany of Athena [1549ff., see 7.8.2]. At the end of her speech a brief dialogue in trochaic tetrameters, which signal impending movement, cover the final farewells to Delphi as Ion and Creusa start on their momentous journey to Athens [1606–22, see 4.8.2 and 4.8.3].

This makes a rather bald, monotonous survey; but an awareness of Euripides' techniques may help to bring out the way that he makes this final act full of suspense and variety, which mirrors the states of mind of the agents, passionate 'children' of Fortune, but here a bountiful Fortune. He varies delivery, the relations and moods of the characters, the visual centre of the scene, and thus makes a finale which moves towards its goal through a darting fragmentation, apparently directionless, but in the event coherent.

All of *Bacchae* up to line 433 is taken up (roughly speaking) with [9.9.1] exposition. All of the play after line 976 may be regarded as the aftermath of the catastrophe and takes the conventional form of a messenger followed by the corpse and next of kin. The central portion, 434–976, consists of three acts, each of them essentially a confrontation between Dionysus and Pentheus. But the outer two (434–518, 912–76) are both unusually brief, and both are structurally simple without major subdivisions and bounded by the entrances and exits of the protagonists. And they make a contrasting pair [see 8.9.1]. But the central act, 576–861, is twice as long as the outer two put together. Furthermore, it is in its turn articulated into two outer sections and a long central section. In the first part (576–641) there are the lyric 'palace miracles' followed by the Stranger's trochaic account of Pentheus' response to them. The central part (642–809) consists of the messenger from the hills and Pentheus' response to him. The final coda (810–61) shows Dionysus' psychic capture of his opponent.

This clearly symmetrical construction makes into drama both Pentheus' failure to acknowledge repeated proofs of Dionysus' divinity and the reversal which follows on his proven incorrigibility. This view has been particularly well argued by Anne Burnett. The first clear evidence given to Pentheus is the 'conversion' of Cadmus and Tiresias [see 5.9.1]: this he rejects uncompromisingly, and he retaliates with force (345ff.). Next he is offered the argument and the behaviour of the Stranger. But this makes no new impression on him, and in the end he resorts to force again (503ff.). So now Dionysus lays on more obvious and violent proof in the form of the 'palace miracles'. But when Pentheus emerges at 642 he is unchanged: 'Have every gate-tower in the city walls locked fast on my orders' (653). But Dionysus does not finally condemn his cousin yet. First he is given a chance to *learn* from the messenger from the hills [see 4.9.3]. This wonderful speech, the centrepiece of the central scene, is the richest, clearest, most irrefutable proof that the Bacchants are not a threat to morality, and that Dionysus is a god and one who can effortlessly sweep aside his enemies. We wait in suspense for Pentheus' response to the speech: can even the most callow and stubborn of tyrants fail to be moved? He turns, as always, to the armed attendants at his side:

> This bacchic outrage catches hold like fire,
> and now it's close – an insult to true Greeks.
> We want no hesitation. You, go to the gate,
> order a parade ready for dispatch –
> all heavy infantry, all light swift horse,
> all light-armed foot, and well-trained archery.
> We march to war against the bacchanals. (778–85)

But even now Dionysus offers Pentheus one more chance. In the dialogue 789–809 he offers to bring the women back without force, though also, of course, without repudiating Dionysus. Mrs Burnett writes 'here at the heart of this play of destruction, the divinity has offered his victim peace (804), rescue (806), alliance (808), and blessedness.' This is rather to overstate the generosity of Dionysus' bargaining, but she is surely right to stress the place of this dialogue as a last chance for Pentheus, a final bid, beyond what may be expected, to make him see the error of his ways. Pentheus' fatal reply is 'Ho there, bring out my armour. And stop talking you' (809).

This time he has obdurately turned his back on the last of his last chances. He has rejected words and reason in favour of force for the last time, and now his choice rebounds against him. The next word of the play is 'ah' [see 7.9.3] the monosyllabic turning point. In the final dialogue of this long act Dionysus ensnares his dangerous marauding beast of an opponent. Pentheus puts up some token resistance, but he is gently, helplessly enmeshed in cruel bonds from which there is no escape but to be torn to pieces. The next act, which concludes this central sequence, displays him reduced to a harmless circus animal on his way to the amphitheatre – the mountain where his mother hunts.

10 Emotion and meaning in the theatre

Let but Sophocles *bring you Ajax on a stage . . . and tell mee
if you have not a more familiar insight into anger than finding
in the schoolemen his* genus *and difference.* (Sidney, An
Apology for Poetry)

Rather than put together an interpretation of each of the nine plays, I
shall attempt, by way of synopsis, to characterize what kind of effect
Greek tragedy has – used to have, may have – on a member of the
audience. I have tried to bring out a view of each play as I went along
and I can only ask anyone who wishes to concentrate on one in
particular to go through the chapters accordingly. What still needs to
be brought out is the feel of the dramatic experience, the way that
tragedy works on its audience. This attempt calls for a basic consideration of the nature of the art-form, and some of the most familiar
doctrines about it will have to be cleared from the air. The life-breath
of Greek tragedy often seems stifled by antiquarian patronizing and
by text-book clichés, clichés which I find trotted out in the
programme-notes to almost every modern production.

My working assumption throughout has been that the tragedians
were free in their use of theatrical techniques, that they chose to
convey their meaning by certain actions and sequences of action
rather than others, and that this artistic choice directs us to their
purpose. But most critics have written not of freedom but of constraints, limitations, rules. In some ways Aristotle's *Poetics* sets the
example for this approach, though at least Aristotle was being pre-

scriptive, not descriptive. But in his wake more petty and more authoritarian critics have so extended and rigidly codified the 'rules' of Greek tragedy as to obscure and even deny its lively freedom. Overgeneralizations and simplifications have become common text-book doctrine; and instead of illuminating tragedy these clichés have mortified and alienated it. Some will have to be cleared out of the way in order both to justify the claims of this book and to approach finally the experience of the audience of a Greek tragedy. This negative progress will, I hope, constantly be bringing our positive goal nearer.

To react against the imposition of rules by critics is not for a moment to deny that the Athenian theatre was in many respects highly con-ventional. Innumerable conventions governing diction, tone and propriety defined the genre and sustained its elevation. Others regu-lated, and at the same time made familiar, the technical medium.[1] Some may strike us as awkwardly restrictive (e.g., those governing the handling of the chorus or stichomythia); others are still dramatic common sense and seem too obvious to notice (e.g., only one charac-ter speaks at a time, characters normally speak on entry). Very few of these 'laws' are unbreakable. Two conventions, for instance – both with sound practical justification – are that the chorus should not go off in the middle of the play, and that wounds and death should not be presented on stage. Yet there are counter-examples to both within the nine plays taken in this book, the former in *Eum* and *Ajax*, the latter in *Ajax*, *OT* and *Hipp*. These unwritten laws are not really restrictions or limitations, they are rather the familiar framework which supports any great cultural florescence. When the artist has accepted forms and his audience shares a complex of expectations, then, since the audience is more sensitive and receptive, the art form can be accordingly more highly developed. So the circumspections are liberating (most, if not all, worthwhile human activities need rules). It is only after the flowering is over that the rules become a bondage and the art tends either towards lifeless imitation (like the tragedy of later antiquity) or towards an indiscriminate formlessness (like today?). These flexible defining rules of the game are not like the stiffly distorting overgeneralizations I am complaining of.

Take this, for instance: 'all the important *action* in Greek tragedy takes place off stage: on stage it is merely spoken and sung about.' If this book has not scotched that common misconception then it has achieved nothing. My claim is, on the contrary, that it is the action which takes place *on* stage which *is* important, and is part of what the play is about: the action off-stage is only of interest in so far as it is given attention on stage. The error comes about from a simple-minded preconception of what constitutes action; it only counts the huge violent events of narrative history – battles, riots, miracles, natural disasters and so forth. This is to miss the point that the stuff of tragedy is the individual response to such events; not the blood, but the tears. It is the life-sized actions of this personal dimension which are the dramatist's concern, and which he puts on stage. (It is above all the film which, for better or for worse, has obscured this distinction.)

I move on to a more evidently attractive fallacy, and one which has, in fact, influenced our contemporary theatre: that Greek tragedy is in one way or another a *ritual* event. This is, I think, true only in so far as all human activities are 'rituals', a use of the word which renders it virtually meaningless. On any useful definition of ritual, Greek tragedy is simply and demonstrably not a ritual. The whole point about ritual is that it should always be the *same*: it is the aim of its performers to repeat the rigmarole as perfectly, as identically as possible.[2] Whatever its origins (see p. 23) Greek tragedy as we know it retains no such repeated elements, neither in part nor in whole. Of course there are all the conventions just discussed above, but they promote diversity, not repetition. Many attempts have been made to find invariable ritual elements in Greek tragedy, but all have failed and all (so far as I can see) are bound to fail. Probably the best known is the struggle, death, lament and rebirth of the 'year spirit', a pattern of fertility ritual which Gilbert Murray extended to Greek tragedy. But not one single tragedy we have can be claimed without distortion actually to follow this pattern; in particular Greek tragedy does not go in for resurrection or rejuvenation.

Now there certainly are some ritual procedures during the course of the events of the plays, for example supplication [5.7.1], claiming surety [8.8.2] or the hunting *kōmos* [6.9.2]; but these are used *within* the plays, they are not imposed on them from without. Greek tragedy reflects and exploits the rituals of the real world, of course: but it is not itself a ritual. When the playwright set about composition, in other words, he did not have to follow any imposed ritual formula or sequence.

I would go further and suggest that it was a necessary precondition of the great age of Greek tragedy that the drama should *not* have been a ritual. It had to be human and various, beyond the control of repeated superstition, ancestral taboo, actions stylized and codified beyond anything mimetic – it had to exploit ritual, not just conserve and subserve it. This break with the repetitiousness of ritual may well have been one of the great achievements of tragedy's creators. The impulse among modern critics to impose ritual patterns was largely inspired by the rise of comparative anthropological studies.[3] For when it was seen how rituals, including some semi-dramatic rituals, are so extremely important in primitive societies, it was an obvious step to expect ritual patterns in Greek tragedy. What this approach, which is still active, underestimates is the extent to which classical Greek culture had gone beyond the 'primitive', and moved on in the direction, whether or not one regards it as a beneficial progress, taken since by Western civilization.

But a further argument is advanced by those who claim that tragedy was a ritual, the fact that the tragedies were performed as part of the programme of the city festival of Dionysus, an annual event of several days which included many traditional ritual events – processions, sacrifices, etc.[4] The plays were performed within the sacred area of Dionysus, in the presence of his priest, and were preceded and followed by fixed rituals. All true. But the fact is that these circumstances have left no trace whatsoever on the tragedies themselves, no trace of the Dionysiac occasion, the time of year, the priests, the surrounding rituals, nothing. We could not tell one single thing about the Festival from the *internal* evidence of the plays; it is all supplied by external evidence.

Unimaginable? We may go to a secular play or concert which is part of a church festival, is given in a church and is even preceded by some prayers from the priest; but does that make the performance a ritual or attendance a religious experience? You have only to contrast it with the lessons, litany and liturgy of a church service. But surely, it may still be claimed, tragedy was, none the less, a religious experience for the audience, seeing that they were participating in a sacred festival. Is going to the panto a religious experience since it is part of the annual festival commemorating Christ's birth (or marking the winter solstice, if you prefer)? For the Athenians the great Dionysia was an occasion to stop work, drink a lot of wine, eat some meat, and witness or participate in the various ceremonials, processions and priestly doings which are part of such holidays the world over. It was also the occasion for tragedy and comedy; but I do not see any way in which the Dionysiac occasion invades or affects the entertainment. Some Athenians complained that tragedy was 'nothing to do with Dionysus' (cf. our Christmas): but whatever everyone else went for it was evidently not another ritual, nor in any obvious or overt sense for a religious experience. To put it another way, there is nothing intrinsically Dionysiac about Greek tragedy.

Next a dogma which is, if anything, even more widespread and more misleading: that 'they all knew the story already'. This promotes several misconceived inferences: that Greek tragedy was a repository of traditional tales, that the dramatist's composition is 'dictated by the myth', that there is no element of suspense or surprise, that the tragedy is the working out of fate or destiny, that the characters are puppets of the gods. All these clichés I regard as more or less wrong.

Greek tragedy almost invariably drew on stories about the distant heroic age of Greece, the period which in historical terms we now call the Late Bronze Age or 'The Mycenaean Age', those few generations of mighty exploits, turmoil and splendour, which were the setting of most traditional Greek heroic song, both in epic and lyric. But these stories were not history, nor were they canonized in any definitive collection of 'Greek myths'. Their oral transmission 'at mother's knee' was no doubt subject to the huge variations which characterize nearly all such oral traditions, variations of emphasis and mood no less than of narrative content (whatever 'deep structures' the reductionist sage may claim to detect). It is likely, in any case, that the tragedians drew predominantly on literary sources. Here, too, there was almost limitless variation, the product of centuries of re-arrangement and invention, a process which the tragedians themselves continued. Not even the myths of the *Iliad* and *Odyssey* are definitive. The only full coincidence with Homer in surviving tragedy, *Rhesus* and *Iliad* 10, reveals many important divergencies. Or take the myth of Orestes. In the story alluded to several times in the *Odyssey* (and also, it seems, in early lyric; cf. pl. 10) Aegisthus is the chief agent of Agamemnon's murder and chief object of Orestes' vengeance: but the whole shape of the *Oresteia* is moulded by Aeschylus' decision, probably innovatory, to make Clytemnestra the sole murderer and chief victim of vengeance. Then we all know from Sophocles that when Oedipus discovered the truth he blinded himself and went into exile, while Jocaste hanged herself. In the version in *Odyssey* 11 Epicaste (as she is called) hangs herself, but there is nothing about Oedipus' blinding: he rules on in Thebes. And a line in the *Iliad* (23.679) implies that he fell in battle there. Then in Euripides' *Phoenician Women* Oedipus is blind but still in Thebes many years after the discovery of the truth – and Jocaste? She is still alive. Then, again, in Aeschylus' original version of the *Seven against Thebes* Oedipus had no daughters; the death of his sons was the end of his line. Examples like this may be multiplied, and even more so if vase-paintings are brought into play. Very little was immutably fixed.

But even if the myths were much more rigidly laid down than my argument claims, this would still be of minimal consequence for the literary criticism of tragedy, since the mere *story*, such as may be excerpted in a collection of 'Greek Myths', has no significant bearing on the quality of the play. The mere story is shared by good and bad dramatists alike – it may be indistinguishable in Sophocles and in a fifth-rate hack. What matters, for the dramatist and his audience, is the way he has *shaped* the story, the way he has turned it into drama.

The constraint is minimal: the scope for artistry enormous.[5] The area of artistic initiative may be conveyed by a crude catalogue of some of the decisions in question: which brief section is to be taken from the continuum of the myth, which events are to be emphasized or played down, which characters, which aspects, which motifs and images? The identity and role of the chorus, the sequence of events, the exposition, the shape of the acts and of the ending, the use of the lyric, whether choral, monody or lyric dialogue; and last but not least, all the aspects of theatrical and visual technique which have been the subject of this book: all have to be decided on. The list could be extended and elaborated to fill volumes: for these factors are, in effect, the playwright's medium and, thus, our means to literary criticism and interpretation. What we ask is *how* the dramatist has wrought his play, and why he has done it in his particular way, for he had deliberated on this process and made his decisions. The constraint of his myth, in so far as it is fixed, is only of marginal influence. The standard comparison of Aeschylus' *Choephoroi* with the *Electras* of Euripides and Sophocles shows this process of artistic shaping in practice. The range of variation is even better brought out by looking at Aeschylus' *Seven against Thebes*, Sophocles' *Antigone*, and Euripides' *Phoenician Women*.[6]

Now let us look at this issue from the side of the audience. They did not know the 'plot' in advance, for they did not know what version, what variations and innovations the playwright would use – no doubt they were eager to find out. Still less did they know how he would shape his plot, how he would dramatize it: that is precisely what they went to see. In this respect the audience approached the drama, I would maintain, virtually free of preconceptions. It was then the dramatist's task to enthrall their minds, to fill them with the knowledge, thoughts and feelings which he wished to conjure up, and to the exclusion of all others. That is why each tragedy is more or less self-contained in narrative, and includes even the most elementary facts in its exposition – which is quite uncalled for if they 'knew it already'. The dramatist would, naturally, prepare for and foreshadow the course of his plot (hence 'tragic irony'), though even here there is plenty of scope for surprise and suspense. He might even call to mind previous versions of his story, earlier dramatizations or, above all, Homer; he will then arouse complex associations and expectations which he can confirm or vary or contradict. But such allusions should only receive as much attention as the spellbinder allows; and what is not alluded to does not, within the play, exist. Far from knowing it all already, the audience knows what it is told, thinks and feels what it is aroused to think and feel.

A brief paragraph on the related misconception that Greek tragedy basically shows the working of Fate, of men fastened to the puppetry of higher powers – a notion with an enduring fascination, for Thomas Hardy for example.[7] Most cultures have their expressions of fatalism; they are one of our chief sources of solace in the face of the pointless waste of ill fortune: 'che sera, sera', 'God's will be done', 'his number was up', 'it is written'. . . . The ancient Greeks were as prone as any to resort to such notions, though, naturally enough, after rather than before the event, and after disaster rather than good fortune. And like most cultures, for a pattern or purpose behind catastrophe they looked to superhuman forces, personal or impersonal. But this tendency does not, within the whole compass of a drama, preclude the free will of the characters or their responsibility, nor does it render their whole life puppetry. Most of the time they are presented as free agents working out their own destinies – as a rule disastrously, since this is tragedy. But sometimes they are seen in fatalistic terms; and sometimes the two motivations, human and superhuman, are seen conspiring together, both logically sufficient conditions of the outcome, yet both at work. But never, except perhaps in mad scenes, are the characters of Greek tragedy portrayed as automata or marionettes. Even when they are viewed as victims of the gods, they remain human and independent.

Compared with the 'myth fallacy' and the 'ritual fallacy' relatively few critics are the prisoners of my last trap, what might be called the 'propaganda fallacy'. This is the supposition that a Greek tragedy was primarily or significantly shaped by the desire to promote a certain line on a specific contemporary issue (in politics or philosophy or whatever). The advocates of such a view will have for a start to allow that such propaganda is *cryptic*, if it is true that there is not one single specific allusion to a contemporary person or event in all of Greek tragedy.[8] So far as I can see this is in fact the case. There is not one anachronism to be noted as such, no overt rupture of the dramatic illusion of the remote heroic world. To avert misunderstanding, I hasten to grant that in a sense – in the most important sense – Greek tragedy is entirely topical and the mirror of its own times. It was composed for the audience of fifth-century Athenians, not for a Bronze Age audience; and its general preoccupations, moral, social and emotional, are those of its age. Thus, it is a tissue of technical anachronisms in the strictest historical sense: my point is that they are not to be noticed as such, they are admitted only as long as they are congruous with the heroic world of the far past in which the play is set.

As a warning consider these three facts (all in my view beyond dispute, though not, in fact, undisputed). Nowhere in Greek tragedy is there any direct address to the audience or any other reference to it;

nowhere in Greek tragedy does the dramatist use the first person of himself or refer to himself in any way; and nowhere in Greek tragedy is there any reference of any kind to the theatre, to drama, actors, etc. No 'gentle spectators', no 'humble author', no 'all the world's a stage'. All three absences are in direct contrast to the Old Comedy of Aristophanes and to most later drama, which likes to exploit the tension between the world of audience and the world of the play, between these two competing types of reality.[9] This invariable refusal to admit the existence of audience and actors and playwright, or to admit that the play is not the real world, confirms the claim that the dramatic illusion is inviolable. The world of the play never acknowledges the world of the audience: the distancing remains always intact. This is by no means to deny the relevance of the tragedy to the world of the audience; but the relevance is not that of propaganda.

What then *is* the relevance of Greek tragedy to its audience? Now that some more modern dogmas have been cleared aside, we might turn to the ancient Greek sources to see what they thought their tragedies were about.[10] They give us, I think, some views which are interestingly wrong, and some which tally so well with my own experience that I am unable to improve on them.

By far the most substantial fifth-century discussion of tragedy is the second half of Aristophanes' *Frogs*. One theme is particularly persistent: that tragedy *teaches* its audience. 'We poets make men better citizens' (1009f.). 'Boys have a schoolteacher to instruct them, grown-ups have poets' (1054f.). In Plato too this is generally regarded as the dramatist's chief claim. This may seem fair enough – most of us decide that art is didactic in one sense or another – but both Aristophanes and Plato apply the notion in disappointing ways. Thus, they both speak of poets, including tragedians, as though it was claimed for them that they actually taught various practical skills – strategy, sailing, economics, cobbling, or whatever it may be. Plato's Socrates has a good time at the expense of this absurdity: obviously for such expertise you go, not to poetry, but to a technical manual or to a living authority.

Another questionable assumption is that the poet's teaching is contained in the words of certain of his lines, and so can be extracted from the work (like a tooth). Aristophanes scarcely seems to doubt that the 'message' of a play by Aeschylus or Euripides – and the man's personal moral views also – is purveyed by certain sententious lines from his work. The same assumption has been shared by the generations of critics down to the present day who have put together a picture of the dramatist from a patchwork of quotations. Obviously this is a hazardous, if not downright foolish, method, since each quotation has a context within the drama as a whole, a context from which (in any good playwright) it is indivisible. The dramatizer of conflict has to be able to put both sides of a case: which side is his message? Furthermore, admirable sentiments may be put in the mouth of a villain, and objectionable ones in the mouth of a virtuous character who does not act upon them (like Hippolytus' notorious line 'my tongue swore, but my heart did not confirm it'). Sometimes, it is true, a final message is drawn from the tragedy as a whole – messages like 'life is full of unexpected turns', 'call no man happy until he is dead', 'think on a mortal level'. But these are the traditional maxims of the Greeks, the property of every grandfather: one need not go to tragedy to learn these. As always, as soon as the message of a work of art is reduced to a sentence it becomes banal.

But the idea that tragedy teaches is not to be abandoned just because it has been applied sophistically. We might well agree in general terms that, in so far as tragedy teaches, it does so through the work *as a whole*, through the way that human life is portrayed and not merely by individual spoken lines. So the audience learns, in so far as it learns, by way of the whole experience. That is to say, the intellectual burden of the tragedy and its value as teaching has to do with the quality of the audience's experience.

We do have a scrap of fifth-century criticism which seems to be developing this very train of thought. It is a single sentence, a fragment torn from its surrounding discourse, but we know it was written apropos of tragedy: 'The man who deceives shows more justice than he who does not; and the man who is deceived has more wisdom than he who is not' (*ho te apatēsas dikaioteros tou mē apatēsantos, kai ho apatētheis sophōteros tou mē apatēthentos*). These are the words of Gorgias, the Sicilian theorist and teacher of rhetoric, who worked in Athens in the last quarter of the fifth century, and who is best known for his discomfiture in Plato's *Gorgias*.[11] Inevitably any interpretation of this sentence is speculative, but there is one which seems to me to make very good sense, whether or not it is what Gorgias meant. The tragedian who succeeds in enthralling his audience does more justice by the effect this has on his audience than the playwright who fails to captivate them: likewise the member of the audience who succumbs to the spell of the play will through that experience be a better, wiser man than the member who resists and remains unmoved. On any interpretation the key word is, of course, *apatān*, to deceive, trick, beguile (perhaps conveyed by the English word-play that tragedy 'takes in' its audience). It is a balanced paradox, typical of Gorgias' manner, that deceit should be the means of justice and wisdom. It is also a shrewd reply to all those moralists, above all Plato himself, who have complained that fiction is all lies. The deceit, Gorgias implies, is temporary and it is beneficial. Truth and falsity are not the category

relevant to the case: the worth of the work of art depends rather on
whether it is convincing, on whether it interests, enthralls, moves its
audience.

How, then, does this 'deceit' take effect? Gorgias' own views are, I
suggest, worth pursuing; and the following passage, which comes
from his virtuoso apologia for Helen, surely has tragedy in mind. 'All
poetry I consider and define as discourse in metre. There comes over
the audience of poetry a fearful horror and tearful pity and doleful
yearning. By means of the discourse their spirit feels a personal
emotion on account of the good and bad fortune of others.'[12] This
passage alone should be enough to rescue Gorgias from the common
slander that he was merely a word-juggler. Above all he sees that
emotions are at the heart of tragic poetry. And what is more he has put
his finger on one of the most vital and remarkable features of this
experience: that the emotions are generous – altruistic almost – that
we feel disturbed personally for *other* people, for people who have no
direct connection with us and indeed belong to another world from
ours. (What's Hecuba to us?) This outgoing emotion, as opposed to
introverted self-absorption, is characteristic of Greek tragedy, and of
most (perhaps all) great tragedy. This point is well brought home by
the anecdote in Herodotus (6.21) about Phrynichus, a contemporary
of Aeschylus, who produced a tragedy about the sack of Miletus, a
recent outrage on a city closely connected with Athens. Phrynichus,
was prosecuted and fined for reminding the Athenians of their *own*
troubles; this is not the playwright's function.

Can we characterize these tragic emotions? Gorgias' list is, I think,
extraordinarily apt, and far more evocative than Aristotle's terse and
derivative 'pity and fear' (*eleos kai phobos*). Literally Gorgias writes
'ultra-fearful shuddering and much-weeping pity and grief-loving
longing'. The greatest of these is surely pity, however much Plato and
Nietzsche may protest (how deluded Nietzsche was in claiming the
Greeks as his authority for denouncing pity). We feel an overwhelming *compassion* for these other people who undergo the tribulations,
pain and waste which are the stuff of tragedy. Yet this compassion is
seldom if ever separable from other emotions. We pity Agamemnon,
Oedipus, Agaue; yet at the same time we feel horror, alarm (*phrīkē*);
and at the same time we *want* Agamemnon to be murdered, Oedipus
to find out the truth, Agaue to recognize her son's head. We have a
longing (*pothos*) which wants grief (*philopenthēs*): it is such sweet
sorrow. I shall return to the paradoxical pleasure of these doleful
feelings; the important new point for now is that the emotions of the
tragic experience are *complex*, and they are of course ever-shifting.
Perhaps, indeed, the better the tragedy, the more complex and labile
the emotions it arouses. This may be why there are certain strong

emotions which Greek tragedy does not as a rule su
notably hatred and lust. These are domineering and sin
obsessions which do not permit mental companions.

It seems to me, then, that Gorgias is right that tragedy is essentia…;
the *emotional experience of its audience*. Whatever it tells us about the
world is conveyed by means of these emotions. Plato agreed with
Gorgias in this, but he disapproved of the process and regarded it as
harmful. Aristotle agreed with him too, but, contrary to Plato,
regarded it as beneficial and salutory. Plato's objection was that such
emotions are not the province of the highest part of the soul, the
intellectual part. This is the forefather of the error made by so many
later critics who have not acknowledged the centrality of emotion in
the communication of tragedy. They think that if tragedy is essentially an emotional experience, it must be *solely* that; and they think
this because they assume that strong emotion is necessarily in opposition to thought, that the psychic activities are mutually exclusive. But
is this right? Understanding, reason, learning, moral discrimination –
these things are not, in my experience, incompatible with emotion
(nor presumably in the experience of Gorgias and Aristotle): what is
incompatible is cold insensibility. Whether or not emotion is inimical
to such intellectual processes depends on the *circumstances in which it
is aroused*.

The characteristic tragic emotions – pity, horror, fascination, indignation, and so forth – are felt in many other situations besides in the
theatre. Above all we suffer them in the face of the misfortunes of real
life, of course. What distinguishes the experience of a great tragedy?
For one thing, as already remarked, we feel for the fortunes of people
who have no direct personal relation to us: while this does not
decrease the intensity of the emotion, it affords us some distance and
perspective. We can feel and at the same time observe from outside.
But does this distinguish tragedy from other 'contrived' emotional
experiences (most of them tending to the anti-intellectual) for
example an animal hunt, a football match, an encounter group, reading a thriller, or watching a horror movie? Well, the experience of
tragedy is by no means a random series of sensations. Our emotional
involvement has perspective and context at the same time, and not
just in retrospect. Thus the events of the tragedy are in an ordered
sequence, a sequence which gives shape and comprehensibility to
what we feel. And, most important of all, the affairs of the characters
which move us are given a moral setting which is argued and
explored in the play. They act and suffer within situations of moral
conflict, of social, intellectual and theological conflict. The quality of
the tragedy depends *both* on its power to arouse our emotions *and* on
the setting of those emotions in a sequence of moral and intellectual

complications which is set out and examined. Tragedy evokes our feelings for others, like much else; but it is distinguished by the order and significance it imparts to suffering. So if the audience is not moved, then the tragedy, however intellectual, is a total failure: if its passions are aroused, but in a thoughtless, amorphous way, then it is merely a bad tragedy, sensational, melodramatic.

Thus it is that our emotions in the theatre, far from driving out thought and meaning, are indivisible from them: they are simultaneous and mutually dependent. The experience of tragedy can achieve this coherence in a way that the emotional experiences of real life generally cannot because they are too close, too cluttered with detail and partiality, to be seen in perspective. Tragedy makes us feel that we understand life in its tragic aspects. We have the sense that we can better sympathize with and cope with suffering, misfortune and waste. It is this sense of understanding (not isolated pearls of wisdom) that is the 'message' of a tragedy, that the great playwright imparts. This is well put in T. S. Eliot's essay 'Shakespeare and the Stoicism of Seneca', where he argues that it is the quality of the emotional expression rather than the quality of the philosophy which makes literature great, which makes it 'strong, true and informative . . . useful and beneficial in the sense in which poetry is useful and beneficial'. 'All great poetry' Eliot writes 'gives the illusion of a view of life . . . for every precise emotion tends towards intellectual formulation' (notice the phrase 'precise emotion' as in the quotation on p. 1).

'Illusion'? Maybe; but emphatically not because the play is a fiction and the audiences' experiences the product of temporary artifice. (And all for nothing! For Hecuba?) Their experiences, both emotional and intellectual, are none the less real, and become part of the real person. The experience is not erased when we leave the theatre. Tragedy is only an illusion in so far as any claim to make sense of all the evils of our life is an illusion (and perhaps tragedy does not claim this). The 'tragedies' of real life, unlike those of the stage, are often shapeless, sordid, capricious, meaningless. But supposing this to be true (as I do), what then? It is not *human* to be content with this useless, even if ultimate, truth. We *must* try to understand, to cope, to respond. It is in this attempt that tragedy – that most great art – has its place. For it gives the hurtful twists of life a shape and meaning which are *persuasive*, which can be lived with. And that endurance and perspective are none the less real. As Gorgias so neatly put it 'the man who is deceived has more wisdom than he who is not'. And so in the end the 'deceit' is true to life and part of life and makes life the better for it.

By enthralling its audiences tragedy unites emotion and meaning so as to give them an experience which, by creating a perspective on the misfortunes of human life, helps them to understand and cope with those misfortunes. There is nothing new or startling in this conclusion; but if it is along the right lines there is no harm in its being repeated and rephrased. In this book I have tried to show some of the ways in which Aeschylus, Sophocles and Euripides captured their audiences' minds, especially through their eyes, and what direction they gave to the sensibilities which they had under their spell for those few hours. *We* are now the audience of Greek tragedy. Are the actions and emotions and ideas I have been considering irremediably inaccessible? They still have the power, surely, to amaze indeed the very faculties of eyes and ears.

11 Round plays in square theatres

I know that I rebel against most performances of
Shakespeare's plays because I want a direct relationship
between the work of art and myself. (T. S. Eliot)

Is it worth putting on a Greek tragedy in the theatre today? For myself
I can vouch that some of the most memorable theatrical experiences I
have ever had have been watching the Greek National Theatre at
Epidaurus and, on a different scale, David Raeburn's productions at
the JACT Greek Summer School. And I cannot be alone, for during
the last hundred years there has been a huge revival in the staging of
Greek tragedy after a lapse of some 1500 years. At this very moment
there are sure to be productions in repertoire in countries all over the
world, not even exclusively in Western countries with vestiges of a
classical education. The plays in performance, that is, offer much
more than antiquarian or pedagogic edification. One of my inspira-
tions has been the recognition that the kinds of stage actions and
theatrical techniques I have been bringing to light are transferable
more or less directly to the contemporary stage. At this time I cannot
avoid the unwelcome fact that very little of the kind of thing I have
been observing is in practice reflected in contemporary productions.
This is because of the attitude of our directors towards authenticity
and freedom in the production of old plays. This attitude should, I
believe, be scrutinized.

Authenticity or freedom? To attempt as close as possible a *repro-*

duction of the original performance, or to give uninhibited rein to a modern reframing? Or can the dilemma somehow be resolved? This choice faces any director of a Greek tragedy; and, though less obviously, it faces the actors also. Indeed, this fundamental issue of theatrical principle confronts the director and actors of any play from the past, and even of a contemporary play.[1] Only when the playwright himself is director is the problem avoided. Recently I heard a fashionable young director boast that the first thing he told his actors at the first rehearsal of Shaw's *Heartbreak House* was to cross out all the stage directions. This was a particularly whelpish gesture since Shaw lavished attention on his stage directions precisely because he regarded the embodiment of his plays as a vital part of their meaning.[2] But this is only a blatant and wilful instance of an attitude which goes back at least as far as Gordon Craig's *The Art of the Theatre* (1905).

What I have to say about the production of Greek tragedy is applicable generally, but the problem is particularly well defined because the theatre of the golden age in Athens was a playwright's theatre. There was no intermediary, no independent director. Things changed, and during the following centuries the stage was dominated by the virtuoso actor, rather as the nineteenth-century English theatre was ruled by the great actor-managers. Things have changed again, and we are now so accustomed to a director's theatre that it is hard to imagine anything else. It is the director who controls the text and the actors and shapes the whole production (and sometimes even usurps the title – 'Brook's *Dream*, Zefirelli's *Romeo*, Miller's . . .'). Within this director's world the answer to my question 'authenticity or freedom?' is brief and almost unanimous: freedom. The director is expected to use his inventiveness to reinterpret his play and to make it his own by any means at his disposal. He may make passing gestures in the direction of authenticity, but this is not a consistent policy; it is simply one directorial device among many.

We had better put on one side the kind of overt modern adaptations which usually involve the collaboration of a creative writer – Soyinka's *Bacchae*, Ted Hughes's *Oedipus*, Bond's *Lear* and so forth. The play is openly and unashamedly rewritten. Scenes are cut out and rearranged, others are added, 'anachronistic' elements are deliberately introduced, to say nothing of rewriting the style and tone or social and moral assumptions. The production is as good as a new work, inspired, more or less randomly, by an old one. This genre seems to be on the increase, and Greek tragedy is a favourite source. So long as gifted adaptors can be found, may this practice prosper. At least the new play's relation to the original is brought out into the open: it does not pretend to *be* Aeschylus or Marlowe. And the adaptation invites fruitful comparison with its source.

But most productions do not encourage this kind of comparison since they claim to be a production of the original work, and the play is attributed to the author not an adaptor. By and large they keep to the original text,[3] and by doing so they appear to be faithful to their playwright. But the medium of drama is sound and sight, not the printed page. We must ask how deep this textual fidelity goes.

Consider, for a start, how far the work can be transformed by purely aural means, even when the wording of the text is scrupulously preserved. It would not be hard to turn a tragedy into undiluted comedy with no other tool than the actors' *voices*. Even if we disallow tampering with punctuation and with the attribution of parts (though both are common devices in our theatre) we still have at our disposal accents and dialects, manipulation of rhythm and stress, tonal pointers like sarcasm or hesitancy, volume, pitch, interjections, noises (giggles, raspberries, etc.) and, perhaps above all, timing – it is only too easy. Purists often plead that we should 'let the text speak for itself': but how much does this mean when all these aural manifestations lie, not in the text, but in the hands of the director and his actors?

And yet, fundamental though these aural factors are, they are not the chief means for the reinterpretation of old plays today. It is astounding how little the all-conquering strategy has been openly acknowledged, though it is obvious enough – the director's manipulation of the *visual dimension* of the play: setting and scenery, lighting, costumes, props, make-up, the gait and demeanour of the actors, grouping and blocking, stage business in general from the smallest gestures and grimaces to the hugest tableaux, machinery or crowd scenes. This whole dimension has no necessary connection with textual fidelity.

And the least detected yet most pervasive and significant of all these directorial strategies is the *interpolation of stage business*. By 'interpolation' I mean the introduction of visual elements which, while not necessarily in contradiction of the text itself, are not explicitly required or indicated by the text. That is to say they are the invention of the director not of the playwright. Such business usually accompanies dialogue which is about something else, but it is often introduced in some kind of 'dumb show', either in silence or accompanied by music or indecipherable stage noise ('rhubarb', etc.). Anyone not fully aware of this kind of interpolation should simply keep an eye open at the next professional production of Shakespeare to see how far it determines the impact of the performance as a whole.[4] We have learned to accept the device without question as though it were inevitable.

I have seen, for example, an *Oedipus the King* which staged love-making between Oedipus and Jocasta (in Pasolini's film even *after* the discovery of their incestuous relationship). And in productions of *The Bacchants* I have seen the chorus indulge in bloody violence, drug-taking, and erotic orgies. In both cases the interpolated stage business has obvious bearing on contemporary preoccupations but nothing to do with Sophocles or Euripides. Or again, something which seems virtually obligatory in professional productions of Greek tragedy (and even of Shakespeare and his contemporaries) is the interpolation of ritual business accompanied by inarticulate noises in unison, whether war dances or sacrificial hocus-pocus or simply anything which reflects the popular notion of primitive cult. In the case of Greek tragedy this at least has some pretext in the ritual associations discussed and disparaged in the previous chapter. But the point is that in order to make his ritual theatre the director has to *add* visual and aural material of his own.

Inventiveness and novelty in his use of the visual dimension is expected of the modern director. It is the chief topic of publicity, of press reviews, and of discussion in the interval. It is, as a rule, what is *new* about the production. But are most directors and their public aware how far the free invention of stage effects obscures, and even fights against, the author's meaning? I suspect that this freedom is so much taken for granted that the question does not get asked. Some directors (and critics) could not care less about the author: that is at least a frank attitude, though presumptuous and small-minded. But most do respect the creator in that they hesitate to change the author's actual words. But this very compunction shows up the contrariety of uninhibited *visual* invention; for in drama the visual dimension is as essential a vehicle of meaning as the text. Good dramatists (let alone great ones) do not hand over such an important medium to others, they use it to the full themselves. My point is, simply, that the free invention of stage business is the theatrical equivalent of rewriting the text of a poem or novel.[5]

My whole argument in this book has been, broadly, that in Greek tragedy the *significant* stage action, the visual dimension, is recoverable from the words, and that it is part and parcel of the play's meaning as a whole. If there is anything to this, and if we agree that we should respect the author's meaning, then a director should follow the author's instructions, visually and scenically as well as textually. There is, then, a case for his paying very close attention to the author's stage directions, both explicit and implicit.

Now this doctrine, and especially the emphasis in implicit stage instructions, goes against most current theatrical practice. Many contemporary directors bridle against the constraint even of text and explicit stage directions. The tide is probably in the other direction,

towards more independence. All I can do is point out the assumptions that lie behind such liberties. If the director pays no attention –
indeed, pays less than undivided attention – to the author's visual
and scenic meaning, then it is not the author's work he is producing:
he is using it, adapting it, 'improving' on it. Just because the author is
dead and powerless that does not mean his name should be taken in
vain. Such productions should openly admit that they are 'inspired
by' or 'based on' Shaw or Shakespeare or Sophocles. Such adaptations and 'improvements' are a legitimate practice with a long pedigree; but once again the tacit assumptions should be spelt out. The first
is that the director knows better than the playwright what makes
good theatre, that his visual meaning is better than the author's. A
great director might make good this claim, particularly with a minor
playwright; but for ordinary mortals it calls for some self-confidence,
not to say conceit or arrogance. There is no escape from this implication. To allege 'this is what the author would have done if he were
alive today' is mere sophistry for 'this is what I want to do'; and to
allege 'he would approve if he were alive', while more modest, is no
less arbitrary. Second, the practice implies that the director knows
that the original work, the playwright's creation, is unacceptable to
modern audiences, that it needs to be improved and refurbished.
That is not only a slight on the author – who would dare to revamp a
Rembrandt painting or a Shakespeare sonnet? – it is also an insult to
the audience, since it presumes that the audience is incapable of
responding to the original masterpiece and is only fit for a doctored
adaptation. What poses as a popular benefit is in fact dictatorial
patronizing.

Does this polemic drive me to the other extreme, to advocating total
authenticity, a carbon-copy of the first performance (or, rather, the
ideal of what the author meant the performance to be)? That may have
seemed to be my destination, but I wish to argue that that extreme is
scarcely less damaging to the drama than its currently acceptable
opposite.

Objections of two kinds come crowding in. In the first place there is
plain impracticability. There is only one theatre of Dionysus at Athens
and that is altered and damaged beyond recognition. Even less
remains of the Globe. There are no native speakers of ancient Greek,
nor for that matter of Elizabethan English. Even if we take the
demands of authenticity less rigidly, must we perform out of doors
during the day, must men play women's parts, must there be masks,
must the music be played on an *aulos*? And so on. The initial practical
constraints are paralysing. And in any case we do not know nearly
enough to aspire to ideal authenticity. So much remains obscure
about, for example, the sound of ancient Greek, histrionic style,

music, choreography and innumerable details of stage management. There may still be some point in a production which is as authentic as possible, despite the obstacles of impracticability and ignorance: the exercise can be fascinating for scholars, instructive for the uninitiated, and even refreshing and formative of taste. But since compromise and speculation are inevitable, the ideal authenticity is ruined. Such an imperfect patchwork cannot serve as a model for the live theatre.

There are in any case some more fundamental objections. Even if all these problems could be surmounted, the reproduction could still not be authentic because we, the audience, are not authentic. The first performance can never happen twice.[6] For the original audience the play was unprecedented, contemporary, made for them: for us it is not. Even if the carbon copy were perfect in all external, impersonal respects, it can never be the original in human terms, in the terms which really matter. The moral, social, aesthetic, intellectual and emotional world of the playwright's production is gone; the culture of the Athenians and Elizabethans, their familiarity with the conventions of their drama, and the expectations that familiarity gave them, their common aspirations and concerns in life all passed on with them. What was new is now old, what was immediate is now distanced. So though we might (in theory) see and hear a performance indistinguishable from that which they saw and heard, our response would be bound to be different, irreparably different. For we would be witnessing an antiquarian reconstruction of an ancient play.

I am questioning what might be called the 'naive historicist' approach to the culture of the past. This claims that we should catch a sort of mental time machine; that we should entirely cast off our temporal selves and should become a member of the original audience. We should 'hob-nob with the ancients', step into their shoes, get inside their skins. 'You must, so far as in you lies, become an Achaean chief while reading Homer, a medieval knight while reading Malory, and an eighteenth-century Londoner while reading Johnson', as C. S. Lewis put it.[7] But this doctrine is doubly deluded: it is not only impossible, but it is also self-destructive, spiritually suicidal. Impossible, because even if we drink a distillation of every scholarly book there is as a kind of magic potion, there is again the fatal impediment of ignorance – we do not and can not know properly what it is we are meant to be changing into. Self-destructive because we are ourselves. (Even if we caught the time machine we should not become ancient Athenians, we should be twentieth-century visitors from a time machine.) Perhaps this point is best made by the analogy of the field anthropologist. It used to be held that the anthropologist should *become* one of the people he is studying. But how can he when his self is indelibly formed by his alien background and his professional training, when he has his notebook in his pocket and the prospect before him of returning home and writing up his findings? He cannot undo his external, anthropological perspective without ceasing to be an anthropologist. 'No foreign anthropologist can ever be wholly assimilated to another culture; he can never quite become one with and indistinguishable from the people he is studying. Nor is it desirable he should.'[8] And if the student of a living society cannot stop being himself, how much more must this be true of the student of a distant society dead beyond recall?

If we must deny ourselves in order to make contact with the culture of the past, then there is no point. The real interest lies in the interplay of the past with the present: the present – we in our real selves – must be enriched. If a Greek tragedy is worth producing today it must speak to us, engage us and move us today. It is no good if it is only a curiosity for the pious antiquarian.[9] For the original audience the drama was alive and immediate. If we sacrifice this quality, if we stuff the bird and put it in a glass case, then we have lost that very authenticity – that other more important kind – which should have made the whole enterprise worth while.[10] So we have to reject antiquarian historicism just as we rejected the total freedom of independent modernism.

The tension we have arrived at is, in fact, the theatrical equivalent of that same tension which emerged in consideration of literary meaning (pp. 5–6). We must respect the author's meaning, we cannot divorce his creation from his communicative purpose: on the other hand we are now readers and we are necessarily different from the author's original public. It is mere evasion to hypothesize 'if the author were writing today . . .'; but it is no less of an evasion to begin 'if we were his original audience . . .'. The real search is the search for what the author's meaning has to say for us now, his present public. To put it another way, reading is an effort of translation and interpretation so that the life latent within the work may be renewed. It is not a matter of catching time machines; no more is it the same as rewriting or improvising afresh.

Apply this to the theatre. The difference is that there is a further stage of translation intervening between author and audience. The audience, instead of being confronted with a printed text, is faced with a production which realizes – or should realize – the author's work, a work which is not itself until it is put on stage. In that case it is the task of director and actors to attempt to convey the creator's play, not to the original audience, but to their own public. But this translation, this presentation of the living drama is not the same as a *recreation*. The life of the drama was put there by the author and should not be replaced by a director. To rewrite rather than to translate in stage terms is to deprive the audience of its contact with the playwright's work of art, which is, to say the least, to do it an injustice (Eliot had a right to protest 'I want a direct relationship between the work of art and myself').

All this theory leads to some practical prescriptions. The director (and actors) must first of all respect the words of the author. He should translate but not alter. Unintentional failure to convey the creator's meaning may be inevitable; but it is still the director's task to do his best, and not deliberately to change, distort, or 'improve'. Likewise in the sphere of visual meaning: he must try to elicit and present it by translation. The author's explicit and implicit stage directions should be given due emphasis. Moreover, the invention and interpolation of stage business, that is of visual meaning, must be shunned, because this replaces the author's meaning; and even when it does not positively contradict, it distracts and submerges and distorts. To most players of early music these imperatives would seem commonplace: to a modern director in the theatre they might appear intolerably restrictive. But are they? I see these as liberating constraints, limits within which the interpreter may work all the better for knowing what it is he is interpreting. And there remains open all the variety that is the product of critical interpretation and scenic translation.

Now all this may seem rather inexplicit and theoretical when it comes to the details of actual production. Do I or do I not think a modern production should use masks, should have a chorus which dances and sings, should be in modern dress, should have scenery, and so on? I have my own ideas, but these are the kind of issues on which I think neither I nor anyone else can lay down the law. I am only trying to define guidelines, the proprieties which will respect the dramatist and will kindle the life inherent in his work. Negatively this means the faithful director should not tamper with the text and should not invent or add significant scenic business. Positively he should look in the work itself both for the meaning of the words and for his staging. These are great *plays*, not mere scripts, and their stage life is there for the finding. That is what chapters 4 to 9 have been all about. The director is a practical translator, and a translator is a medium, his creativity is intermediary: the 'medium' who makes it all up is an impostor.

It may help, finally, to make explicit the analogy of translation which I have implicitly invoked. We are accustomed to distinguish three kinds of translation: the literal crib, the creative rewriting, and between the two the faithful version – or, as Dryden put it, 'metaphrase, imitation and paraphrase'.[11] The theatrical equivalent of the 'metaphrase' is the antiquarian reconstruction. As with the crib more is lost than is saved by slavish literalism. There is some value in the exercise, particularly as a pedagogic aid, and occasionally some living facet of the original may be reflected that could not have been put across in any other way. But on the whole the crib robs the work of life and movement. The equivalent of 'imitation', of free composition inspired by the original, is the type of production which (I have claimed) is standard practice in the contemporary theatre (a modern adaptation doubles the process). In the field of translation it is well known that such imitations may at the hands of great artists rival and even surpass their originals. We welcome such creative achievements, but it would be intolerable if this were the only sort of 'translation' available. Yet in the theatre we are given little choice. There is no reason why an ambitious director should not attempt an inspired 'imitation' of this sort, provided he realizes what a presumptuous project it is: but it should not be the norm. Most directors are in fact immeasurably inferior craftsmen of the theatre compared with their authors, as is witnessed by all the travesties which litter our stage, insults to the authors whose names they exploit. Furthermore this kind of production, like literary imitation, brings the audience into contact not with the original source but with the imitator.

So we come to 'paraphrase', the middle way. I do not see that fidelity to the author's meaning in the theatre is any more constrictive and inhibitive than in translation. There is no such thing as the perfect translation. Each succeeds and fails in different ways, and we take as the best that which most succeeds in the most important ways; and there is, of course, much scope for discussion of which is the best. The literary translator tries to transfer into his language what he thinks is essential in his original, and his success or failure depends both on his choice of what is essential and on his ability to convey that essence. Dramatic production is more than just an analogy, it is the same process in a different medium. The good translator studies his original as deeply and closely as he can; he has to decide which aspects are the most significant and the most necessary to be conveyed across the linguistic barrier; and then he has to try to do it. To be a good translator is hard work and calls for unusual skill and talent: to be a good director in the theatre is no easier. The director must study the verbal and visual meaning of his original, decide on his priorities, and then attempt to make them into live theatre. This is not the same as the current practice of free invention; but it still leaves enormous scope for the director's skill and talent in interpretation and presentation.

The present is what matters because that is where we are. But we have much to learn from the past, and we have every reason to be humble before the great artistic creations of the past. An age which refuses to learn from the past, or which uses it merely as inanimate raw material without regard for its integrity and life, is an age of tyranny, narrow-mindedness and arrogance. My argument has been that Greek tragedy is far from a fossil forest of platitudes. Its power, its intellectual and emotional life may be revived daily on the stage, or in the theatre of the mind. And it is worth listening to and watching closely, for we have much to learn from this theatre that presents and confronts the very substance of human suffering.

Notes

Chapter 1 The visual dimension of tragedy

1 I have argued the case fully in *The Stagecraft of Aeschylus*, and naturally I hope that those who wish to pursue the matter more deeply will read the introductory chapter of that book. [Where details of books mentioned are not given, see bibliography.]

2 I say 'see and *hear*', though I fear I shall have little to say on the aural dimension of Greek tragedy. This is a huge and little explored subject, and we know very little about the range of tone, timbre, pace and volume of delivery. There is however some consideration of the variety of delivery, particularly in chapter 9, and of the use of silences, sound-effects and noises in chapter 7.

3 This may be seen by comparing Daniel Selzer's article in *A New Companion to Shakespeare Studies* (ed. K. Muir and S. Schoenbaum, Cambridge, 1971) with its equivalent by Granville-Barker himself in the original *Companion* (1934). The chief books (so far as I can tell) are Neville Coghill *Shakespeare's Professional Skills* (Cambridge, 1964), John Russell Brown *Shakespeare's Plays in Performance* (London, 1966), J. L. Styan *Shakespeare's Stagecraft* (Cambridge, 1967), Emrys Jones *Scenic Form in Shakespeare* (Oxford, 1971), Michael Goldman *Shakespeare and the Energies of Drama* (Princeton, 1972). These vary greatly in quality, but all say things worth saying.

4 The modern controversy goes back at least to Eliot's essay 'Tradition and the Individual Talent' (first published in 1919, 3rd ed. 1961). A handy collection of contributions from the 30 years since Wimsatt's and Beardley's 'The Intentional Fallacy' has been compiled by D. Newton-De Molina *On Literary Intention* (Edinburgh, 1976). I recommend the essays by Hirsch, Cioffi and Skinner. I had my own say in *Essays in Criticism* (26, 1976, 341–4). In the more purely philosophical discussion of meaning and intention the 'seminal' essay was P. Grice's in *The Philosophical Review* for 1957. For more recent dis-

cussions see, e.g., J. R. Searle, *Speech Acts* (Cambridge, 1969, 42ff.), P. F. Strawson, *Logico-Linguistic Papers* (London, 1971, 170ff.).

5 It would, of course, take a thousand volumes to give a *total* account of every single factor which goes to make up one person's experience of one minute of one play; just as it would take a historian a thousand volumes to give a total account of the meanest action of the meanest person in the past. That is not, of course, the task in hand: it is to try to single out what is most telling within the totality of the experience.

6 I think, for instance, of Erving Goffman's collection *Interaction Ritual* (New York, 1967) or Michael Argyle's *Bodily Communication* (London, 1975).

Chapter 2 Stage management and stage directions

1 For those who read German both brevity and scholarship are combined in Erika Simon's monograph (1972). John Gould's section on the Greek theatre in the forthcoming *Cambridge History of Greek Literature* will at last supply a brief yet scholarly introduction in English. For the evidence in full we have to go to Pickard-Cambridge's two volumes *The Dramatic Festivals of Athens* and *The Theatre of Dionysus at Athens* (Oxford, 1946). My *Stagecraft of Aeschylus* (1977) contains specialist discussions of some of the problems: see especially appendix B (pp. 434ff.). Flickinger's book is sensible in most matters, and readable. If something really brief and elementary is wanted there are P. Arnott, *Introduction to the Greek Theatre* (London, 1959, 1–62), or H. C. Baldry, *The Greek Tragic Theatre* (London, 1971, 1–73) – though both are somewhat faulty and superficial.

2 Some tragedies were probably re-performed in small theatres at village festivals of Dionysus; but we lack clear evidence.

3 The 'stage question' has been the subject of interminable controversy. Whether or not there was this stage – and I doubt it – it should be understood that I use phrases like 'on stage', 'stage action', etc. without reference to this contentious literal stage.

4 As an introduction I recommend A. M. Dale's lecture 'Words, Music and Dance' in her *Collected Papers* (1969, 156ff.).

5 These generalizations are inevitably simplistic. It may help if I quote verbatim from Colin Macleod's remarks on this paragraph, where he protests that I have made the chorus sound too 'metaphysical': '. . . combine *two* points which form a tension: (1) that they *tend* to move on a wider plane, whether more universal or more probing in the past and future: but also (2) – *which is often how they arrive at* (1) – that they express an emotive response to what's happening: joy, horror, foreboding, puzzlement, speculation (sometimes mistaken or partly mistaken) – they are all-too-human participants (if not agents).'

6 Spitzbarth (1946) attempts, far from successfully, to catalogue all the actors' movements indicated by the text. F. L. Shisler (1945) was able to fill 20 pages with 'stage business used to portray emotion in Greek tragedy'.

7 See P. Arnott, *The Theatres of Japan* (London, 1969, *passim*). For example, Arnott reports that a Nôh actor might by different gestures with his fan convey actions as different as a sword thrust or the pouring of wine.

8 Admittedly the relation of the gestures and poses of vase painting to those of life is a largely unexplored subject. But see G. Neumann, *Gesten und Gebärden in der griechischen Kunst* (Berlin, 1965): this careful monograph does not, in fact, broach the idea that there may have been a separate range of theatrical gestures.

9 I came upon some nice illustrations of this when reading Barrie's *Peter Pan* recently (the written play is very different from the version put on at Christmas time). Thus the final rather embarrassing line of Act III 'To die will be an awfully big adventure' is really subordinate to an observation in the very final stage-instruction of the play in Act V. Peter will never embrace Wendy – he resists the implications of that act of love and domesticity: 'If he could get the hang of the thing' *writes* Barrie 'his cry might become "To live would be an awfully big adventure!"'.' A delightful touch of self-mockery is lost in a

stage direction earlier in Act V. Mrs Darling day-dreams that her children have come home (when in fact they have).

> Mrs D.: So often their silver voices call me, my little children whom I'll see no more.
> Wendy: (perhaps rather silvery): Mother!

10 I discuss these questions more fully, but along the same lines, in The Stagecraft of Aeschylus (1977, 28ff.).

11 I discuss this whole subject fully in The Stagecraft of Aeschylus (esp. 49ff.). For a clear and cool account of the 'Aris-totelian analysis' see A. E. Haigh, The Tragic Drama of the Greeks (Oxford, 1896, 348ff.). Its basic structural anchor is the strophic choral songs, the first one called parodos, the others stasimon. The part of the tragedy before the first choral song is called prologos, the part after the last exodos, and all the parts in between stasima are called epeisodia. While not utterly inappropriate, anyone who tries to analyse a real Greek tragedy along these lines will see how very inflexible and unsatisfactory this can be.

Chapter 3 Introduction to nine plays

1 Plus some 20 satyr plays. Each playwright would produce 3 tragedies and a satyr play for any festival at which he competed: for further details see any of the books cited in p. 183 n. 1. Longish fragments of 2 satyr plays by Aeschylus, both attractive, lewd and lively, have been found on papyrus. They are conveniently available along with the papyrus fragments of his tragedies (all with translation) in H. Lloyd-Jones' Appendix to vol. II of the Loeb edition of Aeschylus (1957).

2 It is generally supposed, on insufficient evidence, that Aeschlus usually composed in connected trilogies (Sophocles and Euripides did so very rarely, if ever). However, it is true that Seven against Thebes and Suppliant Women were parts of trilogies, though they too can stand as separate plays. I leave aside the problems of Prometheus (Bound) which I suspect was composed by the 'School of Aeschylus' on the model of his Prometheus (Unbound).

3 Line-numbers, without division into acts and scenes, are the conventional markers of place in the scholarship of Greek tragedy, and are the same in almost all modern editions and translations.

4 Plus some 30 satyr plays. Over half of one satyr play Ichneutai (Satyrs on the Track) and a few scraps of tragedies have been found on papyrus and are conveniently available in Page's Loeb collection of Greek Literary Papyri (London, 1942, 26ff.).

5 See G. S. Haight, George Eliot (Oxford, 1968, p. 195). Compare John Cowper Powys on the question 'what did he pick up from Hardy?' (Visions and Revisions, London, 1966, xix): 'the Sophoclean power of transubstantiating the burden of any victim's suffering, whether that suffering is mental or physical, till it becomes, by the sheer poetry of its identification with human suffering all the world over, the very bread by which we live and move.'

6 The corpus also contains a satyr play, Cyclops, and one play, Rhesus, which is, I believe, our one-and-only fourth-century tragedy. Euripides was the most popular of the great three in post-classical antiquity, and we have more papyrus fragments of his lost plays than of the other two put together. Some of the most interesting, e.g., Hypsipyle (about 300 lines) and Antiope are in Page's collection (see n. 4); but Phaethon is also intriguing (see p. 140), and so are the 100 or so lines of his Erectheus, first published in 1967.

Chapter 4 Exits and entrances

1 In his justly celebrated essay 'Jacobean Shakespeare' in Stratford-upon-Avon Studies (1, 1960, 11ff., esp. 28ff.).

2 On the concepts and language of the Greek oikos see W. K. Lacey, The Family in Classical Greece (London, 1968, esp. Chapter I).

Since Aeschylus does not use the skēnē building at all in his plays except the Oresteia, it is more than possible

that for most of his career the actors'
changing booth had been off the scene
and out of sight of the audience, and
that it was only in his last few years,
shortly before the *Oresteia*, that it was
erected at the far side of the *orchēstra*,
and its front wall and doors were
drawn in as part of the world of the
play itself. If this is so, then Aeschylus'
dramatic inventiveness is all the more
astonishing.

3 The roof seems the place to watch for
the beacon, though the opening lines
of the play do not, in fact, make this
certain. Later when Clytemnestra tells
of the chain of beacons she had
arranged from Troy (281ff.) she concludes 'And finally this light, offspring
of the fire of Troy, fell upon this roof,
the house of the Atreidai' (310–11).
Agamemnon must fall with Troy, and
this gives a literal reinforcement to the
symbolic chain which links the fates of
the houses of Priam and Atreus. The
physical position of the watchman in
the theatre fits his role as herald of
triumph and disaster.

4 There may have been just twelve
chorus members, one to each couplet;
but for myself I suspect that there were
fifteen in early tragedy, just as in
Sophocles and Euripides. The other
three may have spoken 1344, 1346–7.

5 The precise text of this couplet is uncertain, but its sense is clear. The texts of
ancient tragedy, particularly of Aeschylus, contain many major corrup-
tions and even more minor ones; and I
shall only draw attention to those
places where a significant and relevant
difference is made by emendation. I
should, none the less, stress the vital
importance of textual criticism for the
reading of texts whose very survival
has been so precarious, and which
have passed through stages (especially
before   250   B.C.   and   during
A.D. 500–1200) when they were liable
to serious corruption. For an excellent
introduction to the subject see K.
Dover, *Aristophanic Comedy* (London,
1972, Chapter 1). For more detail, yet
admirable lucidity, see L. D. Reynolds
and N. G. Wilson, *Scribes and Scholars*
(2nd ed., Oxford, 1974, esp. Chapters
1 and 2).

6 Compare Shakespeare, *Coriolanus*
1.i.250, where the Folio has the stage-
instruction 'Citizens steal away'.

7 Contrast Sophocles' *Electra* where the

play of return and revenge ends with
Orestes' entering his paternal home to
complete his quest.

8 This line has been suspected by many
editors, but without justification in my
view. There are interpolations in our
texts of Greek tragedy, mostly added
by actors, in the first century or two of
the plays' transmission, to supply extra
melodrama or sententiousness. I am
among those who hold that there are a
great many such interpolations; but
this is not one of them.

9 The lack of any clear indication of the
stage direction leaves us with possibilities that Apollo may have gone
immediately on the acquittal at 753, or
with Orestes at 777, or some final
speech by him may have been lost from
after 777. See further my *The Stagecraft
of Aeschylus* (1977, 403–7).

10 These elements of the final scene are
well brought out in different ways by
the works of Reinhardt (154ff.),
Peradotto and Macleod.

11 The others are *The Suppliants* of Aeschylus and of Euripides, Sophocles'
Oedipus at Colonus and Euripides' *Children of Heracles*.

12 On the strength of the phrase 'even
when you are unseen' most scholars
suppose that Athena is invisible in the
theatre, or at least that she is above the
skēnē and invisible to Odysseus. But
the gods who appear in prologues are
always on the ground; and Athena has
been following Odysseus, and she
speaks to him almost intimately. Later
she will speak with Ajax with a similar,
but false intimacy (91ff.). The phrase is
verbally ambiguous; but if in performance Athena was in fact standing
close by Odysseus then its sense would
be perfectly clear: on many occasions
Odysseus has been able to recognize
her by her voice alone, but now he first
hears her then turns and sees her.

13 A well-known Greek example of a
'paradox-riddle' ran 'a man and not a
man threw a stone and not a stone at
a bird and not a bird on a tree and not
a tree': answer – a eunuch threw a
pumice-stone at a bat on a giant hem-
lock. An example of the more sophisti-
cated type quoted from the *Oedipus* of a
later tragedian, Theodectas: 'there are
two sisters. One gives birth to the
other, and she having once borne is
given birth by the other one': night
and day. I leave unanswered a riddle

in a later comedy called *Sphinx* by
Euboulos: 'Tongueless it talks, male
and female called the same, dispenser
of its own winds, shaggy though sometimes beardless, talking nonsense,
playing tune upon tune. It is one thing
and yet it may be repeatedly stabbed
and remain unwounded. What is it?'
The best collection of Greek riddles is
to be found in book 10(§§ 448–57) of the
Deipnosophistai of Athenaeus, a dilet-
tante miscellany compiled about A.D.
200.

14 See Lattimore, *The Poetry of Greek
Tragedy* (1958, 96–100).

15 There are good reasons for thinking
that the final lines of the play, 1524–30,
have been added, and perhaps replace
the original ending. Before Colin Macleod dissuaded me I was tempted to
make a case for holding that 1515–23
are also interpolated to replace an ending in which Oedipus went off into
exile on Cithaeron.

16 This staging, which gains dramatic
power from its sudden revelation,
seems to be indicated by the wording
of 211 'the man is not outdoors, but
close within'. The cave is to be
imagined as having a second entrance
out of sight of the audience; see Dale,
Collected Papers (1969, 127–8).

17 Many scholars read back the definitive
version of the prophecy of Helenus
from 1326ff., and maintain that the
desertion of Philoctetes at 1080 is a
bluff, and that the audience is meant to
assume that Odysseus and Neoptolemus will return to fetch Philoctetes
somehow or other. But not only is
there no trace of bluff in the text, it
would also bleed all the emotional
strength out of the great lyric dialogue
(1081–217). This scene, epitome of
Philoctetes' terrible isolation, would
become on this interpretation a tedious
time-filler.

18 It is very rare in Greek tragedy (though
common enough in later drama) for an
entry to be made as though in mid-
dialogue. I have discussed this in an
appendix to my article on *Phil* cited in
the bibliography, where I also argue
that the four lines 1218–21 are interpolated and not by Sophocles. Someone
tried, rather incompetently, to make a
transition across the deliberately
unconnected hiatus.

19 Cf. John Jones, *On Aristotle and Greek
Tragedy* (1962, 219). While he is excellent on this aspect of the last plays,
Jones does not see the importance of
the Trojan plain to *Ajax* [see 6.4.2].

20 In Greek the *theos apo mēchanēs*. It is,
however, far from certain that in
Euripides' own productions, as opposed to later revivals, these gods
actually hovered from the crane-like
flying machine – see Barrett's commentary (1964) on *Hipp* 1283.

21 The word *homilia* ('friendship'), which
is also used in 19, like the words connected with *syneimi* used at 17, 85 and
949, has a slight sexual overtone.
This may be exploited, for Hippolytus'
relationship with Artemis transcends
sex.

22 The attribution of these half-lines is
disputed, but this arrangement seems
to me far and away the best. It may
seem presumptuous to question the
attribution of speeches which are in
our manuscripts and hence in most
editions. But the discovery of early
copies of plays on papyrus show that
changes of speaker were at one stage in
transmission (in fact the first half mil-
lennium or more) marked only by
symbols, and the speaker's name was
not added. This means that all attribution of parts is the work of scribes
and scholars, and that we are at lib-
erty to question them. For fuller discussion see the works referred to in
n. 5 above.

23 Nearly all of Dionysus' speech is lost
through textual damage. There are two
large sections missing from the last
part of *Ba*, some thirty lines between
1300/01 and some sixty from 1329/30.
We are not totally in the dark about the
wording of the missing lines, since
some are preserved on papyri and
some in a Byzantine poem, *The Passion
of Christ*, which is in parts a cento of
Euripidean quotations. But much
remains beyond recovery, and this is a
constant hindrance to criticism of the
play.

24 For example, in this play, at 1113
Pentheus 'begins to understand' his
fate (*emanthenen*), at 1296 Agaue 'realizes now at last' (*arti manthanō*, cf.
mathe in 1281), and at 1345 Dionysus
says 'you saw the truth about me too
late' (*emathete*).

Chapter 5 Actions and gestures

1 Apollo 'of the streets'. His stone or altar stood before the doors of most Greek houses, and was also represented in the theatre before the *skēnē*. For details see Fraenkel's commentary (1950) on *Agam* 1081.

2 This clothing is thrown to the ground in full knowledge of what she is doing and what it means, as a contrast with the purple cloth which deceives in the previous Agamemnon scene [6.1.1]: see Macleod, 'Clothing in the *Oresteia*' (1975). On the contrasting pair of Cassandra to Agamemnon see 9.1.1.

3 These lines may be many children's first encounter with Aeschylus, as they are the epigraph of the first chapter of Richard Adams' extraordinary fable *Watership Down*.

4 For reasons too complex to go into here, I suspect that this dialogue once contained three or four more couplets. Unfortunately, the text of the trial scene may have been extensively interfered with by interpolations, omissions and transpositions. Even if this gloomy conjecture is right, the trial we have has still not been altered beyond recognition.

5 It has been asserted, even by highly reputable scholars, that this speech is addressed directly to the audience; but the second line shows quite clearly that this is false. There is, in fact, in my view not one single place in the whole of surviving Greek tragedy where there is direct audience address, or specific reference to the audience or to members of the audience: see D. Bain, 'Audience Address in Greek Tragedy' in *Classical Quarterly* (25, 1975, 13ff.).

6 See John Gould in *Journal of Hellenic Studies* (93, 1973, 74ff., esp. 86f.). My account of the scene in *Hipp* is a development of this and suggestions made by Colin Macleod.

7 Later bibliographers gave the play its subtitle *Hipp. kalyptomenos* ('veiled') from this incident – this distinguished it from the surviving play which was labelled *Hipp. stephanēphoros* ('carrying a garland') after his first entry, see 6.7.1. For the authoritative discussion of the lost *Hipp* see Barrett's commentary (1964, 15ff.).

8 See D. M. Macdowell, *Athenian Homicide Law* (Manchester U.P., 1963, 8).

9 According to the usual interpretation of the usual text Creusa goes tamely to the altar at 1260, despite her protest in 1255f. Ion then denounces her (1261ff.); tells his companions to seize her, but they – we have to suppose – hesitate (1266–8); and he does not even comment on her supplication at the altar until 1279–81, although it surely calls for immediate comment at the start (the idea that he does not even see her until 1279 is absurd). In order to avoid this flaccid sequence one needs to transpose 1266–8 to follow 1281, and perhaps also to retain the negative in the ms. reading of 1280 so that it means 'she did not flinch before the altar of the god', instead of 'she cowers at the altar of the god'. One might also attribute to Creusa a refusal to supplicate with the words 'but I must face my fate' in 1260, which are usually taken as a weak comment by the chorus-leader 'you must bear your fate'. With this reconstituted text Creusa may go to the altar *after* and not before Ion's speech. None the less, I am far from confident of this conjecture, especially since 1285 evokes no more explicit reaction.

I may add that I am far from happy with the accepted text of 1283 which I have translated 'for my sake and Apollo's, where we stand' – this reflects the near-nonsense of the original. Perhaps it should say something like 'for the sake of my union with Apollo' (for example emending *hin' hestamen* to *homilias*).

10 I am assuming that lines 1364–8 are not authentic.

11 The middle of these three lines is usually treated as a question spoken by the old man. I put forward this rearrangement, which disturbs the regularity of the stichomythia, with grave misgivings.

12 Notice how at their exit (360ff.) the thyrsus has become a walking stick for the doddering 'rejuvenated' old men – thus showing Dionysus as a cruel taskmaster as well as a liberator.

Chapter 6 Objects and tokens

1 The gods of the Greeks were jealous, resentful of any attempt by mortals to rival or encroach on their privileges and prerogatives: the word for such resentment is *phthonos*. The genitive plural 'of the gods' at the end of 945 I have taken with *phthonos* to translate 'divine envy'; it might be taken possessively with the 'sea-wrought purple', and should perhaps be taken with both.

2 'Note the indifference to repetition' remarks one recent commentary of this carefully calculated verbal technique. On the significance of the palace itself cf. 4.1.1.

3 This aspect is well brought out, but to the exclusion of all others, by Jones (1962, 79ff.). Other discussions which I have found most useful are those of Reinhardt (1949, 96ff.); Goheen (1955, 113ff.); Lebeck (1971, 74ff.); and Easterling (1973, 10ff.).

4 Cf. L. Gernet, *Anthropologie de la Grèce antique* (Paris, 1968, 223–4).

5 Despite the conservative majority of scholars, I am in little doubt that Fraenkel (1950, 815ff.) is right to cut out lines 205–11 as interpolation. The only plausible alternative is that 201–4 should be transposed to come after 211.

6 The near-necessity that this should be performed *round* Orestes is strong evidence that the statue was in the orchestra itself. A sober scholar (H. J. Rose), who assumed that it must have been outside the orchestra, observes 'the chorus has now arranged itself in a semi-circle facing the stage. In *real life* they would probably surround the object of the incantation' (my italics)!

7 The whip is assumed on the basis of the ancient subtitle *Ajax 'carrying a whip'* which bibliographers gave the play to distinguish it from another Sophoclean *Ajax* about the other Ajax, which they subtitled *'the Locrian'*. No doubt some later productions in the fourth or third century did have Ajax with the whip; but there is no evidence that Sophocles produced it in this way.

8 I have followed Colin Macleod's suggestion that the flat line 816 ('If I pause to reflect on it . . .') was interpolated, and have omitted it.

9 For those readers who use the Penguin translation, I should point out that the stage-instruction on p. 185 is pure fancy without any foundation in the text. On the contrary it is clear, and essential, that the bow does not leave Philoctetes' hands until 776.

10 For the evidence see Barratt's commentary (1964, 154).

11 This is, by the way, clear evidence against the common myth that the Greeks could not or did not read to themselves in silence: see further Bernard Knox in *Greek, Roman and Byzantine Studies* (9, 1968, 421ff., esp. 433).

12 For a full account of the law concerning *epiklēroi* see A. R. W. Harrison, *The Law of Athens* (vol. I, Oxford, 1968, pp. 132–8).

13 The relevant mythographical details are conveniently put together by Anne Burnett as an appendix to her translation of *Ion* (1971, 142–9).

14 These events were, in fact, the subject of Euripides' tragedy *Erechtheus*. Over 100 lines on papyrus were first published in 1964, after they had been discovered in the wrappings of a sacred crocodile in the Louvre.

15 Similar conclusions are reached independently by R. S. Young, *Hesperia* (10, 1941, pp. 138ff.) and L. Bergson *Eranos* (58, 1960, pp. 12ff.). It is quite likely, as Young suggests, that there was at Athens a well-known painting of the opening of Erichthonius' basket. For the type of basket see the pictures in G. M. A. Richter, *Ancient Furniture* (Oxford, 1926, figs 63 and 244–6). On the sacred basket in the Panathenaia see W. Burkert, *Hermes* (94, 1966, pp. 1ff., esp. 20).

16 For some speculations on the significance of the olive see M. Detienne, 'L'Olivier: un mythe politico-religieux', in *Problèmes de la terre en Grèce ancienne*, ed. M. Finley (Paris, The Hague 1973, pp. 293ff.).

17 Cf. Winnington-Ingram (1948, 24–5, 136–7).

18 I have not added 1243 because I am dubious of its authenticity.

19 On the missing parts of *Ba* see p. 186 n.23. It is generally held that not only the head but all the parts of the body were reassembled on stage in a kind of macabre jigsaw. This Senecan recon-

struction, which would be damagingly crude, is based on what is very probably a misunderstanding or an over-

statement by a late rhetorician called Apsines: see Barrett's commentary on *Hipp* (1964, 44, n. 4).

Chapter 7 Tableaux, noises and silences

1 There is in fact a book, *Shakespeare's Use of Off-Stage Sounds* by F. Shirley (Lincoln, Nebr., 1963).

2 Here at least the term *kommos* is correctly applied – the very word is used in 423. It is often used incorrectly of any lyric dialogue between actor and chorus, a sense it is not given even in the unhelpful *Poetics*, chapter 12 (see p. 184 n. 11). *Kommos* meant a lyric *dirge*, usually – or originally – accompanied by beating the breast or the ground in a fashion associated with oriental lament.

3 I suspect, though I am almost alone in this, that a considerable scene has been lost at this point, and this may, among other things, have formally set out the arrangements. I do not, by the way, see any grounds for introducing a motley crowd of spectators here.

4 Cf. the fuller discussion by Peter Burian, *Greek, Roman and Byzantine Studies* (13, 1972, pp. 151–6). He claims that the supplication at the corpse in effect initiates the hero-cult of Ajax. But that is to be too literal: the historical existence of the hero-cult of Ajax is no concern of Sophocles' play.

5 The staging of Ajax's death presents problems. The corpse must certainly be visible from 1000 onwards; it also seems desirable that the sword should be visible during the death scene. Yet Tecmessa finds the corpse just out of sight (892). Also the actor of Ajax is needed for the final scene of the play (Teucer, Agamemnon, Odysseus), so the corpse during that scene must be

represented by an 'extra'. I think the sword must have been planted just by the *skēnē* door, which represents the 'thicket' of 892. The replacement of the actor may be connected with the way that Tecmessa covers the corpse with a robe at 915f. (see plate 11), and Teucer uncovers it again at 1003. These actions are rather conspicuously marked in the words, and I can detect no more far-reaching significance for them. It remains possible that the actor of Ajax went off to kill himself and that the corpse was only brought on at 1000ff.

6 The word *bios* could mean in Greek both 'bow' and 'life' or 'livelihood'. This 'pun' is exploited in lines 931 and 933; cf. Robinson (1969, 43–4). The translation of 932 is an attempt to reproduce Sophocles' vivid use of extra short syllables in the metre of this line.

7 For a brief account of the institution of the *boē* see Fraenkel's commentary on *Agam* (1950, 614). The word for 'call' in 902 is *kraugē*, but this is sometimes used as equivalent to *boē*. I doubt, by the way, that Barrett (1964, 333, 435f.) is right that a crowd of citizens came to witness the curse at 887ff. The *boē* is for witnesses to the injustice, not the curse; and the only significant arrival in response is that of Hippolytus.

8 Hera came on disguised as a begging priestess in Aeschylus' *Semele*, a play which influenced *Bacchae*.

9 The nearest comparison would be Sophocles' *Oedipus at Colonus*, 1456ff., an even more powerful sequence in my view.

Chapter 8 Mirror scenes

1 Cf. G. E. R. Lloyd, *Polarity and Analogy* (Cambridge, 1966, *passim*).

2 A later producer turned three words in this line into plurals in order to introduce a band of colourful fellow-travellers for Orestes and Pylades. But Aeschylus makes it clear there are just the two of them.

3 A slight emendation of this line (1495) has it mean 'brought low in slavish death'. This may be right.

4 Possibly stage-extras brought out the

constituents of the tableau; or it may well be that the *ekkuklēma* was wheeled out, though I have my doubts since there are no introductory lines in *Agam* or *Cho*. (It is, at least, out of the question that the tableau was revealed inside the skene doors, as some scholars suppose, because this could not have been visible in the Greek theatre.)

5 The problem is hammered out in my *The Stagecraft of Aeschylus* (1977, 369–74).

6 I hope to go further into these arguments in a separate article. I cannot pretend that my interpretation solves every difficulty in Ajax's speech – but nor does any other I know of. For example, he says he will bury his sword where no one will see it (659), which is not strictly true; he insists that friends become enemies, just as enemies become friends (680–3), but in the play all his friends remain his friends. Perhaps the worst problem of all lies in 667 'I shall learn to revere the sons of Atreus'. He will have to be subject to the decision of Agamemnon, but 'revere' is much too strong a word to fit my interpretation, especially in view of lines 839ff.

7 K. J. Dover, *Greek Popular Morality* (Oxford, 1974, p. 119). It is worth looking up all the entries of the word in Dover's index II.

8 The text is disputed; this is an attempt to translate the transmitted wording.

9 This misunderstanding depends on the range of the Greek word *philos*

which can move from 'my own property' as Xuthus means, to 'my beloved', which is what Ion takes him to mean.

10 For a discussion see Fraenkel's commentary on *Agam* (1950, 528). For laying hand on a thing to claim it as property, 'geste quasi-ritual', cf. L. Gernet, *Droit et Société dans la Grèce Ancienne* (Paris 1955, 9ff., esp. 11–12).

11 There are two points of verbal interpretation which worry me here, though they do not seem to worry the editors. First, the deictic pronoun (*tēsde*) in 1405 is taken to refer to the cradle; but this is strangely inexplicit. (It seems no better, however, to refer it to Creusa herself.) Second, in 1406 Ion says 'I am being confiscated by *speech* (*logō*).' I suspect the word is corrupt (possible emendations might be 'by touch' or 'by force' or even 'again'); but, assuming it is sound, the point must be that instead of laying her hand on him according to the legal procedure, Creusa in effect 'claims' him purely verbally.

Chapter 9 Scenic sequence

1 The shift in the roles of enlightener and enlightened is managed by a particularly brilliant variation of the conventional techniques of lyric dialogue in 1072–177. It was common in early tragedy for a series of brief emotional stanzas sung by the chorus to be interspersed by symmetrical snatches of a few lines of speech by a relatively calm actor (this type of lyric dialogue is sometimes known as 'epirrhematic'). Now at the beginning of the Cassandra scene the roles are startlingly reversed: Cassandra sings in her frenzy, while the pedestrian chorus speaks. But as the scene progresses more and more speech lines come into Cassandra's stanzas, while the chorus begins to sing odd snatches of lyric; and, as the old men become more and more involved and alarmed, song comes to dominate speech in their contributions. Thus the roles of singer and speaker go much of the way to being reversed.

2 With the possible exception of some parts of *Rhesus*, a strange play which actually attempts to create a realistic picture of the rush and confusion of a military camp in a crisis.

3 These two speeches, since they are part of the lyric dialogue structure, ought to be of the same length. Quite possibly three lines have been interpolated into the second by an actor, perhaps 971–3.

4 For a simple survey of the actual use of the word in tragedy see Lattimore, *Story Patterns in Greek Tragedy* (1964, 23–6). For a fuller discussion see N. Fisher in *Greece and Rome* (23, 1976, 177ff.).

5 Compare the characteristically rash yet brilliant sixth chapter of Johan Huizinga's *Homo Ludens* (127ff, in the 1970 translation, London). On p. 133 he writes 'The riddle was originally a sacred game, and as such it cut clean across any possible distinction between play and seriousness . . . . As civilisation develops, the riddle branches out in two directions: mystic philosophy on the one hand and recreation on the other.'

6 Compare the doggerel riddle set to Pericles at the beginning of *Pericles, Prince of Tyre*:

I am no viper, yet I feed/On mother's flesh which did me breed.
I sought a husband, in which

labour/I found that kindness in a father:

He's father, son, and husband mild:/I mother, wife and yet his child.

How may this be, and yet in two,/As you will live, resolve it you.

7 There are those who think that Phaedra is off-stage between 600 and 680, and that the Nurse sings 669ff. This not only involves hurried and pointless stage-directions, but loses the point about the lack of communication between Phaedra and Hippolytus, even when in each other's presence.

8 I take 663–8 to be interpolated: see Barrett's commentary (1964).

9 John Gould has written of 'the peculiar dramatic quality of stichomythia, which serves to present moments where forces in opposition meet in an ambiguous tension and a breakthrough is always a felt possibility.'

Chapter 10 Emotion and meaning in the theatre

1 One of my purposes in *The Stagecraft of Aeschylus* (1977) is to elucidate this 'grammar' of dramatic technique. W. Jens' *Die Bauformen der griechischen Tragödie* (1971) is an attempt, far from successful but none the less enterprising, to compile the whole of this 'grammar'. Disciples of Walter Jens at Tübingen contribute sections (of greatly varying quality) on the structure of opening and closing scenes, on the acts and choral songs, speech, stychomythia, lyric dialogue and monody; there are also three parerga on supplication, props, and the significance of on- and off-stage.

2 This point is hammered home by Brian Vickers, *Towards Greek Tragedy* (33ff., esp. 41–2). Vickers' confutation in his section 'Metaphysics and Mystiques' (3–51) of various 'transcendant schemes' which have been vainly imposed on Greek tragedy is one of the best parts of a stimulating, if uneven, book. The most influential account of the Greek theatre as ritual has probably been Chapter I of Francis Fergusson's *The Idea of a Theatre* (Princeton, 1949).

3 I relegate a couple more hobby-horsical reflections to a footnote. Another motive for the search for ritual may be the desire of some to find religious or quasi-religious motives for all valuable human activities so that they are all done to the greater glory of god (even if it is the wrong god). Another more modern motive is the desire of the 'counter-culture' to stress all that is anti-rational, impulsive and 'primitive' in our life. The driving forces of this movement are too complex and too close for analysis, but they include the decline of traditional religion, disillusion with scientific 'progress', Freu-

dian psychology, expression of solidarity with non-Western cultures, and simple revolt against whatever system is nearest at hand. Greek tragedy, they gather, was a 'primitive ritual', so it is annexed as a venerable support for these cultural trends. But the ancient Greeks are treacherous allies. The undeniable powers of the irrational, the cruel and the impulsive are clearly recognized by Greek tragedy, but they are not admired; they are rather forces of destruction and inhumanity.

4 Some details may be found in the books cited on p. 183. The authoritative account is Pickard-Cambridge's *The Dramatic Festivals of Athens* (1968, chapter II, pp. 57–125).

5 This should put in its place a fragment of the fourth-century comedian Antiphanes which has been taken much too seriously. His character is trying to show that comedy is much harder to compose than tragedy because you have to make up the story:

I have only to mention Oedipus, and they know the rest:

that his father was Laius, his mother Jocasta,

who his daughters are and his sons, what he is going to suffer, what he has done . . . .

The crudity of this proves, in a sense, the opposite of what it purports to prove.

6 There is an interesting exercise in comparison to be found in the fifty-second (so-called) *Oration* of Dio Chrysostom (Loeb Classical Library, vol. IV, ed. A. L. Crosby, 338ff.), in which he discusses the three *Philoctetes* plays of Aeschylus, Euripides and Sophocles (only the last survives). The fixed elements

192   Greek tragedy in action

are that Odysseus and others have to fetch Philoctetes from Lemnos to Troy: the differences between the three plays move them worlds apart.

7 This dialogue occurs at the most harrowing moment of *Jude the Obscure* when Jude and Sue have discovered the violent death of their children:

'Nothing can be done' he replied.
'Things are as they are, and
will be brought to their destined issue.'
She paused, 'Yes! Who said that?' she asked heavily.
'It comes in the Chorus of Agamemnon. It has been in my mind continually since this happened.'

To move from the sublime to the less than sublime see the very title of Cocteau's version of *Oedipus, La Machine Infernale* (1934). The prologue voice says, 'Spectator, this machine, you see here wound up to the full in such a way that the spring will slowly unwind the whole length of a human life . . . .'
The radio comedy show *I'm Sorry I'll Read That Again* ended its version of *Oedipus* 'My fate, my fate are killing me!'

8 Aeschylus' *Persians* is the exception which proves the rule. Not only is the play not a tragedy about Athens, but the Persian rulers are given the status and distance of tragic heroes indistinguishable, dramatically speaking, from

the usual figures of the heroic age. Even those who generally agree with my case would until recently have made an exception of *Eumenides* and granted that it contains political propaganda. But it seems to me that Colin Macleod in his article on the unity of the *Oresteia* (1973) is completely convincing in his denial of specific topical allusions and in his claim that the play is political in a much more ideal and time-free sense. On the 'dramatic illusion' of Greek tragedy see the first and last chapters of David Bain's book.

9 See, for instance, Anne Righter, *Shakespeare and the Idea of the Play* (London, 1962, repr. Penguin, 1967).

10 Excellent translations of the more important fragments are collected in the first section of *Ancient Literary Criticism*, ed D. A. Russell and M. Winterbottom (Oxford, 1972).

11 Some fragments of Gorgias are in Russell and Winterbottom (op. cit.), but for a translation of all the little that survives see that by George Kennedy in *The Older Sophists*, ed R. K. Sprague (South Carolina, 1972, pp. 30ff.). The standard text is in Diels, *Die Fragmente der Vorsokratiker* (vol. II, 7th ed., rev. Kranz, Berlin, 1951–4).

12 A phonetic rather than literal transcript brings out Gorgias' use of the letters *r*, then *l*, then *t* to vary the predominant emotional *p*: *prikē peripobos kai eleos poludakrus kai potos pilopentēs*.

Chapter 11 Round plays in square theatres

1 There have been conflicts recently between playwrights and theatres (John Arden and Harold Pinter are two instances) because the writers protest, no doubt justly, that the production will travesty their work. This barrier between the playwright and the production of his work is unhealthy (though I am not claiming, of course, that the playwright is necessarily the best director of his own work).

2 See Shaw's essay 'Rules for Directors', *The Strand* (cxvii, July 1949), to be found in *Shaw on Theatre*, ed E. J. West (London, 1958, pp. 278ff.). Compare B. F. Dukore, *Bernard Shaw, Director* (London, 1971, p. 65): 'All changes and cuts, Shaw insisted, were the prerogative of the author, who understood the

relationship of each line to the total fabric of the play.' Fools rush in. . . .

3 Of course cuts and minor textual alterations are commonplace. This may be innocuous, always provided it is realized that (unless they have bibliographical backing) they amount to a claim to be able to *improve* on the author.

4 Peter Brook is probably the most purposeful and perverse, and influential, manipulator of the visual dimension. The removal of *A Midsummer Night's Dream* from the court and wood to the circus rehearsal room was so thoroughgoing, the depravation of *King Lear* so ruthless. Alfred Harbage in *Conceptions of Shakespeare* (Harvard, 1968, pp. 73–4) recalls how at the end of

the blinding scene the compassionate lines of the two servants were cut and instead they pushed Gloucester on his dark way. 'It was not a big push. It was a small push. But all great works are precariously balanced, and small pushes can topple them.'

Two recent, though very different, books provide plenty of material on modern directorial methods with Shakespeare: J. S. Styan, *The Shakespeare Revolution* (Cambridge, 1977), and R. Berry (ed.), *On Directing Shakespeare* (London, 1977).

5 I should make it clear that I am talking about the kind of unique and significant stage business which has been the subject of this book: not about the constant background details of gesture, posture and positioning – vital though these are for the overall success of a production. But they are not so much a matter of positive interpretation as of technical stage competence, and they do not necessarily call for a director. For some stimulating ideas on the dispensability of the director see John Russell Brown's *Free Shakespeare* (London, 1974).

6 In the performance of old music the current trend, contrary to the theatre, is towards greater and greater authenticity in every respect (this threatens curious contradictions in the production of opera). It is widely found that this authenticity enriches the works, that we prefer the sounds, however alien at first hearing, which are the sounds the composer intended. Music is, however, quite different from the theatre, since its medium is relatively free of the barriers of language and culture and since it is almost purely aural. None the less even musical authenticity must have its limits (quite apart from ignorance): there too the first performance can only happen once.

7 *A Preface to Paradise Lost* (Oxford, 1942, p. 64). Lewis seems to have thought that Homer's audience consisted of Achaean chiefs – sufficient illustration of the pitfalls of his doctrine. The phrase 'hob-nob with the ancients' comes from Charles Segal's article –

well worth reading – 'Ancient Texts and Modern Literary Criticism' in *Arethusa* (1, 1968, pp. 1ff.).

8 J. Beattie, *Other Cultures* (London, 1964, p. 89).

9 I was distressed to find Granville-Barker regarding this as the only way of staging Greek tragedy: 'There are few enough Greek theatres in which Greek tragedy can be played; few enough people want to see it, and they will applaud it encouragingly however it is done. Some acknowledgement is due to the altruism of the doers!' (*Prefaces, First Series,* 1927). On the other hand I note this from *On Dramatic Method* (London, 1931): 'We can play the *Agamemnon* in the very theatre for which Aeschylus wrote it, but it cannot mean to us what it meant to his audience. We can rebuild Shakespeare's Globe, but can we come to accepting its conventions as spontaneously as the Elizabethans accepted them?' This realism is, despite appearances, more positive than the defeatist attitude of the earlier quotation.

10 The danger, the fatal flaw, of the historicist approach is fascinatingly reflected in Milman Parry's brilliant essay 'The Historical Method in Literary Criticism' written in 1934, two years before his death at the age of 33 (to be found in *The Making of Homeric Verse,* Oxford, 1971, pp. 408ff.). Parry foreboded, quite rightly as it turned out, that his discoveries about the nature of Homeric composition would distance Homer fatally from his critics and turn him into a lifeless curiosity. Reacting against the pernicious anti-historical exploitation of literature in the 1930s he was unable to break this conflict which distressed him deeply – little though it has troubled his followers.

11 There is a helpful, if idiosyncratic, review of the history of the theory of translation in Chapter 4 of George Steiner's *After Babel* (Oxford, 1975). Though Steiner seeks to supersede the traditional three-fold model, it remains more concrete and applicable than his abstracts.

Select bibliography

*(This is a selection of the works which I have found most
relevant and helpful for the subject of this book. So it
does not contain every item mentioned in the notes, and
it does contain many that are not. It does not claim to
include all the most important works on all aspects of
Greek Tragedy.)*

General

D. BAIN, *Actors and Audience*, Oxford, 1977.

W. BARNER, 'Die Monodie' in *Die Bauformen der griechischen Tragödie*,
ed W. Jens, Munich, 1971, pp. 277ff.

A. M. DALE, *Collected Papers*, Cambridge, 1969, esp. chapters 3, 9, 14
and 19.

J. DINGEL, *Das Requisit in der griechischen Tragödie*, unpublished dissertation, Tübingen, 1967: there is a severely abridged version in
Die Bauformen der griechischen Tragödie, ed W. Jens, Munich, 1971,
pp. 347ff.

T. S. ELIOT, *Selected Essays*, London, 3rd ed., 1951.

R. C. FLICKINGER, *The Greek Theater and its Drama*, Chicago, 4th ed.,
1936.

H. GRANVILLE-BARKER, *Prefaces to Shakespeare*, London, 1927–48.

E. JONES, *Scenic Form in Shakespeare*, Oxford, 1971, esp. chapter 1.

J. JONES, *On Aristotle and Greek Tragedy*, London, 1962.

H. D. F. KITTO, *Form and Meaning in Drama*, London, 1956.

W. KRANZ, *Stasimon*, Berlin, 1933.

R. LATTIMORE, *Story Patterns in Greek Tragedy*, London, 1964.

R. LATTIMORE, *The Poetry of Greek Tragedy*, Baltimore, 1958.

A. W. PICKARD-CAMBRIDGE, *The Dramatic Festivals of Athens* (2nd ed. revised by J. Gould and D. M. Lewis), Oxford, 1968.

J. DE ROMILLY, *L'évolution du pathétique d'Eschyle à Euripide*, Paris, 1961.

T. G. ROSENMEYER, 'Gorgias, Aeschylus and *apate*', in *American Journ. of Philology*, 76, 1955, pp. 225ff.

T. G. ROSENMEYER, *The Masks of Tragedy*, Texas, 1963.

W. SCHADEWALDT, 'Furcht und Mitleid?' in *Hellas und Hesperien*, Zürich, 2nd ed., 1970, vol. I, pp. 194ff.

W. SCHADEWALDT, 'Antike Tragödie auf der modernen Bühne' in *Hellas und Hesperien*, Zürich, 2nd ed., 1970, vol. II, pp. 622ff.

F. L. SHISLER, 'The use of stage business to portray emotion in Greek tragedy', in *American Journ. of Philology*, 66, 1945, pp. 377ff.

E. SIMON, *Das antike Theater*, Heidelberg, 1972.

A. SPITZBARTH, *Untersuchungen zur Spieltechnik der griechischen Tragödie*, Zürich, 1946.

W. STEIDLE, *Studien zum antiken Drama*, Munich, 1968.

J. L. STYAN, *Shakespeare's Stagecraft*, Cambridge, 1967.

O. TAPLIN, *The Stagecraft of Aeschylus*, Oxford, 1977.

B. VICKERS, *Towards Greek Tragedy*, London, 1973.

P. WALCOT, *Greek Drama in its Theatrical and Social Context*, Cardiff, 1976.

U. VON WILAMOWITZ, *Einleitung in die griechische Tragödie*, Berlin, 3rd ed., 1921.

Aeschylus

E. R. DODDS, 'Morals and politics in the *Oresteia*', in *The Ancient Concept of Progress*, Oxford, 1973, pp. 45ff.

P. EASTERLING, 'Presentation of character in Aeschylus', in *Greece and Rome*, 20, 1973, pp. 3ff.

R. F. GOHEEN, 'Aspects of dramatic symbolism', in *American Journ. of Philology*, 76, 1955, pp. 113ff.

A. LEBECK, *The Oresteia*, Center for Hellenic Studies, Washington D.C., 1971.

C. W. MACLEOD, 'L'Unità dell'Orestea', in *Maia*, 25, 1973, pp. 267ff.

C. W. MACLEOD, 'Clothing in the *Oresteia*', in *Maia*, 27, 1975, pp. 201–3.

J. J. PERADOTTO, 'Some patterns of nature imagery in the Oresteia', in *American Journ. of Philology*, 85, 1964, pp. 378ff.

K. REINHARDT, *Aischylos als Regisseur und Theologe*, Bern, 1949.

W. SCHADEWALDT, 'Der Kommos in Aischylos' *Choephoren*', in *Hellas und Hesperien*, Zürich, 2nd ed., 1970, vol. I, pp. 249ff.

O. TAPLIN, 'Aeschylean silences and silences in Aeschylus', in *Harvard Studies in Classical Philology*, 76, 1972, pp. 57ff.

P. VIDAL-NAQUET, 'Chasse et sacrifice dans l'*Orestie*', in *Mythe et Tragédie en Grèce ancienne*, Paris, 1972, pp. 133ff.

R. P. WINNINGTON-INGRAM, 'Clytemnestra and the vote of Athena', in *Journ. of Hellenic Studies*, 68, 1948, pp. 130ff.

Sophocles

E. R. DODDS, 'On misunderstanding Oedipus Rex', in *The Ancient Concept of Progress*, Oxford, 1973, pp. 64ff.

G. M. KIRKWOOD, *A Study of Sophoclean Drama*, Cornell, 1958.

B. M. W. KNOX, *Oedipus at Thebes*, Yale, 1957.

B. M. W. KNOX, *The Heroic Temper*, Berkeley, 1964.

B. M. W. KNOX, 'The *Ajax* of Sophocles', in *Harvard Stud. in Class. Philology*, 65, 1961, pp. 1ff.

K. REINHARDT, *Sophokles*, Frankfurt, 3rd ed., 1947.

W. SCHADEWALDT, 'Experimentalle Philologie' in *Hellas und Hesperien*, Zürich, 2nd ed., 1970, vol. I, pp. 483ff.

D. B. ROBINSON, 'Topics in Sophocles' *Philoctetes*', in *Classical Quarterly*, 19, 1969, pp. 34ff.

O. TAPLIN, 'Significant actions in Sophocles' *Philoctetes*', in *Greek, Roman and Byzantine Studies*, 12, 1971, pp. 25ff.

J. P. VERNANT, 'Ambiguité et renversement. Sur la structure énigmatique d'*Oedipe-Roi*', in *Mythe et Tragédie en Grèce ancienne*, Paris, 1972, pp. 101ff.

T. VON WILAMOWITZ, *Die dramatische Technik des Sophokles*, Berlin, 1917.

Euripides

S. BARLOW, *The Imagery of Euripides*, London, 1971.

A. P. BURNETT, *Catastrophe Survived*, Oxford, 1971.

A. P. BURNETT, 'Human resistance and divine persuasion in Euripides' *Ion*', in *Classical Philology*, 57, 1962, pp. 89ff.

A. P. BURNETT, 'Pentheus and Dionysus: host and guest', in *Classical Philology*, 65, 1970, pp. 15ff.

D. J. CONACHER, *Euripidean Drama*, Toronto and London, 1967.

G. M. A. GRUBE, *The Drama of Euripides*, London, 1941.

B. M. W. KNOX, 'The *Hippolytus* of Euripides', in *Yale Class. Stud.*, 13, 1952, pp. 1ff.

W. LUDWIG, *Sapheneia*, unpublished dissertation, Tübingen, 1954.

K. REINHARDT, 'Die Sinnekrise bei Euripides', in *Tradition und Geist*, Göttingen, 1960.

A. RIVIER, *Essai sur le tragique d'Euripide*, Paris, 2nd ed., 1975.
H. STROHM, *Euripides*, Munich, 1957.
R. P. WINNINGTON-INGRAM, *Euripides and Dionysus*, Cambridge, 1948.

Recommended texts and translations
(*includes commentary)

AESCHYLUS

texts   *E. Fraenkel (Oxford, 1950: *Agam* only).
D. L. Page (Oxford, 1972).
*A. Sidgwick (Oxford, 1895–1905).
H. W. Smyth (Loeb Classical Library, Harvard and London, 1957).
U. von Wilamowitz (Berlin, 1914).

translations   *R. Fagles (London, 1976; Harmondsworth, 1977).
R. Lattimore (*The Complete Greek Tragedies* [CGT] ed. D. Grene and R. Lattimore, Chicago, 1959–60).
*H. Lloyd-Jones (*The Prentice-Hall Greek Drama Series* [P-H], Englewood Cliffs, 1970).
L. MacNiece (Oxford, 1936: *Agam* only).
H. W. Smyth (Loeb Classic Library, Harvard and London, 1957).

SOPHOCLES

texts   A. Dain (Paris, 1955–65).
R. D. Dawe (Leipzig, 1975: *Ajax* and *OT*).
*R. Jebb (Cambridge, 1893–8).
A. C. Pearson (Oxford, 1924).
*W. B. Stanford (London, 1963: *Ajax* only).

translations T. H. Banks (New York, 1966: *Ajax* and *Phil*).
D. Fitts and R. Fitzgerald (London, 1951: *OT* only).
*T. Gould (*P-H*: *OT* only).
D.Grene (*CGT*: *OT* and *Ajax*).
*R. Jebb (Cambridge, 1893–8).
J. Moore (*CGT*: *Ajax* only).
E. F. Watling (Harmondsworth, 1947–53).

EURIPIDES

texts   *W. S. Barrett (Oxford, 1964: *Hipp* only).

*E. R. Dodds (2nd ed., Oxford, 1960: *Ba* only).
L. Méridier and others (Paris, 1947–61).
G. Murray (Oxford, 1902–13).
*J. Roux (Paris, 1970–2: *Ba* only).

translations W. Arrowsmith (*CGD*: *Ba*).
*A. P. Burnett (*P-H*: *Ion*).
D. Grene (*CGD*: *Hipp*).
*G. S. Kirk (*P-H*: *Ba*).
D. W. Lucas (London, 1949: *Ion*).
F. L. Lucas (*Greek Drama for Everyman*, London, 1954: *Hipp* and *Ba*).
R. F. Willetts (*CGD*: *Ion*).

Index of passages discussed

l indicates the line number of the text of the play, *p* the page number of this book.

Aeschylus

AGAMEMNON

l. 1–39	*p.* 32
218–247	81, 185
351–487	80–2
585–614	33
783–850	102–3, 123
851–974	33, 78–83, 124, 141–2
975–1034	37, 81–2, 104, 142
1035–1330	33, 36, 59–60, 82, 103–4, 142–3, 187, 190
1331–1371	33–4, 103, 143, 185
1372–1576	81–2, 125–6, 143–4
1577–1673	34–5, 144–5

CHOEPHOROI

l. 1–21	*p.* 35–6, 51, 83, 145
164–305	83–4, 188
306–552	61, 104–5, 189
652–718	35, 105, 123–4, 144
719–782	82, 144–5

CHOEPHOROI—*contd.*

783–854	35, 144–5
869–930	35, 60–1, 103, 105–6, 124–5, 144–5
973–1020	81, 125–6
1021–1076	35–6, 85, 127, 145–6

EUMENIDES

l. 1–63	*p.* 61–2, 85, 146
94–139	36–7, 106–7, 146
140–234	36–8, 40, 127, 146
235–275	36–9, 84, 127, 146
276–306	38, 107–8
307–565	38, 84–5
566–708	63, 85, 106
708–777	38–9, 62–3, 107, 185, 187
778–915	38–40, 63, 82, 146–7
916–1047	37, 39–40, 85, 147–8

OTHER PLAYS 23, 163–4, 185, 189, 192

Euripides

BAKCHAI

l. 1–63	*p.* 55–6
170–209	74–5
210–369	75, 98, 100, 157, 187
434–518	98, 100, 138–9, 157
576–641	119–20, 157
642–861	57, 100, 120–1, 157–8
912–976	76, 139, 157
1169–1329	56, 99–100, 186
1330–1392	56, 120

HIPPOLYTOS

l. 1–120	*p.* 51, 93–4, 134–5
141–266	69, 94, 116, 135–6, 155
267–361	69–70, 94, 116
362–524	116, 155
565–668	70–1, 155, 191
669–789	95, 155–6
790–855	94, 114–15, 156
856–980	95, 115–16
1045–1101	95, 117, 135
1342–1441	51–2, 135–6
1442–1466	52, 71–2

ION

l. 1–81	*p.* 51, 136
82–183	95–6, 136–7
184–251	53–4
510–675	52–3, 72, 117–18, 137–8
725–922	54–5, 73, 118–19

923–1047   54–5, 74, 97
1250–1319   72–3, 156, 187
1320–1394   73–4, 97, 117, 137, 156
1395–1436   73–4, 97–8, 137–8, 156, 190
1437–1509   54, 73–4, 96, 157
1510–1622   54–6, 117, 151

OTHER PLAYS   27–8, 70, 72, 95, 140, 163–4, 185, 187–8

Sophocles

AIAS

l. 1–133   p. 40–1, 85, 108, 131, 185
333–429   63, 85, 87–8, 108–9
430–595   63–4, 129
646–692   64, 85–6, 109, 127–31, 190
719–814   41–2, 127
815–865   86–8, 127–8, 130–1, 148–9, 188
866–973   109, 148–9, 189
974–1162   65, 87, 109, 148–9, 181
1163–1184   65, 88, 108, 149
1185–1222   108, 149
1223–1315   149–50
1316–1420   41–2, 150

OIDIPOUS (TYRANNOS)

l. 1–150   p. 43, 88, 109–10
216–462   43–5, 110
513–697   46, 150
698–862   65, 150
863–949   43, 88–9, 151
1054–1085   45, 111, 151–2
1086–1109   45, 152
1110–1185   45, 65–6, 152
1287–1306   89, 110, 131
1369–1530   45–6, 66, 110–11, 186

PHILOKTETES

l. 1–218   p. 46–7, 49, 89, 113, 186
219–342   47–8, 90, 113
461–675   67, 90, 113
676–729   49, 153
730–864   67, 91, 112–13
865–926   67–8, 91–2, 133–4
927–962   50, 92, 113–14, 189
963–1080   68, 92, 114, 131–2
1081–1217   48–50, 68, 92, 153–4, 186
1222–1401   49, 68, 92–3, 132–3, 154, 186
1402–1471   49–51, 68–9, 93, 134, 154

OTHER PLAYS   20, 25, 110–11, 164, 185, 188–9

General index

acting style, *see* conventions
Adams, Richard, 187
altar, *see* suppliancy
anthropology, 7–8, 83, 161–2, 177–8
aria, 28, 95–6, 118–19, 135–6, 155
Aristophanes, 1–2, 18, 27, 35, 101–2, 166
Aristotle, 2, 20, 27, 122, 140, 159–60, 169
audience, 2–3, 5, 10, 125, 128, chapter 10,
 187
authenticity, author's intention, etc., 3,
 5–6, 175–8, 182, 193 *and passim*

blindness (and sight), 43–4, 66–7, 80,
 110–11
Brecht, Bertolt, 1, 141
Brook, Peter, 173, 192–3
Burnett, Anne, 157, 188

Chekhov, Anton, 1, 102
chorus, 12–13, 19–20, 34–6, 41, 60–1, 118,
 126–7, 142, 147–8, 156, 160, 183
conventions, 13, 15–16, 160, 191
Corneille, Pierre, 12
costume, 13–14, 17, 47–8, 59, 74, 76, chapter 6, 103, 187
Craig, Gordon, 173

dance, 12, 84, 95–6, 105, 127, 188

delivery, 13, 15, 20, 174, 182
Dionysus, *see* festivals
director, role of, 1, 17, chapter 11, 193
doorway, 33–5, 47, 105, 120, 124, 131,
 136
dramatic illusion, *see* audience
dumb-show, 17–18, 40, 174

eavesdropping, 70–1, 132–3
ekkyklema, 11–12, 101, 108, 110, 115, 189
Eliot, George, 26
Eliot, T. S., 1, 8, 170, 179, 182
embrace, *see* recognition scenes
emotion, tragic, 1, 14, 26, 66, chapter 10,
 and passim
enigma, *see* riddles
entrances and exits, 20, chapter 4, *and passim*
Epidaurus, theatre at, 10, 15, 172
exile, 24, 34–5, 39–40, 45–6, 56, 135, 145,
 185
exodus, see procession
extras, 13, 17, 88, 102, 109, 134–5

Fate, fortune, free will, etc., 28, 45, 51, 60,
 75, 143–4, 151–2, 157–8, 165, 192
festivals (esp. of Dionysus), 10, 13, 23, 162,
 183

Globe Theatre, 14, 176, 193
gods, 29, 38–41, 51–3, 70–1, 79–80, 100, 119–20, 188, *see also mēchanē*
Gorgias, 167–70, 192
Gould, John, 183, 187, 191
Granville-Barker, Harley, 4, 182, 193

hand, clasping, 66, 112, 133
Hardy, Thomas, 165, 184, 192
historicism, *see* authenticity, etc.
Homer, 52, 64–5, 87, 163–4, 177
house, 10–11, 16, 32–3, 46, 56, 80, 103, 117, 123, 184–5
Huizinga, Johan, 190
hunting imagery, 37–8, 41, 94, 99, 107, 127, 139
hybris, 79, 149, 190
hymn, *see* prayer

interjections, *see* noises
interpolation of stage-business, *see* director, role of

Knox, Bernard, 115, 128, 188
kommos, *see* lyric dialogue

legal terminology, procedure, etc., 38, 62–3, 71, 76, 106, 115, 138, 188
Lewis, C. S., 177, 193
lyric dialogue, 19–20, 47–8, 70, 73, 85, 92, 104–5, 143, 147, 149, 153–5, 186, 189–90

Macleod, Colin, 46, 183, 185–8
Marceau, Marcel, 16
Marlowe, Kit, 58
mask, 14–15, 85, 89, 95, 99, 127
mēchanē (esp. 'God from machine'), 12, 16, 52, 54, 56, 117, 120, 186
metre, use of, 20, 54, 134, 136–8, 156–7
mirror scenes, *see* reversal
monody, *see* aria

naturalism, *see* convention
Nietzsche, F. W., 168
Nôh theatre, 16, 183
noises (esp. off-stage), 47, 60, chapter 7, 156, 158

palace, *see* house
Parry, Milman, 193
Pasolini, Pier Paolo, 175
Phrynichns, 12, 168
pity, *see* emotion, tragic

place, sense of, 49–50, 87–8
Plato, 2, 166–9
pollution, 36, 38, 56, 66–7
Powys, J. C., 184
prayer, 33, 83, 86, 88, 110, 119–20
procession, 39–40, 42, 127
prologue, 47, 55–6, 146, 148
propaganda, 25, 165, 192
props, 11, chapter 6, 125–6, *and passim*

rapid scenes, 144–6, 154
recognition scenes, 72–4, 97–8, 137–8, 156
Reinhardt, Karl, 4, 128, 185, 188
responsibility, *see* Fate, etc.
revenge-return, *see* exile
reversal, 61, 100, chapter 8, 142–4
riddles, 44, 82, 104, 129, 141, 152–3, 185–6, 190–1
ritual, 83, 161–2, 175, 190–1

sacrifice, 60, 76, 103, 139, 143
sequence of scenes, structure, etc., 19–21, 31–2, 49, 128, chapter 9, 164, 169–70, 184, *and passim*
Shakespeare, William, 1, 4–5, 14, 17, 32, 58, 77, 102, 105, 122–3, 125, 141, 145, 175–6, 185, 190–3
Shaw, G. B., 1, 17, 28, 173, 192
silences, 34–5, 38, 43–4, 90, chapter 7, 135
skēnē, *see* house
sōphrosynē, 130–1, 135
stage-directions, 4, 16–19, 173, 179, *and passim*
statues, 84, 93–4, 107
Steiner, George, 193
stichomythia, 19, 124, 156, 191
structure, *see* sequence of scenes
suppliancy, 39, 65, 69–70, 72–3, 88–9, 108–9, 117, 126, 136, 187, 189

tableaux, 65, chapter 7, 125–6, 149
text, 1–2, 16–17, 174–5, 185
Thespis, 23
threshold, *see* doorway
time, handling of, 36, 142
translation, 179–80, 193

violence, 65–6, 75, 139, 158, 160
voice, *see* delivery

witness, 95, 106, 115
wreath, 93–4, 98